The New Age of Catastrophe

The New Age of Calgary sphe

The New Age of Catastrophe

Alex Callinicos

polity

Copyright © Alex Callinicos 2023

The right of Alex Callinicos to be identified as Author of this Work has been asserted in accordance with the UK Copyright, Designs and Patents Act 1988.

First published in 2023 by Polity Press

3

Polity Press
65 Bridge Street
Cambridge CB2 1UR, UK

Polity Press
111 River Street
Hoboken, NJ 07030, USA

All rights reserved. Except for the quotation of short passages for the purpose of criticism and review, no part of this publication may be reproduced, stored in a retrieval system or transmitted, in any form or by any means, electronic, mechanical, photocopying, recording or otherwise, without the prior permission of the publisher.

ISBN-13: 978-1-5095-5416-4
ISBN-13: 978-1-5095-5417-1 (pb)

A catalogue record for this book is available from the British Library.

Library of Congress Control Number: 2022943050

Typeset in 10.75 on 13 Adobe Janson
by Fakenham Prepress Solutions, Fakenham, Norfolk NR21 8NL
Printed and bound in Great Britain by TJ Books Ltd, Padstow, Cornwall

The publisher has used its best endeavours to ensure that the URLs for external websites referred to in this book are correct and active at the time of going to press. However, the publisher has no responsibility for the websites and can make no guarantee that a site will remain live or that the content is or will remain appropriate.

Every effort has been made to trace all copyright holders, but if any have been overlooked the publisher will be pleased to include any necessary credits in any subsequent reprint or edition.

For further information on Polity, visit our website:
politybooks.com

To Julia
With boundless love

Contents

Preface and Acknowledgements ix

Introduction 1
1 Antechamber to the Present 15
2 The Destruction of Nature 30
3 Economic Stagnation 61
4 Hegemonic Decline and Geopolitical Antagonism 86
5 Revolt and Reaction 118
6 Pulling the Emergency Cord 149

Notes 180
Select Bibliography 226
Index 230

Preface and Acknowledgements

Louis Althusser entitled his autobiography *The Future Lasts a Long Time*. But this future – the one we are all now living – has arrived in a series of sudden jolts – proliferating wildfires, floods, and heatwaves, the onset of COVID-19, the far-right seizure of the Capitol, the renewed threat of nuclear war, the cost-of-living crisis. Our lives have changed irreversibly. The book before you is an attempt to make sense of this future and to identify ways in which we can avert the worst.

Louise Knight suggested that I write this book and has kept me firmly on the straight and narrow. I have enjoyed the return to Polity and am very grateful for the help of Inès Boxman and Manuela Tecusan.

I first set out some of the arguments that are now fully developed in this book in an article titled 'Neoliberal Capitalism Implodes: Global Catastrophe and the Far Right Today' and published in the spring 2021 issue of *International Socialism*. I am grateful to the editor, Joseph Choonara, for allowing me to draw on this article and to him, Richard Donnelly, Gareth Jenkins, Sheila McGregor, John Rose, and Mark Thomas for their valuable comments on it in draft. Preparing my Farewell Lecture at King's College London in March 2022 was helpful for refining the overall thesis of the book. My thanks go to Ramon Pacheco Pardo, who organized this pleasant event, and to all those who attended.

In completing the book I have greatly benefitted from feedback on various drafts from two anonymous reviewers and from Dariush Moaven Doust, Martin Empson, and Louise Knight. But my toughest critic has been, as ever, Lucia Pradella. I hope the book is now closer to what her high intellectual and political standards demand, but I fear it probably still falls short. My thanks to all for their help.

Twitter is, notoriously, a venue for the expression of malice and for self-congratulation, but I must confess that I have found it very valuable as a source of analysis, information, and references while working on this book. I also benefitted from my old standby, the *Financial Times*. Hegel wrote: 'Reading the morning newspaper is the realist's morning prayer.' Well, the *Financial Times* has been the object of my devotions for fifty years now.

Too many lives have been lost during the pandemic – not always from COVID-19, but all without our being able to mourn them properly. I would like to remember here Mick Brooks, Mario Duayer, Jane Elderton, Steve Hammill, Leo Panitch, Ed Rooksby, Chanie Rosenberg, David Sanders, and Neale Williams. And then, as I was correcting the proofs of this book, I learned of Mike Davis's death. He was at once a brilliantly original and often highly unorthodox Marxist writer and, as he said himself, an old-school working-class socialist. His influence on the pages that follow is pervasive, and I mourn his passing.

But in dedicating this book I look mainly forward, not back. The appearance of my adorable daughter Julia, who turned five while this book was being finished, has filled my life with joy. The other day she asked whether humans would be become extinct, like the dinosaurs. So I'm dedicating *The New Age of Catastrophe* to Julia, as a contribution to the fight to ensure that we were right to answer her question with a 'No'.

Introduction

The world lives in the shadow of catastrophe. The COVID-19 pandemic has underlined that even invoking a crisis of capitalism is insufficient for grasping the gravity of our present plight. We are confronted with a crisis of civilization: the forms of living that were made possible by the development of industrial capitalism in the early nineteenth century and that became increasingly generalized in the twentieth century are no longer viable, indeed they are hurtling us towards societal collapse. The most important long-term driver of this process is, of course, climate change, whose effects have become so visible in the past few years through floods, wildfires, and storms. The pandemic, moreover, has drawn attention to how the colonization of nature, accelerated by capitalist globalization, has increased the probability of viruses making the leap from other species to humans.

But the threat doesn't come merely from what we like to think of as 'natural' catastrophe. On 27 February 2022 Vladimir Putin, president of the Russian Federation, reacted to the western financial sanctions imposed on the Russian economy to punish his invasion of Ukraine by announcing that he was putting Russia's nuclear forces on alert. Short of going nuclear, Russia's war on Ukraine, like the wars in Syria and Yemen before it, sent millions of people fleeing to other countries, displaced millions more internally, and subjected the civilian population to intense bombardment and – in too many cases – to the murderous attention of the invading troops.

The exceptional is becoming normal

Catastrophe is indeed no longer exceptional; it is becoming normal. This is penetrating mainstream planning. In December 2020 the Brookings Institution published a call for the incoming administration of Joe Biden to set up a commission on COVID-19 comparable to the inquiries into the Kennedy assassination and the 9/11 attacks. The author, Elaine Kamarck, says that the commission should address the question of how we should prepare for low-probability but high-intensity events. These 'black swan' events (as they are called) are supposed to be rare and unpredictable – they fall outside the normal pattern of events – but to have a large and destructive impact. But they 'seem to be increasingly prevalent in the 21st century'. For example, 'climate change is going to make natural disasters more frequent and more deadly.'[1]

William H. McNeill, author of a pioneering study of the role played by disease in human history, has argued that catastrophe – by which he means 'some sequence of events that disrupts established routines of life and inflicts suffering or death on many' – is intrinsic to the human condition: 'Ever since civilization arose, leaving decipherable records that allow us to understand something of what people have experienced, catastrophes have been chronic and all but continual.'[2] In an interesting study of the mathematics of catastrophe, Gordon Woo has extended the concept far beyond human history, making it embrace volcanic eruptions, earthquakes, tsunamis, and other physical phenomena. Woo suggests that what tends to be common to the very wide range of events he studies is fluctuations in complex systems that can be destabilized and that change in a non-linear fashion, giving rise to black swans, thanks to small alterations in their initial conditions.[3]

Marxists have preferred a more historically specific and more political focus than the one offered in either of these approaches, thematizing the immanence of catastrophe in the capitalist mode of production and its culmination in imperialism. It was classically formulated by Rosa Luxemburg in 1916, in her *Junius Pamphlet* against the First World War:

> We stand today, as Friedrich Engels prophesied more than a generation ago, before the awful proposition: either the triumph of imperialism and the destruction of all culture, and, as in ancient Rome, depopulation, desolation, degeneration, a vast cemetery; or, the victory of

socialism, that is, the conscious struggle of the international proletariat against imperialism, against its methods, against war.[4]

Socialism or barbarism, in other words.[5] And indeed Eric Hobsbawm calls the period between 1914 and 1945 'the Age of Catastrophe' – the two world wars, the Great Depression, the victories of Mussolini's Fascism and National Socialism, the Stalinist Terror, and the Holocaust.[6] Luxemburg had an almost visceral sense of the profundity of this chain of disasters, of which she was an early victim, battered to death by a proto-fascist militia in January 1919. Another victim of the far right, Walter Benjamin, writing, in Victor Serge's words, at 'midnight in the century' – just after the outbreak of the Second World War, when it seemed as if Hitler and Stalin were triumphant – famously summed up the era when he said '"the state of emergency" in which we live is not the exception but the rule.'[7]

After 1945, watched over by the United States, advanced capitalism rebuilt itself in Western Europe and Japan, and the world economy experienced its greatest boom. For a quarter of a century the western working class experienced full employment and an expanding welfare state. Catastrophe receded in the advanced capitalist states – although in Korea in the early 1950s, in Indonesia in the mid-1960s, and in Indochina till the end of the 1970s it remained a terrible reality, as it did also in those parts of the global South afflicted by famine.

The postwar boom collapsed amid worker insurgency in the late 1960s and early 1970s. Neoliberalism was the riposte, and it marked what David Harvey calls 'the restoration of class power' to 'economic elites'.[8] It inflicted a series of severe defeats on the organized working class, restructured production, thereby facilitating the industrialization of parts of the South (a process that had, however, started much earlier and was promoted by decolonization), and relentlessly commodified all spheres of life. The US victory in the Cold War and a revival of economic growth, driven by the development of financial bubbles that stimulated consumption and investment, gave a degree of plausibility to Francis Fukuyama's claim that, with the fall of the Stalinist regimes, history had ended in the triumph of liberal capitalism.[9] Facilitated by the increasing digitalization of life, consumption soared – especially among upper-middle strata and the ballooning rich and superrich in the North and in the economically successful parts of the South. Liberal democracy spread, in form at least, beyond its postwar core zones of North America, Western Europe, and Japan.

This era of good feeling – from a western perspective at least – was punctured first by the 9/11 attacks on New York and Washington and the terrible wars the United States waged in Afghanistan and Iraq, and then by the global financial crisis (GFC) of 2007–9. It is now definitively over. Through the decades after 1945, catastrophe loomed as a shadow on the horizon. J. G. Ballard was the great poet of catastrophe of this era, his novels and short stories ceaselessly imagining situations that unfolded amid the ruins left by some vast, obscure disaster. It became clear a long time ago that, short of the ultimate catastrophe of nuclear war that hung over the Cold War era and that has now become an imminent threat again, the main danger comes from the way the blind process of capital accumulation destroys the natural world, of which humans are but a dependent part.

Chief among these forms of destruction (though definitely not the only one, as COVID-19 has taught us) is climate change. The chaos that experts and activists have long warned that global warming would bring is now here. Take Cyclone Idai, which caused widespread flooding and deaths in East Africa in March 2019. I was brought up in Zimbabwe (then Southern Rhodesia) in the 1950s and 1960s. We used to take seaside holidays in Beira, a sleepy port city on the coast of neighbouring Mozambique. Idai put Beira under six metres of water, destroyed nine tenths of the city, and killed a thousand people. And this event belongs to a much larger pattern. According to the UN, six million people were affected by flooding in East Africa in 2020, five times the number four years before.[10]

Disasters such as these are becoming normalized. The burning of the Amazon in 2019 caused widespread shock. Since then we've had wildfires and flooding in Australia and repeated wildfires on the west coast of North America (they brought darkness at noon in San Francisco in September 2020) and in Greece. Of course, rich countries such as the United States and Australia can cope better with disasters of this magnitude. But, as the pandemic shows, decades of privatization and austerity have pared down state capabilities, making it harder for governments to respond effectively (assuming that they have the will to do so, as those of Donald Trump and Boris Johnson plainly did not).

The pandemic has also dramatized a feature of plagues and famines that is as old as class society. The poor are far more vulnerable to catastrophe because they lack the resources to buy their way out of danger. As Jean-Paul Sartre puts it, '[t]he Black Death acts only as an *exaggeration* of the class relations; it *chooses*. It strikes the wretched, it spares the wealthy.'[11] The mortality figures for COVID-19 have been coded for 'race' and class. The other side of the equation can be found, for example, in an increased demand for luxury yachts. There the rich can shun centres of infection and continue to run their businesses online and accumulate yet more wealth in the sun. This is at odds with the relentless pressure placed on many workers to risk their lives daily during the pandemic. In these contrasts we see what the Argentinian Marxist philosopher Natalia Romé calls 'the normalization of barbarism', which penetrates the very pores of society.[12]

The Marxist thinker who addressed catastrophe most systematically was Theodor Adorno. A German Jew, he was able to escape Europe after the Nazi seizure of power, unlike his friend and mentor Benjamin, who committed suicide when prevented from fleeing Vichy France in September 1940. Adorno returned to Germany from American exile in 1950, but never forgot. In his philosophical masterpiece *Negative Dialectics* he writes: 'The world spirit, a worthy object of definition, would have to be defined as permanent catastrophe.'[13] Adorno makes it clear that by 'world spirit' he is referring, ironically, to capitalism.

At the centre of his imagination of catastrophe was Nazism and the Holocaust. In a brilliant passage written in exile, Adorno invokes the German V-1 pilotless flying bombs to upend Hegel's famous description of Napoleon riding victorious through Jena as 'the world-spirit on horseback' – the instrument of History in bringing Reason and reality into alignment:

> Like Fascism itself, the robots career without a subject. Like Fascism they combine almost utmost technical perfection with total blindness. And like it arouse moral terror and are wholly futile. 'I have seen the world spirit', not on horseback, but on wings and without a head, and that refutes, at the same stroke, Hegel's philosophy of history.[14]

Capitalism, having overstayed its welcome, has become a 'permanent catastrophe'. Today this chronic condition has its source in a multidimensional crisis of capitalism, what the economic historian Adam Tooze has called a 'polycrisis':[15]

- BIOLOGICAL: the consequences, already noted, of capitalism's increasingly destructive relationship with nature. They confront us personally with what Jem Bendell, in a widely read and disturbing paper, calls 'climate tragedy',[16] as well as with plagues, of which COVID-19 may be only the first;

- ECONOMIC: the global financial crisis and its aftermath – what Michael Roberts calls the 'Long Depression' – which has been exacerbated by the impact of the pandemic and of the Russo-Ukrainian War;[17]
- GEOPOLITICAL: the liberal international order constructed by the United States after the Second World War and globalized after the collapse of the Soviet Union is widely accepted to be in crisis. Geopolitics was already in flux, thanks to the US defeats in the Greater Middle East and the increasing challenge to US hegemony mounted by China – the biggest economy in the world, by some measures – and by Russia, a militarily formidable challenger to the western powers in Europe, in the Middle East, and in sub-Saharan Africa. Two academic studies of the COVID-19 pandemic written from a liberal perspective – Colin Kahl and Thomas Wright's *Aftershocks* and Tooze's *Shutdown* – both blame the collapse of international cooperation in dealing with the virus on the rivalry between the United States and China.[18] The extreme dangers that geopolitical instability poses were brought home by Russia's confrontation with the West after its invasion of Ukraine in February 2022.
- POLITICAL: the emergence of the far right, for the first time since the 1930s, as a serious political player on a global scale. The electoral squeeze suffered since the GFC by what Tariq Ali calls 'the extreme centre' – the centre-right and centre-left parties that have managed the neoliberal economic policy regime since its emergence in the late 1970s – gave the far right its opening.[19] This has contributed to the intensification of geopolitical competition, for example through the support that many far right politicians gave Putin. The disastrous consequences of their advance are seen in the mismanagement of the pandemic by Trump in the United States, Bolsonaro in Brazil, and Modi in India. The failure of Trump's re-election campaign and of his followers' attempt to seize the Capitol in Washington DC on 6 January 2021 doesn't mean that the threat of the far right has gone away, as the growing intransigence of a Republican Party dominated by Trumpism shows. The right's continuing advance has been underlined by the US Supreme Court's highly partisan decision to strike down the *Roe vs Wade* judgement, which recognizes a constitutional right to abortion.

The severity of this multiple crisis is understood by at least sections of the western ruling classes. After taking office as Joe Biden's Secretary of the Treasury in January 2021, Janet Yellen wrote to her staff about the 'four historic crises' he had identified: 'COVID-19 is one ... the country is also facing a climate crisis, a crisis of systemic racism, and an economic crisis that has been building for fifty years'.[20] But my argument goes beyond this kind of descriptive registration of the polycrisis. One could put it like this. The past twenty years or so have seen a series of shocks to the international system – 9/11, the wars in Afghanistan and Iraq, the GFC, the pandemic, and now the Ukraine War. But the language of 'shocks', which in mainstream economics means disruption external to the system, is misleading. These events, destructive and unpredictable (at least in their detail) though they may be, are immanent in the system, arising from its internal logic. They demonstrate that it has hit the buffers.

This book

The unifying theme of this book, then, is the exploration of this new global conjuncture in its different but interrelated dimensions. I draw on the Marxist critique of political economy, as I have done for fifty years now. What is distinctive to this approach, if we compare it to contemporary liberal scholarship – exemplified notably by the work of Adam Tooze, who also engages closely with the very recent past (the GFC in *Crashed*) and now with the present (the pandemic in *Shutdown*)?[21] Tooze offers very well orchestrated and well researched narratives of the interaction of economic and geopolitical processes under stress and of the efforts of liberal elites to manage these processes; I touch on his work at several points in this book.[22]

What is missing from these narratives, however, is, as Fredric Jameson would put it, 'the methodological imperative of totalization': the aspiration to integrate the different aspects of our situation into a structured totality – an aspiration that Jameson, inspired by Georg Lukács and Jean-Paul Sartre, claims distinguishes Marxism. It is a total*ization* rather than a finished whole, because realizing this aspiration is always incomplete, is a process.[23] And what it reveals is the contours of the capitalist mode of production. It is this system that defines our horizons and unifies the different dimensions of the multiple crises we confront. Marx conceptualizes it in *Capital* as an economic system whose relations of production are constituted by two interrelated antagonisms: the exploitation of wage labour by capital and the competition between rival capitals (whether firms or states).[24] These antagonisms give rise to a blind and unending process of competitive accumulation that, as I try to show in what follows, drives simultaneously environmental destruction, the Long Depression, and the growing geopolitical rivalries. By comparison, even the best mainstream scholarship tends to fragment the totality – for example, by treating economic globalization and climate change as distinct processes rather than closely interconnected phenomena.

This conception of capitalism as what Sartre called a 'developing totalization' informs the structure of this book as an exploration of ascending levels of this totality.[25] We thus can map the different dimensions of the multiple crisis onto Marx's representation of the structure of the social whole in his 1859 Preface to *A Contribution to the Critique of Political Economy*:

> In the social production of their existence, human beings inevitably enter into definite relations, which are independent of their will, namely relations of production appropriate to a given stage in the development of their material forces of production. The totality of these relations of production constitutes the economic structure of society, the real foundation [*Basis*], on which arises a legal and political superstructure and to which correspond definite forms of social consciousness.[26]

Accordingly, in the course of this book, we move from economic base to ideologico-political superstructure (see Figure 1). I take inspiration here from Antonio Gramsci, who was greatly influenced by the 1859 Preface and whose work I regard as a continuation of Marx's critique of political economy.[27]

Biological	Productive forces = labour process = metabolism of labour and nature
Economic	Relations of production = exploitation + competitive accumulation
Geopolitical	Imperialism = intersection of economic and geopolitical competition
Political	Crisis of extreme centre and rise of far right
Ideological	'Race', gender as terrains of contestation

Figure 1   Dimensions of the crisis

Chapter 1 offers a prelude, the earlier 'age of catastrophe', as a benchmark for understanding the present – not, it must be emphasized, because history is repeating itself, but because it helps us to identify what is different in the present, and also what is (or could be) the same. Chapter 2 commences the main argument by exploring the relationship between labour and nature, which is the bedrock of any social formation; the transformations that this relationship undergoes are expressed in the development of humankind's productive powers. The dominant feature of the permanent catastrophe today is the accelerating destruction of nature since the middle of the twentieth century and its increasingly dangerous consequences – the onset of climate chaos and, now, COVID-19 (with what it may presage). I draw here on one of the main achievements of Marxist scholarship in the past couple of decades, namely the attempts, notably by John Bellamy Foster and Mike Davis, to develop still further Marx's critique of capitalism's destruction of nature. I also examine the ways in which states have sought to manage the pandemic – essentially through a combination of coercion and technological fixes – and what this suggests about the forms of what Michel Foucault calls 'governmentality', through which elites will seek to address future catastrophes.

Chapter 3 moves to focus on how capitalist relations of production, constituted by the antagonisms between labour and capital and between competing capitals, also underlie the combination of extreme economic instability with a phenomenon that some mainstream economists label 'secular stagnation', which has come to dominate global capitalism since 2007–8. This naturally leads to the much debated question of whether the neoliberal economic policy regime pioneered in Chile, the United States, and Britain during the 1970s is on the way out (to preview my decisive response: yes and no). Chapter 4 turns to consider imperialism, understood as arising at the intersection of the economic and political competition that develops under capitalism. Today this competition takes the form of growing geopolitical rivalries, combined with transnational economic integration: at a global level, between the United States and the West, generally, against China and Russia; regionally, in the struggles of various Middle East states, for example, to fill the vacuum left by the United States' partial withdrawal after defeat in Iraq (these struggles are now spreading to sub-Saharan Africa and Central Asia). The destructive power of these conflicts has been brought into focus by the war in Ukraine.

With Chapter 5 we turn to what Marx calls 'the legal and political superstructure' and 'the legal, political, religious, artistic or philosophic

– in short, ideological forms in which human beings become conscious of this conflict [in the economic base of society] and fight it out'.[28] The interaction between geopolitical instability and the rise of the far right is a major theme of this chapter, which analyses the contemporary spectrum of populist racism and outright fascism and the factors responsible for their spread. These trends are most dangerously expressed at the very centre of the capitalist system in the United States: this country's archaic constitution is cracking under the strain of the struggle between a Republican Party where the far right is increasingly making the running and a Democratic establishment still deeply embedded in the neoliberal imperialism of Bill Clinton and Barack Obama.

Given the importance of 'anti-gender' ideology and racism, both old (anti-Semitism) and new (Islamophobia), to the far right, there is a natural transition to my exploration of gender and 'race' as terrains of struggle in Chapter 6 (of course, there is much more to gender and 'race' than this ideologico-political contestation; above all, there is their role in the social reproduction of capitalism).[29] This discussion thus provides a good starting point for the concluding exploration of the politics of catastrophe, also in Chapter 6. Plainly, it is no longer controversial that existing human civilization is now unsustainable. To assert that an essential precondition to attaining sustainability is to rid the world of the capitalist mode of production is a little more disputable, but this is what I argue.

Here, too, there is a disagreement between and Tooze and me. He writes:

> Far from being a culmination, 2020 is merely a moment in a process of escalation ... In an earlier period of history this sort of diagnosis might have been coupled with the forecast of revolution. If anything is unrealistic today, that prediction surely is ... The chief countervailing force to the escalation of global tension in political, economic, and ecological realms is therefore crisis management on an ever-larger scale, crisis-driven and ad hoc.[30]

Tooze is right that anti-capitalist revolution is not on the immediate agenda. But revolution is not a null category in the present – the Middle East still reverberates with the turbulence unleashed by the risings of 2011 and their continuations in Algeria and Sudan. Moreover, refusing to admit the possibility of revolution has the effect of naturalizing capitalism. All that is left, then, is to trace, in the dense and confining labyrinths of the existing power structures, the narrow paths that the liberal crisis manager tries to negotiate – paths that indeed seem to be narrowing still, as the plight of the Biden administration shows us.[31]

Conceptualizing capitalism as a developing totalization is therefore intimately connected with insisting that the world doesn't have to be the way is, that there are other possible worlds, some of which would represent an improvement on the present one. Adorno puts it very well:

> The only philosophy that can be responsibly practised in the face of despair is the attempt to contemplate things as they would present themselves from the standpoint of redemption. Knowledge has no light but that shed by redemption: all else is reconstruction, technique, mere technique. Perspectives must be developed that displace and estrange the world, reveal it to be, with its rifts and crevices, as indigent and distorted as it will appear one day in the messianic light … beside the demand thus placed on thought, the question of the reality or unreality of redemption itself hardly matters.[32]

Adorno undoubtedly understands redemption after Benjamin's essay 'On the Concept of History' (1939–40), where redemption is equated with (though not reduced to) revolution, conceived of not as the inevitable fruit of progress but as a defiant Messianic irruption into 'the homogeneous and empty time' of capitalist normality.[33] This seems to me – as it has to other Marxist admirers of Benjamin, for example Michael Löwy and the late Daniel Bensaïd – the only way to think about revolution in this era of catastrophe.[34] I'm still more optimistic about the reality of revolutionary redemption than Adorno ever managed to be. But, as he says, this isn't the point now. We are likely to get the measure of the multidimensional crisis we face only if we track down its source in capitalism, conceived of, as it was by Marx, as a historically contingent and transitory mode of production. There is of course a risk in totalizing in this way, namely that this becomes an exercise in dogmatic deduction. My wager is that this is not inevitable.

It makes a difference, though, how we go about totalizing. Louis Althusser, Sartre's great opponent in the French Marxism of the 1960s, warns against 'expressive totality', that is, against seeing capitalism, for example, as having a core that radiates through all the different aspects of the whole. To this he counterposes what he finds in *Capital*: a structure of determinations where each has its own causal role but all are articulated together in a complex unity. Rejecting, like Benjamin, the idea of 'a conception of historical time as continuous and homogeneous and contemporaneous with itself', Althusser argues that what he sees as different levels have their own time each; and he cites

> what Marx, discussing the capitalist mode of production in *Capital*, calls the type of intertwining of the different times (and here he only mentions the economic level), i.e., the type of 'dislocation' (*décalage*) and torsion of the different temporalities produced by the different levels of the structure, the complex combination of which constitutes the peculiar time of the process's development.[35]

Althusser goes on to say that 'the specific unity of the complex structure of the whole' consists in 'the real historical present: the present of the conjuncture'.[36] Elsewhere he discusses Lenin's writings on the Russian Revolution of February 1917: he understands them as the analysis of a revolutionary conjuncture: 'a vast accumulation of "contradictions" comes into play *in the same court*, some of which are radically heterogeneous – of different origins, different sense, different *levels* and *points* of application – but which nevertheless "merge" into a ruptural unity'.[37] One of the valuable features of this discussion of what Althusser calls 'overdetermination' is that it refuses to deduce important historical events from the abstract dialectic of the forces and relations of production but rather sees them as arising from the contingent conjunction of multiple determinations. Althusser was talking about revolution (this was the 1960s after all), but it seems to me that this historical method can also be applied to far from revolutionary moments, such as the present conjuncture.[38]

The reference to *historical* method isn't just a rhetorical flourish. 'Always historicize!', as Jameson famously put it.[39] This book historicizes in two ways: first and more generally, I trace the roots of the multiple crises, which is necessarily a historical undertaking; secondly, I develop a systematic historical comparison between the present historical moment and the first age of catastrophe (1914–45), an era of inter-imperialist wars and revolutions in which classical fascism developed and made its disastrous bid for global dominance.

The unifying theme connecting the two eras is the interplay of revolution and counter-revolution; here I am indebted to the historical work of Arno Mayer, which culminates in his book *The Furies*. I also follow in the footsteps of Walden Bello, author of a pioneering study of the far right on a global scale, which also frames its rise as counter-revolution.[40] The First World War shattered what had seemed to be solid social structures, releasing powerful revolutionary energies;

fascism, alongside other forms of reactionary politics, sought to push back or divert these energies. The damage caused by the neoliberal variant of capitalism since the late 1970s has stimulated the development, over the past twenty years or so, of mass movements of resistance that have been particularly powerful in the global South; the growth of the contemporary far right has to be understood in part as a response.

The pattern underlying both ages of catastrophe is to be sought with the help of the Marxist theory of imperialism, which is found, first of all, in Marx's *Capital* itself.[41] Here I stand on the shoulders not just of Marx himself, but of the great figures who further developed this theory in the early twentieth century: Rudolf Hilferding, Rosa Luxemburg, V. I. Lenin, Nikolai Bukharin, and Henryk Grossman.[42] But I have sought myself to develop and clarify the theory, conceptualizing capitalist imperialism as a formation at the intersection of economic and geopolitical competition and analysing the different historical forms it has taken.[43] I believe that this theory is indispensable to understanding the interrelation between the tendencies to economic crisis that prevail today and the growing and very dangerous geopolitical rivalries, particularly between the United States, China, and Russia. I will have a lot more to say about all this is in chapters 1 and 4.

Writing at the end of the 1930s, Max Horkheimer famously declared that 'whoever is not willing to talk about capitalism should also keep quiet about fascism', which he argued realized in extreme form the tendencies inherent in the capitalist mode of production.[44] Thirty years later, Nicos Poulantzas commented: 'Strictly speaking, this is incorrect: it is he who does not wish to discuss *imperialism* who should stay silent on the subject of fascism.'[45] While it's a mistake to counterpose imperialism and capitalism, since one is the outgrowth of the other, it's true that, as the liberal historian Richard Overy stresses in his recent study of what he calls 'the Great Imperial War, 1931–1945', both the Fascist and the National Socialist regimes were driven by the sense that, as latecomers to Europe's digestion of the rest of the world, Italy and Germany had forcibly to wrest their rightful share of the spoils from more established colonial powers, such as Britain and France.[46]

But bringing together imperialism and fascism underlines that one needs also to talk about racism. Imperialism in its colonial phase in the late nineteenth and early twentieth centuries imagined humankind as a hierarchy of races in which those at the top, victors in the social Darwinian struggle to survive, had the right to rule over the rest. Hitler's regime took this ideology to the limit in its attempt to exterminate the Jews and in its plans for imperial domination of the Eurasian continent. Racism of course survived the Nazis. Indeed, the huge global Black Lives Matter protests during the first COVID-19 wave, in the summer of 2020, dramatized how the racial antagonism has come to express, in concentrated form, all the conflicts and injustices of contemporary society. It's not entirely surprising that this dimension of the pandemic is neglected in the liberal studies by Kahl and Wright (who focus instead on the repression mounted by 'authoritarian' regimes, to a greater or lesser extent in conflict with the western powers) and by Tooze. In contrast, I address the racial antagonism extensively in Chapter 6. I would like to acknowledge the inspiration of two classics of African–American Marxism: W. E. B. du Bois, *Black Reconstruction in America*, and Angela Y. Davis, *Women, Race, and Class*.

Triangulating imperialism, racism, and fascism has been done before, notably by Aimé Césaire (see the next chapter), and also by Hannah Arendt in *The Origins of Totalitarianism*. Rereading this great work, I was, by turns, impressed with its sheer brilliance and with the way in which Arendt draws on radical critics such as Luxemburg, Benjamin, and J. A. Hobson to achieve her own synthesis; depressed by her capitulation to anti-Black racism in the (hugely inaccurate) account of colonialism in Africa; and disappointed by the way in which a deep and insightful engagement with the specificity of National Socialism gets lost in the final chapters, as it is hypostatized as a critique of 'totalitarianism' fit for the Cold War, with Nazism and Stalinism fused as western liberalism's 'other'.[47] All this underlines the importance of practising a scholarship that is at once rigorous and engaged, and of writing from the standpoint of a redemption understood, as it was by the young Marx, as fulfilling 'the *categorical imperative to overthrow all conditions* in which the human being is essentially debased, enslaved, neglected and contemptible'.[48] It is for others to judge how well I have achieved this.

1

Antechamber to the Present

Imperialism at bay

The last time catastrophe visited humankind at large was during the first half of the twentieth century – it was, in Arno Mayer's words, 'the general crisis and Thirty Years War of the twentieth century': the two world wars, the Great Depression, fascism, the Stalinist terror, and the Holocaust.[1] The technologies of industrialized warfare and the gigantic armies they made possible led to slaughter and devastation on a hitherto unimaginable scale, as well as to terrible cruelty, amplified by the techniques of the assembly line and bureaucratic rationality.[2] A characteristic figure of the time, the revolutionary–conservative writer Ernst Jünger, whose wartime diaries fastidiously record the distance he took in private from the Nazi monster he had helped to conjure up – wrote after a visit to the Eastern Front in March 1943: 'the war in the East has reached a magnitude that Clausewitz could never have imagined ... It is a war of states, peoples, citizens, and religions, with brutal escalation.'[3]

Aimé Césaire, a very different kind of writer, points out that the horrors visited upon Europe during the Second World War represented the return home of techniques of extermination pioneered in its colonies:

> Yes, it would be worthwhile to study clinically, in detail, the steps taken by Hitler and Hitlerism and to reveal to the very distinguished, very humanistic, very Christian bourgeois of the twentieth century that

without his being aware of it, he has a Hitler inside him, that Hitler inhabits him, that Hitler is his demon, that if he rails against him, he is being inconsistent and that, at bottom, what he cannot forgive Hitler for is not the crime in itself, the crime against man, it is not the humiliation of man as such, it is the crime against the white man, the humiliation of the white man, and the fact that he applied to Europe colonialist procedures which until then had been reserved exclusively for the Arabs of Algeria, the '********' of India, and the '********' of Africa.[4]

To understand this first age of catastrophe, we need a theory of imperialism. Modern capitalist imperialism is what happened when, towards the end of the nineteenth century, the process of capital accumulation led to an integrated global economy driven by the rhythms of industrial production and financial circulation in the advanced capitalist states, where economic and military power is increasingly concentrated. As a result, geopolitical competition between states, perennial in some form since the emergence of class societies, is subsumed under the logic of capital. This takes the form of an intersection between economic and geopolitical competition, as both David Harvey and I argue.[5] Individual capitals, which, increasingly, operate globally, need the support of their states to prosecute their interests, and the process that William H. McNeill calls 'the industrialization of war' demands that states promote capitalist development in order to secure the modern weapons systems and means of communication required to project power.[6]

The consequent fusion of economic and geopolitical rivalries devastated the first half of the twentieth century. It helped to fuel territorial competition among the Great Powers in the world outside Europe that was being incorporated into their colonial empires, but also in south-eastern Europe, where the First World War broke out in the summer of 1914. Informing these conflicts was the structural tension between Britain, the hegemonic capitalist power, and the United States and Germany, which had overtaken it industrially and were building navies that threatened its main means of global power projection. The proximity of the challenge from Germany made this country the target of British strategy, helping to ensure that alliance-building and arms races ended in general wars – twice.

This period – roughly between 1914 and 1945 – had three defining features:

(1) *An epoch of inter-imperialist war*: the two world wars (1914–18, 1939–45) of course dominated the age. They destabilized existing economic, political, and social structures and undermined their legitimacy, provoking a polarization between the extreme left (the Communist International) and the extreme right (authoritarian conservatives and fascists). The failure of the First World War to resolve the underlying antagonisms made a second and even more terrible edition highly likely.

(2) *The most severe economic slump in the history of capitalism*: the Great Depression of the 1930s was organically connected with the inter-imperialist rivalries that exploded in the two world wars. Antonio Gramsci traced the source of imperialist expansion to Marx's tendential law for the rate of profit to fall: 'Capitalist Europe, rich in resources and arrived at the point at which the rate of profit was beginning to reveal its tendency to fall, had a need to widen the area of expansion of its income-bearing investment; thus, after 1890, the great colonial empires were created.'[7] Britain's inability to manage the financial instability created by the First World War precipitated the deepest systemic crisis the capitalist mode of production has ever experienced. This intensified inter-imperial rivalries and only began to be overcome as the Great Powers switched to war production in the late 1930s.

(3) *Revolution and counter-revolution*: the destruction and privations of the First World War created the context for the first socialist revolution, which took place in Russia in October 1917, and for a wave of revolutionary upheavals inspired by it, which swept through the most powerful European state, Germany, and reached as far as China in 1925–7. This in turn immediately unleashed a powerful reaction from the right: first the Russian Civil War, and then the counter-revolutionary violence in Germany in which Rosa Luxemburg and Karl Liebknecht perished. The First World War produced large numbers of socially dislocated young men who had become habituated to violence, many of whom were mobilized in reactionary paramilitary forces, from the Black and Tans in Ireland to the Freikorps in Germany and on its borderlands. The early fascist organizations recruited heavily from them.

It is important to understand that this dialectic of revolution and counter-revolution was global. This is why it is too limiting to describe the period as 'the European Civil War', as Enzo Traverso does (among others), in a suggestive interpretive essay.[8] The chapter of revolutionary upheavals began in Mexico in 1910, while the end of the First World War was marked by a wave of colonial risings. Imperial domination was challenged by new revolutionary movements, often linked to the Comintern – in India, China, and Southeast Asia.[9] China – at stake in the three-way struggle between the nationalist Guomindang, the Communist Party of China (CPC), and, from 1931 onwards, Japanese imperialism – was the most important battlefield outside Europe. The 1925–7 Chinese Revolution ended in a bloody breakdown of the alliance between the Guomindang and the CPC against the warlords and colonial powers – whose consequences are dramatically evoked by André Malraux in his novel *La Condition humaine*.[10] Anti-communism was an important source of ideological legitimation for the Japanese military leadership's disastrous attempt to conquer China between 1931 and 1945.

In continental Europe, ruling-class politics was dominated by counter-revolution, especially once the onset of the Great Depression had further destabilized existing structures. The tendency was towards authoritarian right-wing regimes that, to a greater or lesser extent, broke with the parliamentary forms at work in the leading liberal capitalist states, France and Britain, and relied instead on repression imposed by the military and the police. Mark Mazower writes:

> in most of Europe by the mid-1930s – outside the northern fringe – liberalism looked tired, the organized Left had been smashed and the sole struggles over ideology and governance were taking place within the Right – among authoritarians, traditional conservatives, technocrats and radical right-wing extremists. Only France continued its civil war between Left and Right through the 1930s, until that was ended by Vichy. But civil war had already erupted briefly in Austria (in 1934) and more protractedly in Spain before ending in right-wing triumph. In Italy, Central Europe and the Balkans, the Right held sway. Regimes varied from the royal dictatorship of King Carol in Romania, through the military men ruling Spain, Greece and Hungary to the one-party states in Germany and Italy.[11]

We see thus a spectrum of reaction, the different forms of what Nicos Poulantzas calls the 'exceptional capitalist state' (for example fascism, military dictatorship, and Bonapartism).[12] Leon Trotsky, the great Marxist observer, alongside Gramsci, of this period in European politics (alas, their twin victimization, by Stalin and Mussolini respectively, meant that both lost the ability to influence events) had something similar in mind when he described Bonapartism as a regime of military–police dictatorship. As soon as the struggle of two social strata – the haves and the have-nots, the exploiters and the exploited – reaches its highest tension, the conditions are established for the domination of bureaucracy, police, soldiery. The government becomes 'independent' of society ... if two forks are stuck symmetrically into a cork, the latter can stand even on the head of a pin. That is precisely the schema of Bonapartism.[13]

Trotsky was thinking of the final governments of the Weimar Republic in Germany. Between 1930 and 1933, chancellors Heinrich Brüning, Franz von Papen, and General Kurt von Schleicher sought successively to manage the economic crisis mainly by implementing austerity, so as to appease the banks; and to this purpose they used President Paul von Hindenburg's emergency powers to rule by decree, thereby bypassing the Reichstag.[14] Parliamentary government became a façade behind which bureaucrats and generals called the shots, in close alliance with the big bankers and landowners. This amounted to counter-revolution *from above*: forcibly imposing on the mass of the population (workers, peasants, and petty proprietors) a capitalist solution to the economic crisis with the help of the repressive apparatuses of the state.

The prevalence of authoritarian right-wing regimes reflected the fact that, as Mayer puts it, 'down to 1914', and indeed for another twenty-five years in Central Europe, 'the interwoven landed and service nobilities throughout Europe continued to be dominant in the ruling classes', despite the continent-wide financial dominance of the advanced liberal capitalisms of Britain and France.[15] Counter-revolution therefore came as an extension of the political and social order that existed at the time.

Ways of escape

Fascism, by contrast, represented counter-revolution *from below*. It emerged only rarely in its pure form (in Spain, for example, the fascist Falange was subordinated to Franco's military dictatorship), in Italy under Mussolini and in Germany under Hitler, effectively outflanking the authoritarian conservatives. It is not an accident that, aside from liberal France, which managed to fend off fascism until the imposition of the Vichy regime after the military defeat of 1940, Germany and Italy were the two most industrialized economies in continental Europe. But both societies were shaped by the uneven and combined development of global capitalism, experiencing what Ernst Bloch called, in the mid-1930s, the 'contemporaneity of the non-contemporaneous' – the coexistence of social forms that represented different historical times: the steel mills of the Ruhr or the car plants of Turin alongside the Junker landed estates of East Prussia or the great latifundia of southern Italy.[16]

Robert Paxton has given a superb account of fascism, which he defines as 'a form of political behaviour marked by obsessive preoccupation with community decline, humiliation, or victimhood and by compensatory cults of unity, energy, and purity, in which a mass-based party of committed nationalist militants, working in uneasy but effective collaboration with traditional elites, abandons democratic liberties and pursues with redemptive violence and without ethical or legal restraints goals of internal cleansing and external expansion'.[17]

This definition is consistent with the classical Marxist account of fascism, provided above all by Trotsky.[18] The dynamic of fascism, particularly in the purest case of National Socialism, involved especially these features:

(1) a political style that promised a revolutionary rupture with the present;
(2) an ideology that counterposed a racially defined 'national community' to destructive outsiders – crucially 'cosmopolitan Jewish finance capital' – and was characterized by virulent anti-Marxism;
(3) the construction of a mass movement with a paramilitary wing recruited especially from the petty bourgeoisie (small shopkeepers, petty producers more generally, the relatively privileged white-collar 'salariat' of the inter-war years, professionals);
(4) a tendency to radicalization that found its fullest expression in the pursuit of imperial conquest and in the wartime Nazi attempt to exterminate the Jews of Europe.

At the time, Bloch recognized in Nazi ideology the mass appeal of a kind of pseudo-revolutionary romantic anti-capitalism, which rejected modernity in the name of an idealized past:

> Apart from nastiness and speechless brutality, apart from stupidity and panic-stricken deceivability, which are illustrated by every hour and every word of the Germany of terror, there is an element of an older, romantic contradiction to capitalism, which misses things in

present-day life and longs for something vaguely different ... The temporal alienation of this contradiction facilitates both the deception and the pathos of 'revolution' and reaction at the same time.[19]

Plainly what Paxton calls 'traditional elites' – capitalists, landowners, generals, and bureaucrats – would not lightly contemplate the idea of parties of this kind coming to power. They were only prepared to take the risk of supporting them *in extremis*, when confronted with a working class that, although weakened by defeat (the failure of the German Revolution of 1918–23 and of the Italian factory occupations of September 1920), still retained too much organization and militancy for a Bonapartist 'regime of military–police dictatorship' (in Trotsky's characterization: see pp. 19–20) to deal with it effectively.

The fascist mass movements, fused and driven by a reactionary utopian ideology, provided the impetus and the capacity for extreme violence that were needed to crush and atomize the organized working class. John Foot writes that, in the violent rampage of the Fascist *squadristi* – the Blackshirts – against the left and trade unionists in 1920–22, '[a] novel and highly effective form of political activity was being experimented with for the first time – a *militia party*'.[20] But, it bears emphasizing, both the Italian Fascists and the German Nazis came to power thanks to the support, however reluctant or self-deluding, of the ruling classes. Neither Mussolini nor Hitler won a free election, but they came to office constitutionally, although they then moved to crush the left and to concentrate power in their hands. Fascism in power thus combines counter-revolution from above with counter-revolution from below.

The greatness of Trotsky's writings on Germany lies in his understanding of the specificity of fascism amid the spectrum of bourgeois reaction and of the mortal threat that fascism represented to the workers' movement. But his insight into the dynamics of fascism stopped with the seizure of power. To some extent, this reflected his acute understanding of the conflicts between fascist parties and the ruling class, combined with the assumption that such conflicts would be resolved in favour of the latter: 'German fascism, like Italian fascism, raised itself to power on the backs of the petty bourgeoisie, which it turned into a battering ram against the organisations of the working class and the institutions of democracy. But fascism in power is least of all the rule of the petty bourgeoisie. On the contrary, it is the most ruthless dictatorship of monopoly capital.'[21]

Trotsky predicted that, 'as the Italian example shows, fascism leads in the end to a military–bureaucratic dictatorship of the Bonapartist type'.[22] In fact, as I pointed out some years ago, 'far from finishing up as a military dictatorship, the Nazi regime massacred the generals after the July 1944 plot' to assassinate Hitler. As I argued, the relationship between National Socialism and German capital 'is best characterized as a conflictual partnership. It was based on a limited convergence of interests between the Nazis and sections of German capital (particularly those associated with heavy industry) who shared common objectives, notably the destruction of the organized working class and a[n] imperial programme of expansion into the East.'[23] In his important study of the Nazi economy, Adam Tooze describes the relationship in the same terms: 'Partners: The Regime and German Business'.[24] He notes the benefits that Nazi rule brought to German capital thanks to the crushing of organized labour, the reassertion of the rights of management, and the rearmament boom:

> profits were rising rapidly after 1933 and this opened attractive future prospects for German corporate management. At first the profits were used to undo the damage done by the Depression. Then from the late 1930s onwards, they financed an extraordinary investment boom such as had never before been seen in German industrial history. What Hitler's regime positively enabled German business to do was to recover from the disastrous recession, to accumulate capital and to engage in high-pressure development of certain key technologies: the technologies necessary to achieve the regime's twin objectives of increased self-sufficiency (autarchy) and rearmament.[25]

The radicalization of the Nazis in power was driven by a variety of considerations: ideology, namely what Daniel Guérin calls '"anti-capitalist" capitalism';[26] Hitler's objective of waging a war of imperial expansion; competition between different parts of the regime; and the imperatives of economic management amid a global depression characterized by the fragmentation of the world market. But one aspect of this radicalization was the construction of a considerable state capitalist sector, which simultaneously supported and constrained private capital. Moreover, the relentless pursuit of the extermination of the European Jews, which in no way corresponded to the needs of German capital or to the priorities of waging a two-front war, highlighted the political autonomy of the Nazi regime; this autonomy was expressed particularly in the growing power of the ideologically driven police–military bureaucracy that was the Schutzstaffel (SS).[27]

The dynamic behind what drove National Socialism into the Second World War was not some personal idiosyncrasy of Hitler's. The three 'nation-empires' that formed the core of the Axis – Germany, Italy, and Japan (where the expansionist wing of the military substituted for the fascist movements dominant in the other two) – all sought 'national autonomy, which meant in effect releasing the nation from a situation in which its development seemed limited or framed by the existing international order – "Great power intervention and oppression" as one Japanese pamphlet put it'.[28] All three believed that they had been cheated at the Paris Peace Conference at the end of the First World War – Germany because it had been punished by the victors, Italy and Japan because they had been denied what they regarded as their share of the spoils. Meanwhile, the empires of the two victorious European liberal powers, Britain and France, reached their greatest territorial expansion, notably thanks to their dismantling of the Ottoman Empire and sharing out of its Arab possessions.[29]

The financial crash of 1929–31 and the austerity measures demanded by economic orthodoxy to maintain the gold standard undermined the credibility and effectiveness of the liberal international order that had been constructed in Paris. Territorial expansion therefore became more attractive, for example to some sections of German capital.[30] To quote Overy again,

> Empire-building was designed to transcend the limitations imposed by the existing global economic and territorial structures by acquiring additional 'living space' to cope with population pressure and land shortages, securing access to resources of raw materials and food, and establishing an economic bloc where trade and investment would be controlled by the imperial centre rather than the business community. The three states shared a growing commitment to state planning, and a hostility to the Western model of liberal capitalism and the Western values that sustained it.[31]

Territorial expansion meshed with more immediate economic priorities in the case of the National Socialist regime: in 1936–7 the Nazi rearmament boom was threatened by chronic scarcities of foreign exchange and raw materials, limits that Hitler believed could be overcome only through annexation and conquest.[32] This drive to an economic autarky premised on imperial expansion was reinforced by fears of the kind of blockade the Entente powers had imposed on Germany and its allies during the First World War.[33] And the stunning military successes that Germany and Japan enjoyed in the early stages of the Second World War allowed them to construct sizeable but happily short-lived empires in the territories they had seized.[34]

Dealing with the three outsiders' territorial ambitions was hugely complicated by the Russian Revolution, which meant that one of the traditional Great Powers was now hostile to the existing economic and political system and accordingly shunned by the other leading states. As the international crisis escalated in the second half of the 1930s, British and French policymakers were unable seriously to contemplate an alliance with the Soviet Union. As Jonathan Haslam puts it, '[r]ivalry between the great powers after 1917 was acutely affected by a battle of ideas that reached above and beyond the normal preoccupations of diplomatic practitioners accustomed to the European states system from 1815 to 1914. In this sense, the twentieth century more closely resembled the era of the wars of religion of early modern Europe or of the French Revolution than that of the nineteenth-century Concert of Europe.' [35]

Accordingly, Hitler was able to mobilize a European coalition of reaction to mount his climactic act of aggression, the invasion of the Soviet Union on 22 June 1941. As Mayer puts it, 'the Nazis loudly proclaimed that the war against Soviet Russia was a *Glaubenskrieg* [war of faiths] against "Judeobolshevism", which initially earned them considerable sympathy and support among conservatives, reactionaries, and fascists throughout the Continent'.[36] This anti-communist crusade pitched Europe into the depths of barbarism, as the Nazis seized the opportunity to exterminate Jews, Sinti, and Roma and to line up other 'inferior races' for the same fate. But in the end, of course, the three nation-empires were defeated by the alliance, previously shunned by European policymakers, between the last liberal powers left standing – the United States and Britain – and the Stalin regime in the Soviet Union.

The Allied invasion of Italy prompted Mussolini's own colleagues, in alliance with the old regime represented by King Victor Emmanuel III, to remove Mussolini in July 1943 (though he was rescued and propped up until April 1945 by the Nazis), while National Socialism perished with the invasion and parcellation of Germany, the physical destruction of the German military and much of the country's infrastructure, and the death of its main leaders. As Paxton succinctly puts it, 'the Italian and German fascist regimes drove themselves off a cliff in their quest for ever headier successes'.[37]

Gramsci argues that the 'organic crisis' of the capitalist mode of production that exploded during the First World War provoked not only the October Revolution and the attempts to imitate it elsewhere but also efforts from the side of capital to reconstruct the system in order to allow it to survive. Gramsci uses the concept of passive revolution to understand these responses. Passive revolution consists in 'molecular changes which in fact progressively modify the pre-existing composition of forces, and hence become the matrix of new changes'. The process involves attempts to defend the existing capitalist mode of production and avert its overthrow by incorporating some of the pressures to socialize the productive forces, all of which reflects 'the necessity for the "thesis" [capitalism] to achieve its full development, up to the point where it would even succeed in incorporating part of the antithesis itself [socialist revolution] – in order, that is, not allow itself to be "transcended" in the dialectical opposition'.[38]

In the era of counter-revolution and global depression between the world wars, passive revolution took two main forms: fascism, which combined elements of economic intervention with the systematic repression of the workers' movement; and the complex that Gramsci calls 'Americanism and Fordism'. The latter reached its climax with Franklin Roosevelt's New Deal – the reorganization of liberal capitalism, which had failed in Europe, on the basis of mass production and the transformation of proletarian subjectivity in order to accommodate its rhythms.[39] Looking back from the 1970s, Louis Althusser offers a somewhat similar take. One contemporary left-wing intellectual, Paul Mason, has called for a return to the Popular Front strategy pursued by communist parties in the mid-1930s of constructing alliances between the organized working class and the liberal bourgeoisie. Interestingly, in the light of this advocacy, Althusser sees the resulting governments in France and Spain as contributing to the reorganization of capitalism that was needed to overcome the Great Depression and the broader crisis of imperialism:

> The most extraordinary thing in this whole unconscious process, however, is the way in which imperialism has succeeded in overcoming its own crisis. ... a very precise policy of economic exploitation: monopolistic concentration, a close-knit alliance between the state and the monopolies, central direction of the economy (of production and circulation) in the service of the monopolies, and the like. What

occurred in this way in the fascist states' economies ... also occurred in the popular democratic states, but *under the domination of counterposed political forms* ... The Popular Fronts, much like (important differences notwithstanding) Roosevelt's New Deal, thus served as instruments in the most gigantic process of monopolistic concentration in history – unintentionally, of course.[40]

There is, moreover, an important qualification to be made of Gramsci's analysis, which he wrote in 1933, when both the Depression and these political responses were at an early stage. He could not know that neither fascism nor the New Deal were to overcome the economic crisis. It wasn't just Germany that grappled with economic difficulties; recovery in the United States was punctured by a sharp recession in 1937–8. The resolution came only with the Second World War, in which liberal imperialism in the shape of the United States defeated fascist imperialism. J. K. Galbraith put it pithily: 'The Great Depression of the thirties never came to an end. It merely disappeared in the great mobilization of the forties.'[41] Fascism may have been a response to the greatest capitalist crisis, but it wasn't a solution.

The persistence of imperialism

The Second World War was thus a global struggle between two rival imperialist projects that US 'corporate liberalism' – to use Kees van der Pijl's formula – won.[42] One of its main consequences was the weakening of the European colonial empires, all but one of which collapsed in the two decades after 1945 (the exception, Portugal's African colonies, survived until the Carnation Revolution of 25 April 1974). For Overy, the defeat of the Axis powers, followed as it was by decolonization, marked the end not just of the Thirty Years War but of the imperialism that had precipitated it: 'territorial empires that involved direct subjugation and loss of sovereignty of the indigenous population ... The hegemonic status enjoyed by the two superpowers was not based on this form of territorial empire and it has not been revived since 1945.'[43]

Overy thus equates imperialism with formal territorial empires that are based on conquest and annexation. But this leaves out of account what John Gallagher and Ronald Robinson famously call the 'imperialism of free trade': at the height of its power in the mid-nineteenth century, Britain used its competitive manufacturing industries and the financial supremacy of the City of London, underpinned in particular by the Royal Navy, to dominate economically regions that were not formally part of its empire – for example southern China, the US South, and much of Latin America.[44] US Open Door imperialism in the twentieth and twenty-first centuries is in many ways a generalization of this type of liberal informal empire: open global markets would allow US capital and commodities to flow freely, enabling US corporations to dominate thanks to their superior organization and their workers' high productivity, reinforced after 1945 by Washington's central role in managing the international financial system and by the military muscle of the Pentagon and its vast global network of bases.[45]

Thus imperialism – a historically evolving system, like capitalism itself – did not end in 1945 but entered a second phase, that of superpower imperialism (1945–91). Europe and, to a significant extent, the world were partitioned between two rival superpowers, each with its bloc of allied and dependent states; the Soviet Union constructed its own 'informal empire' in Central and Eastern Europe on the basis of military conquest and its client states' largely enforced adoption of monopolistic rule by the local communist parties. The Cold War era allowed the United States to brigade together the advanced capitalist states in an institutionalized liberal capitalist international order; the high levels of arms spending required by the global contest with the Soviet Union made possible the longest and most sustained boom in the history of capitalism, between 1948 and 1973.[46]

The Cold War, moreover, encouraged the US-sponsored reconstruction of capitalism in continental Europe and Japan; this helps to explain why the socioeconomic base of the Axis regimes largely survived, and indeed flourished, in the era of corporate liberalism. In West Germany, for example, the business dynasties that had fed Hitler's war economy and profited hugely from the Aryanization of Jewish wealth and the exploitation of slave labour re-emerged as pillars of the Federal Republic during the postwar *Wirtschaftswunder* (economic miracle) and beyond.[47]

The most important difference from the classical imperialism of 1870–1945 was that the Soviet Union and the other Stalinist states were state capitalist societies.[48] Thanks to the disintegration and demoralization of the working class that had made the 1917 Revolution, a new party bureaucracy crystallized and usurped state power, which it used to control the means of production. The dynamic of capital accumulation was imposed through geopolitical competition from without: consumption was constrained in order to concentrate investment in the heavy industries that sustained the Soviet Union's military power against its western rivals. The Great Terror that unfolded in the second half of the 1930s reflected the strains of Russia's rapid forced industrialization, which involved the expropriation of the peasantry and a leap in the rate of exploitation; it replaced the revolutionary generation of 1917 with a more pliable managerial elite.

The Stalinist regimes presided over largely closed national economies that were only partially integrated in the world market, which was dominated by western capitalism. Meanwhile the triumph of the struggle for decolonization between the late 1940s and early 1960s – at the price of tremendous, costly struggles in countries as different as China, Vietnam, Kenya, and Algeria – created what proved to be the main terrain for superpower competition, leading to major proxy wars between the United States and the Soviet Union in Korea (1950–3) and Afghanistan (1979–89). C. Wright Mills captures the resulting polarization of the international system in slightly hyperbolic but vivid terms:

> In the two superstates the history-making means of power are now organized. Their facilities of violence are absolute; their economic systems are increasingly autarchic; politically, each of them is increasingly a closed world; and in all these fields their bureaucracies are world-wide. These two continental behemoths of our epoch have gone 'beyond nationalism' to become centres of blocs of previous sovereign power. They have relegated the European scatter of nations to subsidiary importance; they regulate the pace, and often even the possibility of industrial development among the underdeveloped peoples of the world. International power, in short, has been centralized.[49]

Nevertheless, illustrating Althusser's conception of differential temporality, the dialectic of revolution and counter-revolution, so dominant in the first half of the twentieth century, was still at work during the long boom and its aftermath. But it was overdetermined by Cold War geopolitics. In Hungary in 1956, Soviet troops ultimately crushed the popular revolution initiated by youth and workers. The Cuban Revolution of 1958–9 overturned a dictatorship that presided over a US semi-colony, but, to survive the blockade and attempts at counter-revolution organized by Washington, its leaders turned to the Soviet Union for military protection and economic support. In Indonesia in the autumn of 1965, an abortive left-wing coup led to the slaughter by the army and right-wing militias of 500,000 Communist Party militants – an act that even the Central Intelligence Agency (CIA) (which, along with the rest of the US government, backed and facilitated the repression) described as 'as one of the worst mass murders of the 20th century'.[50] The CIA was also implicated, along with the Brazilian junta, in the military coup that brought down the left-wing Popular Unity coalition in Chile in September 1973. In the second half of 1976, peasant and student movements in Thailand were crushed by the army and right-wing paramilitaries.[51] The greatest European workers' movement of these years, Solidarność in Poland in 1980–1, was crushed by yet another military coup, this time backed by Moscow.[52] In counterpoint, the defeat of the United States in Vietnam represented the climax of the anticolonial movement and was rapidly followed by another severe blow to US hegemony: the Iranian Revolution of 1978–9.[53]

In the late 1960s and early 1970s the advanced capitalist states experienced a form of youth radicalization that spilled over into mass strikes carried out by a working class strengthened by a generation of full employment. But the southern European peak of this radicalization in the mid-1970s was contained mainly through different kinds of reformism rather than the kind of coercive interventions seen in Indonesia and Chile.[54] The breakdown of the boom amid stagflation, worker insurgency, and the Vietnam War provoked the neoliberal turn at the end of the 1970s (see Chapter 3). As a result, the postcolonial states were forced to accept market discipline and their politico-economic subordination to the US-dominated liberal international liberal order – a process facilitated by Washington's counter-revolutionary campaign against leftist regimes in the South.[55] This order became genuinely global after the collapse of 'real socialism' in the Soviet Union and its client states in 1989–91. *Pace* Fukuyama, however, history not only continued, but rushed us towards new catastrophes.

2

The Destruction of Nature

The future is here

The last age of catastrophe represented the climax (to date) of humankind's capacity for violence. One study finds that 45 'high-fatality wars' between 1899 and 1978 'resulted in 86 million fatalities (of which World War II accounted for about 50 million)'.[1] Another estimates that 73 per cent of the 150 million or more war-related deaths since 3000 BC took place in the twentieth century.[2] The twenty-first century has already seen plenty of organized violence, notably in the wars the United States has waged for the Greater Middle East and in the other wars that have raged chiefly in various parts of Africa and now in Ukraine. But the main driving force of catastrophe today is the progressive destruction of nature by fossil capitalism.

As we have seen, the triumph of liberal imperialism over its fascist rivals helped to unleash, in the context of the Cold War, the greatest and most sustained boom in the history of capitalism (1948–73). But the mid-twentieth century is also the historical moment when what Earth system scientists call the Great Acceleration took off.[3] Their famous hockey stick graphs record the levels of CO_2, stratospheric ozone, marine fish capture, tropical forest loss, methane, ocean acidification, nitrous oxide, surface temperature, shrimp aquaculture, land domestication, coastal nitrogen, and terrestrial biosphere degradation, all starting to shoot up around 1950. These figures provide the basis for proposals to recognize a new geological epoch, the Anthropocene, to mark the extent to which human activities are now changing the rest of nature.

According to Ian Angus, 'capitalism's worst depression and most destructive war set the stage for the economic and social changes that have pushed the Earth System into a new and dangerous epoch'.[4] The gigantic military machines that clashed in the Second World War ran on oil. Japan's attack on Pearl Harbor was prompted by President Franklin Roosevelt's decision to cut off the supply of oil in summer 1941. The disastrous German siege of Stalingrad in 1942–3 was motivated by Hitler's preoccupation with seizing the oil wells of the Caucasus. The emergence of the United States as the greatest military power in history depended on its control of vast oil reserves; at the end of the war, Washington drove to extend that control by displacing Britain as the dominant imperial state in the Middle East, although until the early 1970s it relied on waning British military power to maintain order in the region.[5]

Washington's postwar Marshall Plan for European economic reconstruction was used to encourage a shift to the US pattern of oil-based energy consumption, allowing US companies to supply much of the fuel for the Long Boom. According to Helen Thompson, 'perhaps around 20% of Marshall aid went in one way or another on oil payments'.[6] As Angus puts it, '[t]he Great Acceleration would not have been possible without cheap oil – as a commodity in its own right, as the raw material for plastics and other petrochemicals, as the enabler for high-energy manufacturing processes, and above all as the fuel for hundreds of millions of cars, trucks, ships, and planes'.[7] The climax of the first age of catastrophe was thus the antechamber to the present one.

Forty years later, the very dangerous effects of the Great Acceleration, above all the impact of rising CO_2 emissions on global temperatures, were sufficiently visible for the United Nations to establish the Intergovernmental Panel on Climate Change (IPCC) in 1988. This was followed in 1992 by the Earth Summit in Rio de Janeiro, which agreed on the UN Framework Convention on Climate Change, thereby initiating the tortuous negotiating process punctuated by successive conferences of the parties (COPs), most recently in Sharm el-Sheikh in Egypt in November 2022. Another thirty years on, it is clear that this process is a complete failure.[8] CO_2 emissions have risen by 60% since 1990. As Andreas Malm puts it, 'the more knowledge there is of the consequences, the more fossil fuels are burnt'.[9] The latest IPCC report on the physical evidence for climate change, published in August 2021, starkly warns: 'Global warming of 1.5°C and 2°C will be exceeded during the 21st century unless deep reductions in CO_2 and other greenhouse gas emissions occur in the coming decades.'[10] Even on its most optimistic scenario, where global warming is kept to 1.5%, the report predicts more extreme weather events – heatwaves, storms, and droughts.

The *Financial Times* quotes a study published in *Science* in September 2021, which found that 'people born in 2020 would experience between a two- and sevenfold increase in extreme weather events during their lifetimes, particularly heatwaves, compared with people born in 1960'.[11] As these studies were published, wildfires were raging in the US Pacific Northwest and in Greece. Indeed, 2021 was the fourth-warmest year on record for the United States, which 'suffered 20 severe natural disasters that inflicted damage costing more than $145bn, according to the US National Oceanic and Atmospheric Administration'.[12] A subsequent IPCC report on the impact of climate change (published the same day that Vladimir Putin announced he was activating Russia's nuclear forces) estimated that between 3.3 and 3.6 billion people live in 'contexts that are highly vulnerable to climate change'. This vulnerability 'is higher in locations with poverty, governance challenges and limited access to basic services and resources' and is aggravated by injustices 'linked to gender, ethnicity, low income or combinations thereof'.[13]

The imminence of climate catastrophe has been expressed vividly in a widely downloaded paper by the British academic Jem Bendell. He proposes that 'we consider the implications of it being too late to avert a global environmental catastrophe in the lifetimes of people alive today'. Bendell argues that we must do this because,

> unfortunately, data collected since [2014] is often consistent with non-linear changes to our environment. Non-linear changes are of central importance to understanding climate change, as they suggest both that impacts will be far more rapid and severe than predictions based on linear projections and that the changes no longer correlate with the rate of anthropogenic carbon emissions. In other words – 'runaway climate change'.[14]

Non-linear processes are characteristic of complex systems where change doesn't always take the form of gradual increases, but can be self-reinforcing and therefore accelerating.[15] The warming of the Arctic is an example. This is a consequence of rising temperatures; but, by reducing the amount of ice sheet that reflects back the rays of the sun, it speeds up global warming, thus leading to further reductions.

But the warming of the polar region could also release methane – a much more powerful climate gas than CO_2 – which is currently trapped in surface or subsea permafrost. The scariest example Bendell gives is of a 2010 study that warns 'how the warming of the Arctic could lead to a speed and scale of methane release that would be catastrophic to life on Earth through atmospheric heating of over 5 degrees within just a few years of such a release'.[16]

It is, however, not an individual study but the accumulation of evidence that comes from different sources and covers different areas – for example the destruction of biodiversity, or the effects of rising temperatures and sea levels on agriculture – that prompts Bendell to conclude:

> The evidence before us suggests that we are set for disruptive and uncontrollable levels of climate change, bringing starvation, destruction, migration, disease and war ... The words I ended the previous paragraph with may seem, subconsciously at least, to be describing a situation to feel sorry about as we witness scenes on TV or online. But when I say starvation, destruction, migration, disease and war, I mean in your own life. With the power down, soon you wouldn't have water coming out of your tap. You will depend on your neighbours for food and some warmth. You will become malnourished. You won't know whether to stay or go. You will fear being violently killed before starving to death.[17]

A study by the US Army arrives at quite similar conclusions, pointing to the severe risks that climate change poses to the United States itself in the relatively short term (mid-twenty-first century). It warns that '[m]ost of the critical infrastructures identified by the Department of Homeland Security are not built to withstand' the increased frequency of extreme weather events. The ageing US energy grid is particularly vulnerable:

> If the power grid infrastructure were to collapse, the United States would experience significant
>
> - loss of perishable foods and medications
> - loss of water and wastewater distribution systems
> - loss of heating/air conditioning and electrical lighting systems
> - loss of computer, telephone, and communications systems (including airline flights, satellite networks, and GPS services)

- loss of public transportation systems
- loss of fuel distribution systems and fuel pipe-lines
- loss of all electrical systems that do not have back-up power.[18]

Fossil capitalism and the rush to the abyss

This amounts to the collapse of the conditions of modern life as they have evolved in the twentieth and early twenty-first centuries, leading in all probability to large-scale mortality. So what has brought us to this pass? A group of scholars working on climate change recently concluded: 'In various guises and to differing degrees, the centralization of power and the privileges that accompany it have coalesced around a particular worldview' that has 'evolved into a wider global Zeitgeist whereby development and progress are reduced to economic growth and defined by increasingly narrow financial metrics and indices'.[19]

But the source of this Zeitgeist can be identified more precisely. In his important study *Fossil Capital*, Malm argues that British manufacturing industry's switch from water power to coal-fired steam in the early nineteenth century occurred in the context of the structural crisis that industrial capitalism experienced in Britain from the mid-1820s onwards. This crisis was solved through technical change (for example, the self-acting mule) that undermined the collective power of skilled workers. Water power was cheaper than steam, but immobile; using steam to run the new machines gave capital much more flexibility – in particular by allowing it to place production in cities with large concentrations of unemployed, whose bargaining power was weak. 'Steam won because it augmented the power of some over others.'[20] Using steam also required much less cooperation among capitalists, thereby avoiding the collective action problems involved in large-scale water projects.

The switch to steam power was the point at which the carbon economy became embedded, humankind 'only developing the fossil economy in the blip of the *last two centuries*'. And even though oil overtook coal as the prime source of energy in the twentieth century, coal has played a major role in the industrialization of China in the last generation. More generally, Malm contends,

> where capital goes, emissions will immediately follow. This is the class content of carbon leakage. ... the stronger global capital has become, the more rampant the growth of CO_2 emissions – indeed, one might argue that the decisive capitalist victory in the long twentieth-century struggle with labour was crowned by the post-2000 rush towards

catastrophic global warming. Counting from 1870 to 2014, a fourth of all cumulative CO_2 omissions were belched out in the last fifteen years of the period.[21]

The relentless rise in CO_2 omissions thus has its source in fossil capitalism.[22] As I have already noted, Marx argues that the capitalist mode of production is constituted by two antagonisms: the exploitation of wage labour by capital; and competition between individual capitals – what Robert Brenner has called 'the "vertical" (market and socio-political) relations between capitalists and workers' and 'the "horizontal" competition between firms that constitutes the capitalist system's economic mainspring'.[23] Malm stresses the first antagonism, but the second is also very important.

Capitalism is a system of competitive accumulation. Its individual units, typically firms but sometimes states, seek to maintain and, if possible, increase their profitability by introducing technical innovations that reduce their costs of production below those of their rivals. This leads to a process of concentration and centralization of capital, which results in economies' domination by larger and fewer firms. It also underlies the chronic tendency towards regular and disruptive economic crises (see Chapter 3). But the pressure to minimize costs also encourages firms to focus on whatever measures will increase profitability and to ignore or conceal the 'negative externalities' (in economists' jargon) generated by their investments, that is, the damage these may cause to their workers, to consumers, and to the broader social and physical environment. The ultimate criterion of capitalist success, the rate of profit, measures the return on the capital advanced to purchase machinery, raw materials, and so on and to employ workers. The damage that the investment may cause doesn't figure in these monetary calculations.

Climate change must be the biggest negative externality in human history. But the process of environmental destruction is intensified by capitalism's tendency to commodify nature, turning the earth itself and the resources it is host to into marketable assets. Marx diagnosed this process, at work in the capitalist agriculture of his day, including in the colonies.[24] The tendency has been greatly reinforced in the neoliberal era: the global reach of capital has been hugely extended at the same time as deregulation has relaxed restrictions on polluting activities, especially in the global South. The very remedies that have been implemented to extend the domain of price calculation and to quantify the costs of environment degradation – for example, through the development of carbon trading and through the concept of 'natural capital' – facilitate the further commodification of nature and expose the absurdity of applying cost–benefit analysis to processes that threaten the collapse of human civilization.[25]

Even if the severity of the threat is increasingly acknowledged, the 'horizontal' contradiction between capitals and states places huge obstacles in the way of addressing it. Thus efforts to reduce greenhouse gas emissions are mediated through what the climate scholars see as 'an international political–economic system that is based largely on state sovereignty and competition'.[26] The leading powers approach the problem from the perspective of their geopolitical positions and of the interests of the main firms domiciled in their territories.

The most powerful fossil fuel corporations (sectors such as oil, gas, coal, automotives, and chemicals) are based mainly in the United States, Europe, and East Asia. But states' access to energy diverges significantly. The United States approaches self-sufficiency, thanks to the emergence of the shale industry, which uses hydraulic fracking to extract oil and gas from bedrock – a profoundly negative development from an ecological point of view. Europe depends heavily on gas imported from Russia. Sizeable coal industries are important elements in China's and India's growth models, while the other biggest energy suppliers, Russia and Saudi Arabia, have of course a lot to lose from decarbonization and are military heavyweights in their regions. More fundamentally, every state has an interest in displacing onto others the costs of moving to a carbon-neutral economy. Finally, in climate negotiations the formal equality of states is undercut by the huge inequalities in power, particularly between the North and the South.

This was symbolized dramatically in the last session of the COP26 conference in Glasgow in November 2021. As the *Financial Times* explains,

> In the final hours of the summit, a plan to approve the COP26 text was thrown off track when India and China objected to the phrase about the 'phase out' of unabated coal power, referring to power plants that do not capture carbon dioxide emissions, as well as all fossil fuel subsidies.
>
> After a huddle between the US, EU and China, a compromise was reached on a pledge to phase 'down' rather than phase 'out' coal.
>
> But many vulnerable and small island nations objected to the weaker language, saying it would imperil their future by resulting in greater emissions and further global warming.[27]

Hence the perpetually repeated drama of hope and disappointment, at every COP. Nevertheless, the process of capitalist adaptation to climate change is already under way. On the one hand, the fossil fuel corporations remain central to the functioning of contemporary capitalism. Thus the major US banks – probably the most important single cluster of capitalist interests on the planet – are deeply implicated in financing fossil fuel investments. In 2019 a coalition of NGOs headed by the Rainforest Action Network produced a report showing that, since the December 2015 Paris Agreement, which was supposed to cut CO_2 emissions sufficiently to keep global temperatures from rising in this century by more than 2°C above pre-industrial levels, bank financing of fossil fuels steadily rose to $612 billion in 2016, $646 billion in 2017, and $654 billion in 2018. The 'worst banks', according to the report, are four US mammoths: JPMorgan Chase, Wells Fargo, Citi, and Bank of America. Barclays, at number six, is the top European bank on the list. JPMorgan Chase takes the lead in financing projects aimed at expanding the extraction of fossil fuels: it is the number one banker of tar sands oil, Arctic and ultra-deepwater oil and gas, and liquefied natural gas and the number two banker of fracking, just behind Wells Fargo.[28]

The activities of the biggest investment banks are the tip of a much larger iceberg. Carol Olson and Frank Lenzmann argue that the fossil fuel supply chain has become thoroughly financialized, as the shadow banking sector – hedge funds, private equity firms, and various kinds of investment fund much less regulated than conventional banks – is very active in speculative trading at the various stages of the process of extracting and distributing oil, gas, coal, and uranium, while oil and gas companies develop their own established 'banking, investment and/or commodity trading subsidiaries'.[29] Capitalism thus continues to be heavily invested in the fossil fuels industries, which lobby very effectively to defend their interests. The climate scholars note how the fossil fuel corporations have shifted their strategy without fundamentally changing the substance of their operations:

> Those opposing decarbonization are increasingly abandoning outright climate denial in favour of hedging strategies, such as diversifying operations to mitigate risks and insistently promoting gas as a transition fuel … the plans typically see significant and ongoing use of oil, and particularly gas (as well as renewable energy, biofuels, nuclear energy, and/or hydrogen), with high levels of emissions compensated through future carbon capture, use and storage, offsets (including afforestation [AF]), and other speculative negative emissions technologies (NETs).[30]

The sheer cynicism involved in all this is underlined by the *Guardian*'s revelation, in May 2022, of short-term expansion plans by oil and gas companies to invest, throughout the rest of the 2020s, in '195 carbon bombs, gigantic oil and gas projects that would each result in at least a billion tonnes of CO_2 emissions over their lifetimes, in total equivalent to about 18 years of current global CO_2 emissions'.[31] Moreover, a green transition would involve writing off the vast amounts of capital sunk in the oil and gas industry: a recent study estimates the value of assets that would be stranded by the policies required to keep global warming at no more than 2°C above pre-industrial levels (which would still involve very disruptive climate change) at $1.4 trillion. This would affect not merely fossil fuel industries but the entire financial system, via pension funds and the like.[32]

On the other hand, firms are responding to the official, sluggish efforts to move towards a net carbon neutral economy by exploring new opportunities for profit. This is easier for relatively new companies that are less heavily invested in the existing energy complex. The situation helps to explain the alignment between the US IT giants – the FAANGs (Facebook, Amazon, Apple, Netflix, and Google) – and Barack Obama's policy, resumed under Biden, of recognizing and managing climate change, although IT companies are heavy producers of CO_2 emissions through their server banks, as are, of course, Amazon's delivery vans. The drive to adapt also affects some of the fossil fuel corporations. The car industry continues to be a massive source of growing CO_2 emissions. But it is also under enormous pressure to restructure, partly because of the rapid growth of the Chinese market, but more fundamentally because of the efforts to develop electric and driverless cars. These efforts were spurred by the European diesel emissions scandal, when Volkswagen was revealed to have programmed its cars to pass official tests but emit far higher levels of nitrogen oxide on the road. This enormous technological transformation offers openings to new entrants – for example Tesla, Google, and now apparently Apple – into an industry long dominated by a handful of transnational giants.

Capitalism's adaptation to climate change also has profound geopolitical implications. The warming of the Arctic doesn't just threaten the future of humankind and of many other species; it opens this ocean to commercial traffic, resource extraction, and intensified military competition among the capitalist states that border on it.[33] More broadly, the intelligence website Stratfor argues that the shift to renewable energy will produce losers – major oil producers such as Saudi Arabia and

Russia. Yet there will also be winners, for example the United States and Germany – but also China:

> In the past decade, China has raced ahead to become the world's unrivalled leader in the manufacture of clean energy products, including solar cells and batteries – of which it makes more than half of the global supply. It is also the world's biggest miner and supplier of rare earth materials, biggest deployer of renewable energy capacity and biggest market for electric vehicles. The country has acquired substantial lithium and cobalt mines abroad to power its push toward renewable energy, while also investing in electric utilities around the world, including in Europe, Africa and South America.[34]

A central dimension of what is best described as the geo-economic struggle between the United States and China, on which Trump embarked but which Biden has continued, is Washington's effort to block Beijing's plans to upgrade its industries from low-wage manufacturing final assembly to hi-tech. This includes the new products crucial to a capitalism that adapts to climate change (see also Chapter 4).[35] Climate change is becoming normalized, integrated into the everyday functioning of the process of competitive accumulation that drives capitalism. Does this mean that the catastrophe foreshadowed by Bendell will be avoided? Absolutely not. In the first place, it is very unlikely that an economic system organized around the blind struggle between 'many capitals' (to use Marx's expression) can make a drastic change in economic priorities quickly and profoundly enough to head off a chaotic climate change. To a system inherently geared to the short term, the costs entailed seem too high; and there is also the fear that capitals based in a state that does take on these costs will be disadvantaged in comparison to their rivals elsewhere.

And fossil fuel interests remain very heavily entrenched, as we have seen, and are at the very core of the capitalist system. It is noteworthy that any disruption to the global economy seems to trigger a return to greater reliance on to the dirtiest fossil fuels. Thus the Chinese government reacted to the surge in natural gas prices and energy supply disruptions in 2021 by supporting an increase in coal mining and burning. Faced with the Ukraine War, Joe Biden sought to contain the rising oil price by encouraging Saudi Arabia and other Gulf producers to increase output and by demanding that the US shale industry increase drilling. Germany tried to compensate for the falling supplies of Russian gas by reopening coal-fired power stations.

Secondly, the natural processes unleashed by the CO_2 emissions generated under industrial capitalism may have already gone too far for any human intervention to stop them. This is where the feedback loops discussed earlier are so important, since they could drive climate change towards levels where human life in anything resembling the forms it has taken these past centuries may become unsustainable. The natural world – of which human societies are a part, but which vastly exceeds them – will have its own say in the outcome.

The plague years

The COVID-19 pandemic is a vivid illustration of the extent of humans' dependence on nature. This dependence is an important theme in the Marxist critique of political economy that has been recovered by John Bellamy Foster and others around the journal *Monthly Review*;[36] and this theme is also developed by ecosocialist feminists.[37] Marx himself calls the labour process at the basis of every social formation 'the appropriation of what exists in nature for the requirements of man. It is the universal condition for the metabolic interaction (*Stoffwechsel*) between man and nature, the everlasting nature-imposed condition of human existence'.[38] Drawing on the research of the great chemist Justus von Liebig, Marx argues that capitalist agriculture has increasingly destructive effects on nature. This reflects the way in which the capitalist process of production, driven by the self-expansion of capital, robs the worker of her labour and the earth of its resources: 'Capitalist production, therefore, only develops the techniques and the degree of combination of the social process of production by simultaneously undermining the sources of all wealth – the soil and the worker'.[39] Large-scale landownership

> produces conditions that provoke an irreparable rift [*einen unheilbaren Riß*] in the framework of social and natural metabolism prescribed by the natural laws of the soil. The result of this is a squandering of the vitality of the soil, and *trade carries this devastation far beyond the bounds of a single country* (Liebig).[40]

Thus Marx – and Engels, who sought to integrate the latest developments in the physical sciences into his unfinished *Dialectics of Nature* – saw humans as beings rooted in nature, with which they interacted through their labour. Mike Davis, however, criticizes them for tending to see solely humans as the active factor in this relationship: 'Marx and

Engels never speculated on the possibility that the natural conditions of production over the past two to three millennia might have been subject to directional evolution or epic fluctuation, or that climate therefore might have its own distinctive history, repeatedly intersecting and overdetermining a succession of different social formations.'[41]

This is a fruitful corrective, as Davis has shown in a series of studies that explore the catastrophes immanent in capitalism as it interacts with complex physical systems subject to non-linear change.[42] Here history happens at the intersection of two dynamic processes: the dialectics of human social formations and the fluctuations of physical systems.[43] Plagues are a good example, since they tend to involve both mutations in viruses and bacteria and changes in human and animal settlement patterns that, together, unleash pandemics. In a pioneering study on 'the history of humanity's encounters with infectious diseases', William McNeill observes that 'one can properly think of most human lives as caught in a precarious equilibrium between the microparasitism of disease organisms and the macroparasitism of large-bodied predators, chief among which have been other human beings'. His warning that 'it is always possible that some hitherto obscure parasitic organism may escape its accustomed ecological niche and expose the dense human populations that have become so conspicuous a feature of the earth to some fresh and perchance devastating mortality' has been amply confirmed since the circulation of the SARS-CoV-2 virus began to be detected in Wuhan in December 2019.[44]

COVID-19 has brought us close to the great pandemics of the past: the outbreaks of bubonic plague in the sixth and fourteenth centuries AD – the latter, known as the Black Death, may have killed 52 million people, 65 per cent of the population of Europe;[45] the 'massive demographic disaster' that afflicted the peoples of the Americas in the sixteenth century when the *conquistadores* brought Europe's endemic diseases with them;[46] and the so-called Spanish 'flu of 1918–19, which is estimated to have killed between 50 and 100m people.[47]

Even before the current pandemic, the classical historian Kyle Harper insisted that 'climate change and emerging infectious diseases have been an integral part of the human story all along'. In *The Fate of Rome*, he argues that the eclipse of Roman power between the fourth and the seventh centuries AD stemmed not from internal contradictions or from external pressures exerted by 'barbarian' peoples beyond the imperial frontiers, but from changes in the natural environment, notably an unfavourable shift in weather patterns and a series of plagues – and, among these, most devastatingly the first appearance in Europe of *Yersinia pestis*, the bacterium responsible for the bubonic plague, under Emperor Justinian in the 540s:

> The Romans built a giant, Mediterranean empire at a particular moment in the history of the climate epoch known as the Holocene – a moment suspended on the edge of tremendous natural climate change. Even more consequentially, the Romans built an interconnected, urbanized empire on the fringes of the tropics, with tendrils creeping across the known world. In an unintended conspiracy with nature, the Romans created a disease ecology that unleashed the latent power of pathogen evolution.[48]

Reading Harper's powerful narrative during the pandemic, I found it hard not to feel that *de te fabula narratur* – the story being told is about you. This is helped by brilliant rhetorical effects such as the description of Hunnic nomads, whose drought-induced move westwards in the late fourth century pushed other 'barbarian' peoples into the Roman Empire, as 'armed climate refugees on horseback'.[49] But Harper's argument has been subjected to searching scrutiny by a group of historians who identify serious weaknesses in how he describes and the interprets the textual and archaeological evidence he cites. They also criticize his approach theoretically, taxing him (and McNeill before him) with 'a strong tendency towards an environmental determinist perspective' that fails to take into account either social structures or human agency.[50]

The impact of the natural environment on human social formations is always mediated by the economic, political, and ideological structures that prevail among them. Marx's idea of a metabolism of labour and nature goes two ways. Harper stresses how the urban character of Roman society created dense population clusters that were particularly vulnerable to disease; Peter Brown, the great historian of Late Antiquity, described the Roman Empire as 'a world of cities'.[51] The Black Death unfolded between 1346 and 1353, in the context of the lengthy crisis of the feudal mode of production that developed around the end of the thirteenth century. After expanding robustly from around AD 1000 onwards, an economic system based on coercive extraction of rents, from the peasantry, by a ruling class of lords could no longer maintain the level of output to support the existing population. This led to ecological collapse and famine, both exacerbated by the lords' efforts to maintain their income by seizing land from one another (the Hundred

Years' War between England and France is a case in point).[52] It was a population weakened by this crisis that perished on an appalling scale as the bubonic plague spread.

Contemporary society has made its own fate to an even greater extent. This is true most obviously of climate change today, which is anthropogenic, that is, human made – more precisely, driven by the dominance of fossil capitalism, as we have seen. But it is also true of the COVID-19 pandemic, which may mark the first in a series of plagues made possible by the way in which industrialized agriculture facilitates the leap of pathogens from their traditional animal hosts to humans. The disastrous effects of modern agribusiness on both humans and the rest of nature have been diagnosed, notably by ecofeminists such as Vandana Shiva.[53]

In a notebook of the mid-1860s, Marx had already described as 'Disgusting!' the developing forms of intensive factory farming in Britain:

> In these prisons animals are born and remain there until they are killed off. The question is whether or not this system connected to the breeding system that grows animals in an abnormal way by aborting bones in order to transform them to mere meat and a bulk of fat – whereas earlier (before 1848) animals remained active by staying under free air as much as possible – will ultimately result in serious deterioration of life force?[54]

We know the answer better now. The continuing capitalist transformation of agriculture provides the context for the work of the Marxist epidemiologist Rob Wallace. He argues that the so-called livestock revolution – the mass production of poultry or pigs in industrial conditions that reduce genetic variation among animals and pack them densely together, thereby weakening genetic and logistical barriers to the spread of disease – in combination with the closely related destruction of the habitats of wild species that may harbour unknown pathogens created the conditions for the development of new pandemics, as was presaged by the SARS-CoV-1 outbreak in 2002–4.[55] Moreover, the different forms of destruction of nature interact. A new study finds that climate change is forcing hitherto isolated species to change habitat and to cluster together in areas of high human population density, thereby dramatically increasing the probability of 'zoonotic spillovers' of the kind that caused SARS-CoV-2 to spread from bats to humans via civet cats.[56]

One of the very interesting features of Wallace's analyses is that they involve precisely the kind of interaction of dynamic processes that I referred to earlier – in this case, the globalization of industrial agriculture (originating in North America, but now well entrenched in southern China, where both SARS and COVID-19 emerged) and the evolution of the extraordinarily Protean influenza virus:

> Even ignoring the routine violations of biosecurity and biocontainment built into the industrial livestock model, we must assimilate the impediment that eliminating the conditions under which many a microbe, influenza included, thrives only establishes niches for new and at times strange strains. If fastidiously sterile First World hospitals are routinely assaulted by drug-resistant pathogens, then feedlots turfed in shit, run by predatory agribusinesses minimizing margins in offshore hovels, stand no chance.
>
> Indeed, the problem of livestock pathogens was already locked in to a Nietzschean syllogism from the get-go. What kills many pathogens makes those left over stronger. The few with the weirdo mutation that lets the virus or bacterium survive a new threat now emerge to survive. Even the very notion of causality appears threatened, with cause and effect effectively reversed. How do we protect ourselves against influenzas and other pathogens that have evolved a counter-response over only the past week to any prophylaxis we could ever imagine?
>
> Influenza's phenotypic variation, generated at mind-boggling mutation rates (2.0×10^6 mutations per site per infectious cycle), embodies the choices with which the virus – if you'll excuse the anthropomorphism – can naturally select a solution to the problems it faces, including those it has yet to even encounter. Along with producing molecular exaptations, the mutations permit escape from learned immune T- and B-cell responses fixated on previous epitopes.
>
> By reassortment, that variation is multiplied at the broader genome level: influenza can trade whose genomic segments like card players on a Friday night. Both H5N1 and … H1N1 emerged as multiple reassortments from across many serotypes.[57]

Of course, it was SARS-CoV-2 that got us, not any form of 'flu. Both are 'single-stranded RNA viruses', though COVID's infamous spike proteins allow it to inject 'its RNA into the infected cell and uses host cell machinery to replicate its genome. Newly synthesized virus particles are then released to infect additional host cells.'[58] Moreover, coronaviruses 'are even more adept shape-shifters than orthomyxoviruses like influenza A', thanks to their facility for splicing together 'different parts of genes (coding for the same protein) from different species'.[59]

One of the most striking features of the pandemic has been the arms race that has developed between the virus and the vaccines; the latter were discovered and began to be produced in the course of 2020, the most successful ones being RNA-based. With billions of humans to play with, SARS-CoV-2 underwent a process of natural selection: new variants emerged with enhanced capabilities of infection, transmission, and immune escape. As I write, the latest variant is Omicron with its proliferating subvariants, but there are plenty more letters in the Greek alphabet awaiting customers. The discovery of Omicron in southern Africa in November 2021 was a particular shock, because this variant represented such a large number of mutations by comparison with strains such as Beta and Delta, which had prevailed earlier. One explanation is that it was incubated in an immuno-suppressed person whose system was too weak to clear the initial COVID infection. The *Financial Times* points out: 'More than half of the world's 37.7m HIV sufferers are in east and southern Africa. In South Africa alone, around 1.9m individuals have HIV that is undetected, untreated or poorly controlled, according to UNAIDs, the UN programme on HIV/Aids'.[60] Therefore this part of the world has a large concentration of immune-suppressed individuals.

Here, then, we return to the other element in the interaction between humankind and nature: the exploitive and competitive structures of the capitalist mode of production. The failure to address the HIV epidemic in southern Africa is one of the starkest examples of global health inequality in the past generation. If the explanation of Omicron's emergence just cited is correct, then the entire world is now paying the price. But in fact injustice is heaped upon injustice. The rapid development of a COVID-19 vaccine, in just 320 days, is a triumph of modern science. But the grossly unequal distribution of the vaccines, overwhelmingly in favour of the rich states of the North over the impoverished global South, is a stark reminder of how our relationship with the rest of nature is mediated by the prevailing social relations. When Omicron appeared, the number of people in high-income countries who had received booster shots was nearly twice that of people in low-income countries who had received two vaccines; 6 per cent of the population in Africa had had two doses, whereas in the G7 the proportion was 66 per cent (see Figure 2). As innumerable experts have pointed out, the failure to ensure that everyone is vaccinated gives scope for the emergence of new variants.

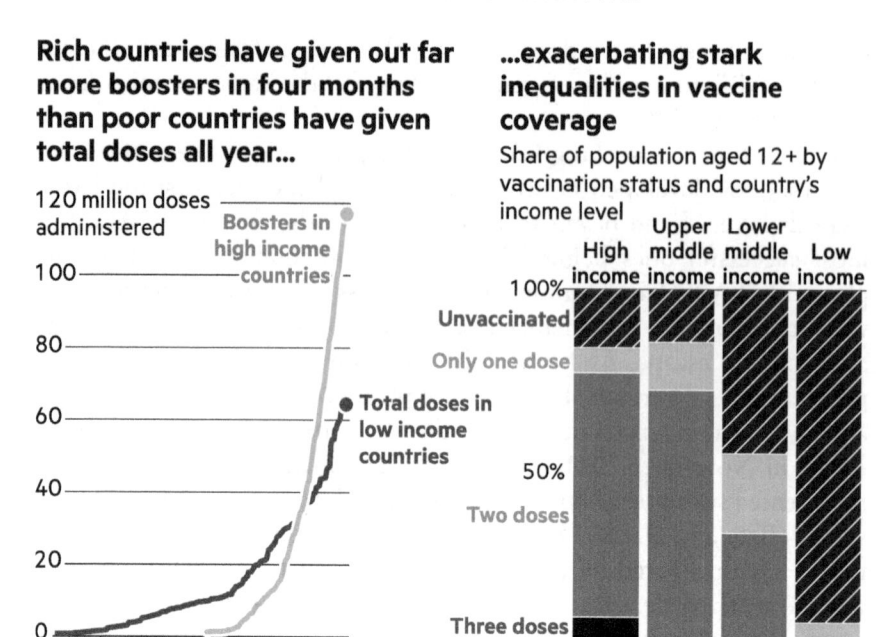

Figure 2 Vaccine inequality (2021)
Source: Hannah Kuchler, Donato Paolo Mancini, and David Pilling, 'The Inside Story of the Pfizer Vaccine: "A Once-in-an-Epoch Windfall"', *Financial Times*, 30 November 2021. Reproduced with permission.

The most successful vaccine, produced and marketed by Pfizer, was estimated to push the company's revenues to $80bn in 2021 – 'a once-in-an-epoch economic windfall', according to one investment banker.[61] Big pharma's highly profitable cornering of the vaccine market has been facilitated by Bill Gates. His COVID-19 ACT Accelerator has dominated the World Health Organization's efforts to distribute vaccines via COVAX and has enforced, in Alexander Zeitch's words, 'his unwavering commitment to drug companies' right to exclusive control over medical science and the markets for its products'. Thus, '[w]hen the director of Oxford's Jenner Institute had funny ideas about placing the rights to its COVAX-supported vaccine candidate in the public domain, Gates intervened. As reported by Kaiser Health News, "A few weeks later, Oxford – urged on by the Bill & Melinda Gates Foundation – reversed course [and] signed an exclusive vaccine deal with AstraZeneca that gave the pharmaceutical giant sole rights and no guarantee of low prices."'[62]

But the problem can't be reduced to the opportunity COVID-19 has given big pharma to amass yet more profits. Colin Kahl and Thomas Wright lament, contrasting the response to the pandemic with the high level of international cooperation among the leading states of both North and South in addressing the global financial crisis of 2007–9,

> Great power rivalry made the pandemic both more likely and harder to contain. The Chinese government was obsessed with regime survival at home and capitalizing on the pandemic to expand its influence abroad. Meanwhile, the Trump administration's decision to frame the international dimensions of its COVID policy almost exclusively through a competitive geopolitical lens eviscerated the prospects for a multilateral response. Every other nation, meanwhile, had to helplessly watch the superpower scrum while largely fending for themselves.[63]

This conflict can't be put down to Trump's idiosyncrasies, great though these undoubtedly are. Indeed, the intensity of US–China competition in 2020 was in many respects a consequence of the earlier global financial crisis, which accelerated the trend towards a global redistribution of economic power from Washington to Beijing. This would have made cooperation more difficult between the declining hegemon and its ascending peer competitor, whoever the two states' presidents might have been. We shall return to the US–China rivalry in Chapter 4. Here it is worth underlining how the divisions of the global capitalist class into competing firms and states impeded a rational and coordinated response in the case of the pandemic, just as it has done for many decades to climate change.

This is one reason why the end of the pandemic, constantly announced and eagerly awaited by humankind, has proved so elusive. 'Herd immunity' – immunizing, by vaccine or past infection, a sufficiently large proportion of the population to limit the further spread of the disease – is in any case a moving target when one is dealing with something as quicksilver as SARS-CoV-2. (A policy of achieving herd immunity as quickly as possible by allowing infections to rise led the British government under Boris Johnson disastrously to delay lockdown at the start of the pandemic, in March 2020.) But the persisting failure to concentrate resources on the task of vaccinating everyone in the world means that the pandemic is likely continue for a while, at the cost of yet more suffering. The epidemiologist Adam Kucharski warns that the build-up of immunity thanks to vaccination and infections will eventually cause the R number (which measures how many others an infectious person will spread the disease to) to fall below 1, leading to a 'honeymoon' period during which infections drop sharply only to rise again later, as immunity wanes and new variants emerge.[64]

Moreover, as Sarah Gilbert, one of the developers of the Oxford AstraZeneca vaccine, predicted in December 2021, 'this will not be the last time a virus threatens our lives and our livelihoods ... the truth is, the next one could be worse. It could be more contagious, or more lethal, or both.'[65] This underlines quite how short-sighted the various dismissals of the long-term significance of COVID-19 are – for example this supposed *bon mot* from the economist Jonathan Portes that reflects the obsession of British elites with the United Kingdom's relationship with the European Union: 'Covid is for Christmas, while Brexit is for life.'[66] The politicians' constant injunction that we learn to live with COVID may be fulfilled in more uncomfortable ways than they realize.

The permanent state of emergency

Thanks to the COVID-19 pandemic, we have a much clearer idea of how catastrophe will be managed. We have seen in particular the role played by expert bodies such as the Centers for Disease Control and Prevention (CDC) in the United States and the Scientific Advisory Group for Emergencies (SAGE) in the United Kingdom and their use of epidemiological models in guiding decisions to lock down or open up. To me, as to many others, how states managed the pandemic recalled Michel Foucault's lectures on biopolitics.[67] By biopolitics he means 'the attempt, starting with the eighteenth century, to rationalize the problems posed to governmental practice by phenomena characteristic of a set of living beings forming a population: health, hygiene, birth-rate, life expectancy, race' – phenomena that formed the context in which liberal political economy, first practised by the physiocrats in the latter decades of the *ancien régime* in France, was constituted.[68]

Although Foucault's troubled relationship with Marxism prevents him for articulating this clearly, biopolitics emerged in a context where the development of capitalist economic structures was destabilizing traditional social relationships and swelling often restive urban populations. At an early stage in the formulation of this analysis, Foucault argues that, 'corresponding to the rise of capitalism', there is '*lower-class or popular illegalism*'.[69] The response came partly through the emergence of 'the disciplines', practices that, through institutions such as the prison, sought to form 'docile subjects'.[70] But this was accompanied by the development of governmentality, 'the ensemble formed by institutions, procedures, analyses and reflections, calculations, and tactics that allow this very specific, albeit very complex, power that has the population as its target, political economy as its major form of knowledge, and apparatuses of security as its essential technical instrument'. With security, the aim is no longer to form the individual: 'individuals, the series of individuals, are no longer pertinent as the objective, but simply as the instrument, relay, or condition for obtaining something at the level of the population'. The problems afflicting the population that security seeks to address – for example, dearth and plague – are specifically urban: 'the fact of the town and legitimate sovereignty had to be reconciled'.[71]

In one particularly interesting passage, Foucault argues that the pursuit of security seeks the 'normalization' of the population:

> In the disciplines one started from a norm, and it was in relation to the training carried out with reference to the norm that the normal can be distinguished from the abnormal. Here, instead, we are having a plotting of the normal and the abnormal, of different curves of normality, and the operation of normalization consists in establishing an interplay between these different distributions of normality and [in] acting to bring the most unfavourable in line with the more favourable. So we have here something that starts from the normal and makes use of certain distributions considered to be, if you like, more normal than the others, or at any rate more favourable than the others. These distributions will serve as the norm. The norm is an interplay of different normalities.[72]

This description of how governmentality acts on distributions within a population now calls to mind the way states have sought, in response to COVID-19, to legitimize decisions to lock down and to require social distancing – or to retreat from such policies – on the basis of the epidemiological models constructed by their expert advisers. Modelling is a widespread scientific practice, which has been used successfully for the past hundred years or so to arrive at a better understanding of how diseases spread and contract. The modellers select variables that reflect the assumptions they make on the basis of (1) their knowledge of the particular virus or bacterium in play and of the characteristics and behaviour of the affected population, and (2) the relevant empirical data, which they use via statistical methods to plot various trajectories.[73]

'A model is a work of fiction', writes the philosopher of science Nancy Cartwright.[74] In other words, the modellers select and simplify in order to make their task of prediction feasible. Rob Wallace points to a deeper problem: 'The modelling of emergencies, however necessary, misses when and where to begin. Structural causes are as much part of the emergency. Including them helps us figure out how best to respond moving forward, beyond just restarting the economy that produced the damage.' He quotes the mathematical epidemiologist Roderick Wallace: 'Context counts for pandemic infection, and current political structures that allow multinational agricultural enterprises to privatize profits while externalizing and socializing costs must become subject to "code enforcement" that reinternalizes those costs if truly mass-fatal pandemic disease is to be avoided in the near future.'[75]

Another way of putting it is that causal explanation is not a matter of simply assembling a set of variables and using modelling to test how they interact, but rather of identifying the deeper 'generative mechanisms' (as Roy Bhaskar calls them) that may have produced these interactions in the first place.[76] But, in cases such as the COVID-19 pandemic, this is, necessarily, an exercise in *critique*, in other words it involves showing the role played by a very specific set of these mechanisms – the historically contingent economic and political structures of contemporary capitalism – in creating the conditions for the outbreak. As Rob Wallace puts it, 'the cause of COVID-19 and other such pathogens is not found only in the object of any one infectious agent or its clinical course, but also in the field of ecosystemic relations that capital and other structural causes have pinned back to their own advantage'.[77] Addressing these causes therefore requires sociopolitical transformation and a new relationship between humankind and the rest of nature.

By contrast, epidemiological modelling, however good the intentions of its practitioners, is not about critique and transformation but about the management of populations, which are treated as objects of a state policy. Foucault's studies of biopolitics don't embrace the emergence in late seventeenth-century England – somewhat earlier that the French developments he analyses – of 'Political Arithmetick', the predecessor of modern statistics and demography, in the writings of John Graunt and William Petty (himself an important early political economist). The two sought to serve the English state's effort to manage increasingly racialized populations in the context of Atlantic colonial expansion, through conquest, dispossession, and forced labour, from Ireland to the Americas.[78] More broadly, epidemiological modelling is one instance of the much more extensive modern practice of using statistical knowledge to manage populations.[79] Today the same kind of probabilistic reasoning used in modelling informs the algorithms employed by companies such as Google and Facebook to extract profit from the vast masses of data that their platforms generate.[80]

The management of the pandemic provoked a splenetic response from the philosopher Giorgio Agamben. Hitherto a poststructuralist influenced, among others, by Foucault, he lapsed back into a more traditional humanism, denouncing the Italian lockdown (the first outside China) as the reduction of human beings to 'bare life', mere physical survival stripped of any spiritual and social dimension. According to Agamben,

> The Great Transformation whose imposition is being attempted is ... the state of exception, that is, the pure and simple suspension of constitutional guarantees. Here there are points of contact with what happened in Germany in 1933, when the new Chancellor Adolf Hitler, without formally suspending the Weimar constitution, declared a state of exception that lasted for 12 years ... While Nazi Germany needed the deployment of an explicitly totalitarian ideological apparatus, the transformation that we are witnessing operates through the institution of a pure and simply sanitary terror and a kind of religion of health.[81]

The concept of a state of exception – which he derives from the theory of sovereignty advanced by the revolutionary conservative jurist Carl Schmitt ('Sovereign is he who decides the exception') – is one of the key themes in Agamben's philosophical reflection.[82] His expenditure of intellectual capital against lockdowns, social distancing, and vaccines has made Agamben a hero for far right COVID deniers and anti-vaxxers. It is hard to respect a polemic that refuses to acknowledge the reality of a virus that took an estimated 18.2 million lives in 2021–2 and that compares the measures taken to protect life to fascism.[83]

But this does not alter the fact that governments have assumed emergency powers to manage the pandemic and have used these powers to impose many restrictions on individual behaviour. A state of exception has prevailed. To assess its significance properly requires considering two types of development. The first (as far as I know, undiscussed by Foucault) is the transformation that governmentality underwent in the twentieth century with the development of the welfare state. This involved simultaneously accommodating pressures for great economic security from the workers' movement and ensuring the reproduction of labour power fit to serve advanced industrial capitalism. These objectives were achieved by organizing collective forms of provision for needs such as unemployment relief, health, and education within a bureaucratic framework that treated the recipients of welfare as objects to be managed.[84] Welfare provision has been restructured and partially privatized in the neoliberal era, but states' responsibility for public health has persisted and provided the framework for their responses to COVID-19.

Indeed, the full story of vaccine development must take into account the role played by governments. The only chink of light in Donald Trump's abysmal handing of the pandemic in 2020, its first year, was the success of Operation Warp Speed (OWS), the improvised partnership between the US government and big pharma that was designed to develop vaccines: coordinated by the military, it pumped billions of federal dollars into the drug companies. By contrast, the European Union, with no experience or capabilities in the area of health provision, fumbled vaccine procurement, and its efforts to displace the blame onto AstraZeneca merely fed anti-vax sentiment. Moncef Slaoui, the ex-GlaxoSmithKline executive whom Trump appointed to head OWS, commented that 'the EU shopped for vaccines like a customer, while the United States basically went into business with the drugmakers'.[85] In this respect, like the global financial crisis, the pandemic underlined the advantages the United States possesses in using its capabilities as a very powerful state to respond rapidly to emergencies and to take financial risks – by comparison with the EU, a bureaucratically managed cartel of states.[86]

Meanwhile the pandemic saw a significant extension of the current welfare regimes, as states in the North introduced large-scale job retention schemes, for example by expanding existing support for short-time working or by introducing wage subsidies. The Organization for Economic Cooperation and Development estimates that, by May 2020, these 'schemes supported about 50 million jobs across the OECD, about ten times as many as during the global financial crisis of 2008–9. By reducing labour costs, JR [job retention] schemes have prevented a surge in unemployment, while they have mitigated financial hardship and buttressed aggregate demand by supporting the incomes of workers on reduced working time.'[87] This was a major addition to the economic responsibilities of states, and one that contradicts the neoliberal doctrine that the rate of unemployment is set by the market. We return to the issues it raises in the next chapter.

The second type of development that we need to consider also precedes the pandemic; it consists, as Ugo Palheta puts it, in the 'authoritarian hardening' of liberal democracies, that is, in

> the successive abandonment of certain fundamental dimensions of liberal democracy by the ruling class itself. Parliamentary arenas are increasingly marginalised and bypassed, as legislative power is monopolised by the executive and methods of government become ever more authoritarian (decree-laws, ordinances, etc.). But this phase of transition from liberal democracy to fascism is above all marked by increased restrictions on the freedoms of organisation, assembly and expression, and on the right to strike, but also the development of state arbitrariness and police brutality.[88]

Palheta has in mind particularly the performance of Emmanuel Macron as French president; he came to office in 2017, proclaiming himself a champion of liberalism against left and right alike. As one anonymous commentator puts it,

> constitutional liberals ... soon condemned his government's decision to write the French 'state of emergency' (introduced after the 2015 Paris attacks) permanently into law. Civil libertarians who had welcomed his arrival were aghast at the repressive tactics used against the yellow vests. Police violence hit protesters and passersby alike, dousing them with tear gas, injuring them with rubber bullets: 25 yellow vests lost an eye or a hand to police weapons. In Marseilles, an elderly woman living close to a protest died after being hit by a police teargas grenade. As the UN and the Council of Europe condemned this brutal crackdown, Macron repeatedly refused to acknowledge that police violence was real. Members of the press, too, have been brutalized by the police and even arrested at protests.[89]

Macron's unleashing of police violence must be partly understood (though not justified) in light of the fact that he saw his main rivals in the 2022 presidential election as coming from the right – indeed, from the far right; this lies behind his government's Islamophobic 'anti-separatism' law and denunciations of the absurd amalgam labelled 'Islamo-leftism'. But this kind of reaction belongs in a more general trend. Thus Boris Johnson's Conservative government in Britain introduced the Police, Crime, Sentencing, and Courts Act 2022, which makes serious inroads into civil liberties, for example by targeting the activities of protesters. The Black Lives Matter (BLM) protests that culminated in the toppling of the slaver Edward Colston's statue in Bristol in June 2020 and the acts of civil disobedience mounted by climate activists such as Extinction Rebellion and Insulate Britain were especially in Home Secretary Priti Patel's sights. In the United States, state legislatures have responded to the BLM rising in the summer 2020 by introducing – and, in many cases, passing – bills that restrict freedom of assembly and exempt drivers, for example, from liability for injuring or even killing demonstrators with their cars.[90]

The trend is a long-term one. In an important study of the policing of protest in the United States, Paul Passavant argues that there was a shift at the end of the 1990s away from the model of 'negotiated management' introduced in response to the inner-city risings of the 1960s. An instance of *'neoliberal authoritarianism'*, which Passavant describes as 'a distinctive state formation', the policing of protest now involves use of excessive violence, which is positively flaunted and celebrated by the ostensible agents of 'law and order'. This is part of a broader effort to suppress disorder in cities that market themselves as venues for financialized capitalism to work and play in; it involves, for example, the use of digital technologies and statistical models to track and identify potential lawbreakers, who are frequent victims of racial profiling, and the increasing deployment of military hardware and tactics.[91] The transformation of policing was summed up by Trump's Defense Secretary Mark Esper when he declared, in a conference call with state governors during the 2020 BLM rising: 'the sooner that you mass and dominate the battlespace, the quicker this dissipates and we can get back to the right normal'.[92]

Even if these trends predate the advent of COVID-19, the global explosion of BLM protests came at the end of the first lockdown and, although that was precipitated by racist police violence, it expressed tensions that had built up during the pandemic – for example, around the greater liability of poor people of colour to fall victim to the virus. The subsequent legislation indicates governments' determination to respond with more of the same, qualified by some concessions to the protesters. Meanwhile, thanks to the management of the pandemic, states' surveillance capabilities have been enhanced, notably through the use of information provided via individuals' smartphones for the purpose of tracing infections and confirming vaccinations. One doesn't have to share the paranoia of Agamben and his anti-vax allies to acknowledge that the police and the security and intelligence agencies are very unlikely to renounce the opportunity of using these capabilities to keep track of those whom they deem to be suspects.

Responding to future catastrophes is likely to lead to further attempts to enhance the repressive powers of states. Populations afflicted by fire or flood will be treated as objects of manipulation rather than as agents with the relevant knowledge when it comes to addressing those threats. A good example is provided by the Greek wildfires of summer 2021, when the conservative government ordered the forced evacuation of the island of Evia; those who managed to evade this directive were able to save their homes and businesses, while the evacuees often lost everything.[93] The greater the disruption to Mark Esper's 'right normal', the more victims are without food or shelter, the more likely the authorities are to resort to coercion, with yet more repressive legislation and appeal to emergency powers.

We can see this very clearly in China, where the pandemic began and where, after initial confusion, the central government under President Xi Jinping responded by closing the borders and imposing comprehensive lockdowns, tight controls over movement, and mass testing and contact tracing. Beijing has persisted in this 'zero-COVID' policy ever since, braving the cost in economically disruptive local lockdowns, which reached a new pitch with the shutdowns, first of Shenzhen and then of Shanghai, in spring 2022. According to the *Financial Times*, '[p]ublic health experts warn that the approach is necessary because of the realities of China's healthcare system: a patchy network of poorly resourced hospitals and a huge elderly population at a higher risk of severe illness, as well as comparatively low efficacy of its domestically-produced vaccines.' But, the article continues, 'keeping China closed for longer also supports Xi's efforts to restructure Chinese society. The CCP [Chinese Communist Party] is orchestrating far-reaching economic and cultural reforms, in part aimed at extending control over the country's business and cultural landscape.'[94]

Chuang, a Marxist collective working on China, offers a more nuanced perspective, in an illuminating early response to the pandemic:

> At a deeper level, though, what seems most fascinating about the state's response is the way in which it has been performed, via the media, as a sort of melodramatic dress rehearsal for the full mobilization of domestic counterinsurgency. This gives us real insights into the repressive capacity of the Chinese state, but it also emphasizes the deeper incapacity of that state, revealed by its need to rely so heavily on a combination of total propaganda measures deployed through every

facet of the media and the goodwill mobilizations of locals otherwise under no material obligation to comply. Both Chinese and Western propaganda have emphasized the real repressive capacity of the quarantine, the former narrating it as a case of effective government intervention in an emergency and the latter as yet another case of totalitarian overreach on the part of the dystopian Chinese state. The unspoken truth, however, is that the very aggression of the clampdown signifies a deeper incapacity in the Chinese state, which is itself very much still under construction.[95]

Let's hope that Chuang is right; certainly the clumsy and brutal lockdown in Shanghai in the spring of 2022 caused much discontent among residents, shut in as they were and cut off from supplies, as well as widespread economic disruption. It's important, however, not to reduce these developments to repression. Foucault famously criticized equating power with repression and insisted that power is productive.[96] He makes the following interesting observation: 'the law prohibits, discipline prescribes, and the essential function of security, without prohibiting or prescribing, but possibly making use of some instruments of prescription and prohibition, is to respond to a reality in such a way that this response cancels out that reality to which it responds – nullifies it, or limits, checks, or regulates it.'[97] This is exactly how epidemiological modelling has operated during the pandemic; behavioural scientists were mobilized to help to anticipate how individuals will react to the introduction or relaxation of restrictions and to advise on how to 'nudge' them in the right direction, whatever that was deemed to be. What is common between this kind of practice and more straightforward repression is the treatment of populations as objects to be managed rather than citizens capable of autonomous initiatives, particularly collectively. There were also other, less planned developments – again, usually extensions of pre-existing trends; for example more affluent households relied on 'platform capitalism' (i.e. on firms such as Amazon or Uber, which have developed extensive digital networks) to deliver the goods, services, meals, and so on that the lockdowns prevented them from obtaining in person. The effect is a significant restructuring of social relations, but one that is going on behind most people's backs.[98]

In a widely noticed book first published during the 1980s, the sociologist Ulrich Beck announced the advent of a 'new' or 'late' modernity: 'risk society' dominated by the imperative of managing the threats created by human intervention in nature. Well, risk society is certainly here now. Beck, however, thought that this late modernity would represent a break from what he calls 'industrial society' – and by this he really means capitalism, with its class divisions.[99] But capitalism and its constitutive class antagonism are still very much with us. This has been very visible during the pandemic. A major new study of the role played by 'race' and class in determining COVID-19 mortality rates in the United States elaborates on this:

> The vast majority of working-class adults are employed in blue-collar, retail or service sales jobs which require onsite attendance and prolonged close contact with others. In addition, working conditions vary with gender and race/ethnicity as well as social class. The most physically hazardous occupations are highly segregated by gender and largely performed by men (e.g. meatpacking) … Moreover, elevated infection risks are amplified across multiple social environmental scales for working-class adults, who may reside in poorly ventilated housing, commute in a crowded carpool, and labour in a poorly ventilated, crowded workplace.[100]

Using the level of educational attainment as proxy for social class, the study found that working-class people aged between 25 and 64 were five times as likely to die of COVID-19 as college graduates. Only 5% of the deaths that occurred in the first year of the pandemic were among white college graduates aged 25 to 64, even though they were 'more than one quarter of the study population … In contrast Hispanic and Black working-class men comprised only 8% of the 25–64-year-old population, but they were 29% of the premature COVID-19 decedents.'[101]

The concentration of COVID infections and mortality in meatpacking plants in the United States during the early months of the pandemic is a stark example of these vulnerabilities; working as they did in the very conditions that help to incubate dangerous pathogens, these plants' low-paid and often migrant workforce were left fully exposed to the virus, usually in rural areas that had already been stripped of health services.[102] A remarkably similar situation was found at the heart of supposedly well-regulated and socially inclusive Rhineland capitalism, in Germany's abattoirs, which rely heavily on subcontractors who supply superexploited migrants.[103]

More generally, workers were often put in harm's way as a result of the campaigns carried out by business lobbies and conservative politicians to end lockdowns and relax restrictions for the sake of 'the economy'. To their credit, mainstream economists have tended to reject the idea that there is a trade-off between health and the economy. But in practice this view has served to legitimize a succession of hasty reopenings, which frequently had to be reversed as some new variant emerged to rip through populations. The pandemic thus has seen a brutal struggle between life and profits. So the chances of dying from a virus that emerged in the context of the globalization of industrial capitalism are shaped by the prevailing class structures. Capitalism features on both sides of the equation. Humankind stands before the rest of nature fractured by social antagonism. And, as we have seen in the grossly unequal allocation of vaccines, this is even more true on a global scale than it is within individual societies.

A study of the COVID death toll in 2020–1 published in *The Lancet* found that 'the highest estimated excess mortality rates were in Andean Latin America, eastern Europe, central Europe, southern sub-Saharan Africa, and central Latin America, with several locations outside these regions having similarly high rates, particularly Lebanon, Armenia, Tunisia, Libya, several regions in Italy, and several states in southern USA'. Mortality, in other words, was concentrated mainly outside the wealthy 'core' of the system, with the main exception of the United States, where the residents of Republican-controlled southern states paid a high price. The countries with the highest number of estimated deaths were India (4.07 million), the United States (1.13 million), Russia (1.07 million), Mexico (798,000), Brazil (792,000), Indonesia (736,000), and Pakistan (664,000).[104]

In mid-2022 the United Nations reported that the number of people living in acute poverty had risen by 77 million since 2019, while three in five workers, mainly in the global South, had seen their real incomes fall in the same period.[105] Meanwhile the rich and super-rich have had their wealth increase even faster, thanks to a flood of central bank money that helped to boost the prices of financial assets, as the vertical rises in individual wealth for the richest in 2020–1 in Figure 3 indicate.

The COVID-19 pandemic thus tells us three important things about what we can expect in the catastrophes to come. First, as we have just seen, the incidence of suffering will reflect the prevailing distribution of economic power: the rich will be shielded, the poor will be exposed. Secondly, managing catastrophe will involve the further development of governmentality; at best, this will mean applying different forms of surveillance, manipulation, and coercion to people for their own good; at worst, there will be further doses of repression. Thirdly, ruling classes will rely on technological fixes to mitigate catastrophe. Vaccines

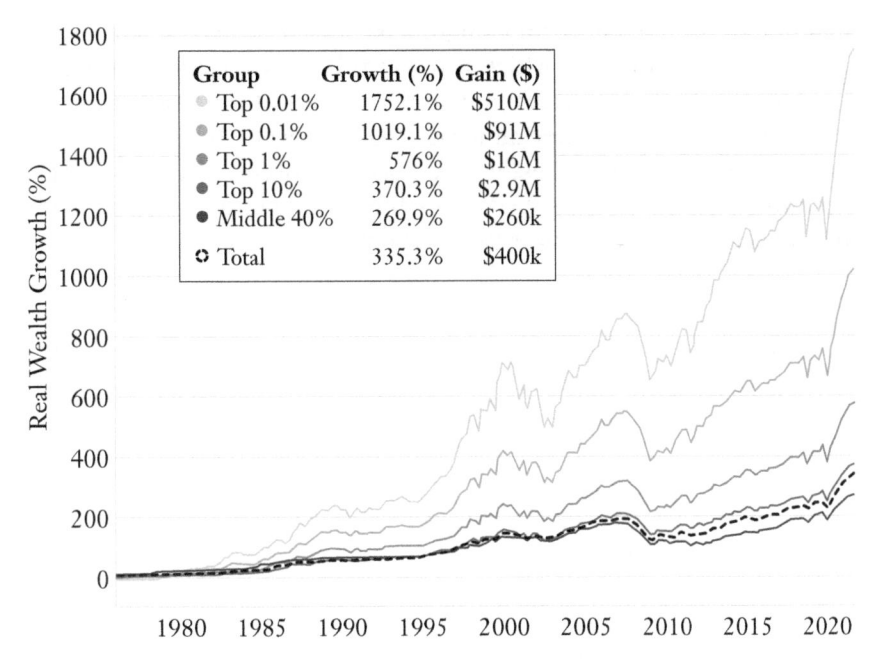

Group	Growth (%)	Gain ($)
Top 0.01%	1752.1%	$510M
Top 0.1%	1019.1%	$91M
Top 1%	576%	$16M
Top 10%	370.3%	$2.9M
Middle 40%	269.9%	$260k
Total	335.3%	$400k

Figure 3 Real wealth growth for individual adults, United States, 1976–2021
Source: Thomas Blanchet, Emmanuel Saez, and Gabriel Zucman, 'Who Benefits from Income and Wealth Growth in the United States?' Realtime Inequality, 1 August 2022. https://realtimeinequality.org.

are a form of technological fix – they seek to suppress infection and its symptoms. They are a relatively benign fix, and the speed at which they were developed in response to COVID-19 is a tribute to the capacities of modern scientific research. Nevertheless, vaccines don't address the underlying problem identified by critical scholars such as Shiva and the Wallaces, namely the disastrous consequences of the global livestock revolution. Indeed, by offering an individualized solution, the vaccination programmes shift our attention from the need to transform our relationship with nature and to invest in better transport and healthcare; and in this way, paradoxically, they feed the anti-vax campaigns of the far right.[106]

Similarly, it is probable that, as climate catastrophes accumulate, the establishment's response will be to encourage us to put our hopes in untested negative emissions technologies and in even more speculative forms of geo-engineering, without sufficient consideration of the environmental costs of these technological interventions and of the undesirable consequences they might have. Once again, this is a way of evading the real solution, which is to get rid of fossil capitalism. But if the destruction of nature is the defining feature of the present age of catastrophe, there are other dimensions to it as well. Two in particular also dominated its predecessor, the period between 1914 and 1945: economic crisis and intensified geopolitical competition. These form the subject matter of the next two chapters.

3

Economic Stagnation

The Long Depression

The twenty-first century is exposing what Chris Harman calls 'the new limits to capital', 'the tendency for the system to undermine the very process of interaction on which it, like every other form of human society, depended': the metabolism of labour and nature.[1] But these years have also seen the global economy descend, especially in the North, into a new phase of slow growth punctuated by moments of extreme instability – notably the global financial crisis of 2007–9, but also the onset of the COVID-19 pandemic in March 2020 and the Russian invasion of Ukraine in February 2022. This proliferation of 'shocks', as mainstream economists like to call them, signals a sea-change: the onset of 'the Long Depression' (in Michael Roberts' words). These shocks have forced a pronounced shift in economic policymaking, away from neoliberal orthodoxy and – to adopt Jens van t' Klooster's label – towards 'technocratic Keynesianism', in which the central banks essentially assume the responsibility of managing aggregate demand, a prerogative of governments during the classic Keynesian era (1945–75). This trend is unlikely to be reversed, despite central banks' retreat to hard-money policies in response to the inflationary upsurge of 2020–2.

This combination of economic instability and stagnation has to be seen in the context of the internal limit to capital, which Marx also identifies. That limit is expressed in the tendency for the rate of profit to fall, which gives rise to a cycle of boom and slump. When we put both limits together, the long boom of 1948–73 and the associated expansion of the welfare state in the North have to be seen against the background of the long-term history of capitalism as a process defined by crisis, impoverishment, and environmental destruction.[2]

Marx's theory of economic crisis is based on what he refers to as the law of tendential fall in the rate of profit. This law follows the same logic that we've seen at work in the destruction of nature discussed in the preceding chapter: the competition of 'many capitals' – the individual units of the system, firms, and states – leads to negative aggregate results. Individual capitals seek to increase their profitability by making productivity-increasing innovations that reduce their costs vis-à-vis those of their rivals. But, in aggregate, the effect is to raise what Marx calls the organic composition of capital, that is, the ratio between capital invested in means of production and capital advanced to pay workers' wages. The rate of profit – the return on the total investment – is a function of the organic composition of capital and the rate of surplus value, which measures the degree of exploitation of workers. Since labour is the source of new value, the average rate of profit tends to fall as a result of the rising organic composition of capital. This 'fall' is only a 'tendential' one, thanks to counteracting effects that either increase the mass of profits by squeezing more surplus value from workers or reduce the mass of capital, causing a rise in the rate of profit in both cases. This logic is at play during economic crises where unprofitable capitals are destroyed and the resulting rise in unemployment reduces workers' bargaining power, forcing them to accept lower wages, speed-up, and the more general deterioration in their working conditions: 'Crises are never more than momentary, violent solutions for the existing contradictions, violent eruptions that re-establish the disturbed balance for the time being.'[3]

Although widely dismissed by mainstream neoclassical economists and also by more heterodox post-Keynesians, Marx's law is now very well corroborated empirically for the period since the Second World War. The latest study, by a group of Marxist economists based at the University of Massachusetts Amherst, concludes: 'there is an unconditional decline in the world profit rate over the past 60 years', which is 'driven by the fall in the output-capital ratio [a proxy for the organic composition of capital], while the profit share [a proxy for the rate of surplus-value] increased.' Between 1960 and 1980, when 'regulated capitalism' prevailed, 'the rate of profit fell sharply, driven by the fall in the output–capital ratio', while during 'the neoliberal period' (1981–2019) 'the world profit rate recovered for a few decades before declining once again'.[4]

G20 rate of profit (%)

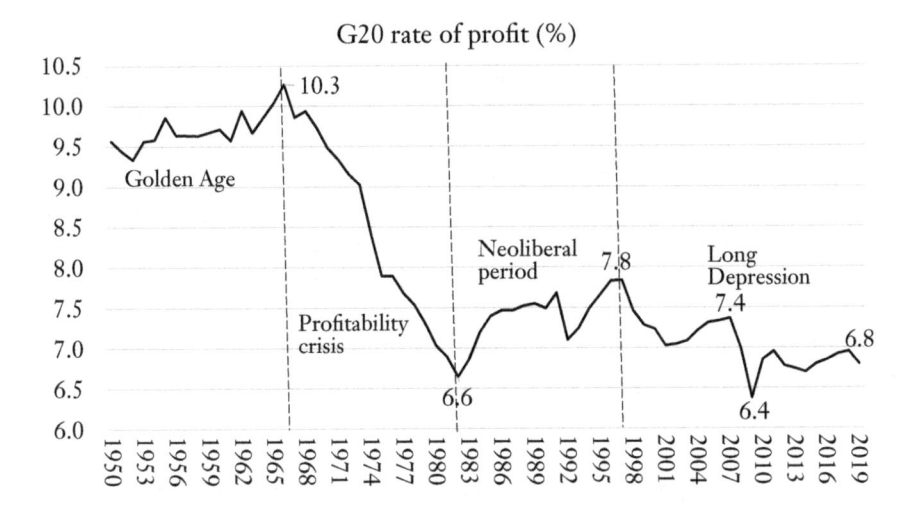

Figure 4 The fall in the rate of profit since the late 1960s
Source: Michael Roberts, 'A World Rate of Profit: Important New Evidence' (22 January 2022), thenextrecession.wordpress.com. Data from Penn World Tables 10.0. Reproduced with permission.

As Figure 4 shows, the turning point for the rate of profit comes in the mid to late 1960s. In the decades after the Second World War, western capitalism benefitted from the unprecedentedly high levels of peacetime arms spending demanded by the Cold War. This permanent arms economy didn't simply help to maintain a high level of effective demand; heavy investment in producing weapons systems, a form of waste production whose output does not feed back into further production as either wage or capital goods, slowed down the overall rate of accumulation and the rise in the organic composition of capital. But by the late 1960s the Cold War had thawed, thanks to détente between the two superpowers. Meanwhile policymakers in the United States, which carried the bulk of the burden of the arms economy in the West, sought to cut back on military expenditure and divert resources into civilian investment in order to enhance the competitiveness of US firms. These were under increasing pressure from rivals in other western economies such as West Germany and Japan, where capital had been encouraged to focus on rebuilding and expanding industries destroyed during the Second World War. The result was a reassertion of crisis tendencies that produced major recessions in the mid- and late 1970s, in an atmosphere heightened by the political and social upheavals of the time.[5]

The neoliberal economic policy regime emerged in response. We shall look at this development more closely in the final section of this chapter; here I focus primarily on its effect on the profitability crisis. As Figure 4 shows, the neoliberal turn saw a recovery in the rate of profit from the very low levels to which it had fallen by the early 1980s. This outcome was achieved crucially by forcing up the rate of exploitation through an offensive against organized labour, which was greatly facilitated by the closure of large swathes of basic industry and the resulting return of mass unemployment. The globalization of production, involving as it did the relocation of manufacturing industry to Asia, Mexico, and Central Europe, also helped to squeeze labour costs.[6]

As Robert Brenner writes of the United States,

> the defence of profitability ... and its partial recovery in the 1990s, has been predicated upon a repression of wages unprecedented during the last century, and perhaps since the Civil War. Between 1973 – when they reached their peak – and 1990, real hourly wages (excluding benefits) for production and non-supervisory workers in the private business economy *fell* by 12%, declining at an annual average rate of 0.7%, and they failed to rise *at all* during the decade of the 1990s, up to 1997.[7]

The late 1990s represent the moment when Brenner's 'partial recovery' of profitability from its low point in the early 1980s came to an end, and indeed started to go into reverse. This provides the background for a recession in the United States and the European Union in 2000–1 and for the outbreak of the global financial crisis in 2007–8, which started once again in the United States and led to the greatest worldwide recession since the 1930s.[8] Both crises began with the bursting of financial bubbles – the dotcom boom on the US stock market in the late 1990s and the US housing bubble in the mid-2000s. This reflected how the dynamics of economic growth evolved during the neoliberal era. On both sides of the Atlantic, one marked feature of this period was the deregulation of financial markets. It promoted a broader process of financialization in which banks (especially in the 'Anglosphere') ceased to act as intermediaries between savers and industrial and commercial firms (which increasingly raise funds directly in the money markets), and actively sought out often speculative and risky opportunities for profit-making.[9]

Central banks, especially the US Federal Reserve Board, became increasingly tolerant of the development of financial bubbles that pushed up the price of particular assets – shares in the late 1980s, and again in the late 1990s, real estate in the mid-2000s. These bubbles acted, in the absence of a robust recovery of the rate of profit, as a mechanism for stimulating effective demand. Riccardo Bellofiore calls this strategy 'asset-bubble-driven privatized Keynesianism'.[10] Through the 'wealth effect' – in other words, the ability of more prosperous households to borrow against the higher monetary value of their assets, and therefore to spend more – aggregate effective demand was maintained at relatively high levels. The atomized decisions of households to borrow and spend achieved the same overall effect in supporting growth and employment that Maynard Keynes had argued that centralized spending by the state would produce. But, as the bubbles ballooned out of control in the 2000s, sucking in the entire western banking system, the conditions were created for a crash that, when it developed in 2007–8, brought down the whole world economy.

The bubbles were fed by the global expansion of credit in the neoliberal era. Guying the opening sentence of Marx's *Capital*, Michael J. Howell writes: 'The wealth of modern capitalist societies appears as an immense collection of stocks, bonds and short-term liquid instruments.' These assets give their holders access to liquidity, that is, to the means to meet their liabilities; hence global liquidity, now greater than global GDP, 'represents the private sector's ability to access cash through savings and credit'. Credit is now substantially the greater source of liquidity, and the main means of gaining access to it are wholesale money markets, which Howell calls 'the "engine room" of Global Liquidity'.[11] These markets, where banks and shadow banks compete with one another and with industrial and commercial firms for funding crucially in dollars, provided the fuel that fed the bubbles of the neoliberal era.

Adam Tooze argues that the global financial crisis of 2007–9 was a crisis of this 'transatlantic offshore dollar system'. The United States and Europe have been bound together since the collapse of the Bretton Woods system in the early 1970s, and especially during the neoliberal era, in 'a financial circulatory system'. Both American and European banks borrow dollars either in the United States or via the offshore dollar market that developed in the City of London from the 1950s onwards, in order primarily to make loans in the lucrative US markets. Indeed, 'the entire structure of international banking in the early twenty-first century was transatlantic. The new Wall Street was not geographically confined to the southern end of Manhattan. It was a North Atlantic system. The second node, detached from but integrally and inseparably connected to New York, was the City of London', which enjoyed the advantage of being less tightly regulated than Wall Street.[12]

But the big Swiss, German, French, and Dutch investment banks that came largely to dominate the City after the deregulating Big Bang of 1986 became, along with smaller and more provincial operations such as the German Landesbanken, more and more heavily involved in borrowing dollars to buy the bundles of mortgages that seemed to offer limitless profits during the US property bubble of the mid-2000s. 'In the process,' writes Tooze, 'the European financial system came to function, in the words of Fed analysts, as a "global hedge fund", borrowing short and lending long'.[13] European banks used this same model when they fed the credit boom that followed the launch of the euro in 1999 and produced property bubbles across the continent.

From this perspective, what was dangerous about the collapse of the property bubble in the United States itself in 2005–6 is that, as the infamous subprime mortgages sold to households unable to repay them turned bad, the markets through which banks lent to each other and issued asset-backed commercial paper (which was based, for example, on these mortgages) shut down in August 2007. The flow of dollars that fed the transatlantic 'circulatory system' stopped. This threatened not just the banks but also the industrial and commercial firms that also regularly sought funding on the dollar markets. The collapse of the Wall Street investment bank Lehman Brothers on 15 September 2008 accelerated but didn't begin this process. But in its aftermath, the funding markets froze completely. The decisive step in halting and reversing the collapse was not so much the bank bailouts mounted by western governments as the determined efforts, orchestrated by the US central bank, to restart the flow of dollars:

> The US Federal Reserve engaged in a truly spectacular innovation. It established itself as liquidity provider of last resort to the global banking system. It provided dollars to all comers in New York, whether banks were American or not. Through so-called liquidity swap lines, the Fed licensed a hand-picked group of core central banks to issue dollar credits on demand. In a huge burst of transatlantic activity, with the European Central Bank (ECB) in the lead, they pumped trillions of dollars into the European banking system.[14]

It is therefore highly significant that these swap lines, which connected the Fed to the central banks of the eurozone, Japan, Britain,

Canada, and Switzerland, were made permanent in October 2013. As Tooze notes, 'prior to the crisis, the transatlantic offshore dollar system had lacked a manifest centre of leadership. Indeed, it had developed "offshore" so as to avoid national regulation and control. After 2008 it was openly organized around the Fed and its liquidity provision.'[15] This at the very least qualifies the claims that 2007–9 marked the beginning of the end of US hegemony. Tooze's analysis in this respect supports the argument of Leo Panitch and Sam Gindin that a crucial dimension of this hegemony is the role that the Federal Reserve and the US Treasury play in orchestrating crisis management by the leading capitalist states.[16]

The problem is, however, that crisis management became permanent. In the wake of the 2007–8 crash, the major central banks kept interest rates at rock bottom (or in some cases negative) and, starting with the Fed, which was followed by the Bank of England, the Bank of Japan, and (last but not least) the ECB, adopted a policy of quantitative easing (QE). In other words, they bought government and corporate bonds as a way of creating new money and pumping it into the financial system. The idea was that this would encourage banks to lend and thereby increase the level of investment and output.

QE is justified by one of the central dogmas of neoclassical economics: the quantity theory of money, according to which the money supply determines the price level. This theory presupposes that any increase in the money supply will be spent. But Marx argues that the money supply fluctuates in response to the needs of the circulation of commodities and therefore of the broader accumulation process, and so economic agents may decide to hoard the money they hold rather than spend it; similar criticisms of the quantity theory are made by Keynes and his followers.[17] Western banks hung on to QE money in order to rebuild their reserves, or lent it to governments and firms in the 'emerging market' economies while they were booming in the immediate aftermath of the crash, pleading that domestic entrepreneurs were reluctant to invest and so had not been knocking on their doors demanding loans. In the longer run, QE, by helping to push up asset prices, has contributed to the obscene rise in the wealth of the rich and superrich (see Figure 3 in Chapter 2).

Concerted state action – not just the action of central banks but also the fiscal stimuli widely introduced in response to the 2007–8 crash – nevertheless prevented the global financial crisis from developing into an economic slump on the scale seen in the 1930s. As the economic historian Barry Eichengreen puts it, 'global GDP dropped by a disastrous 15% between the peak in 1929 and the trough in 1932. In 2008 and 2009, in contrast, it fell by a fraction of 1%, and growth resumed already in 2010. Even in the advanced countries hit hardest, the fall in 2009 was 3.5% of GDP, and growth turned positive again the next year.'[18]

But even mainstream economists such as Lawrence Summers and Paul Krugman acknowledged that the recovery in the United States and European Union was not marked by the sharp increase in output and the relatively rapid resumption of pre-crisis growth rates characteristic of the 'normal' business cycle of boom and recession. This has led to a debate about 'secular stagnation': according to Summers, slow growth in the old 'core' of advanced capitalism represents not a temporary aberration but a structural change.[19] A more radical version of the same idea has been articulated by the post-Keynesian economist James Galbraith (an adviser to Yanis Varoufakis during his brief time as Greek finance minister in the Syriza government in 2015). He argues that the entire economic model on which the United States has based its global hegemony since the mid-twentieth century is exhausted as a result of a combination of economic, geopolitical, and ecological reasons.[20]

One explanation for this protracted period of suboptimal growth since the late 2000s is provided by the failure of the rate of profit to recover significantly from the new low it fell to after the global financial crisis; by 2019 it was falling again (see Figure 4). The onset of the COVID-19 pandemic thus hit a global economy that was already in a vulnerable state. The result was probably the sharpest economic contraction in the history of the United States. According to a Fed economist, 'the cumulative decline in economic activity during the first two quarters of the 2020 recession was somewhat larger than the GNP decline during the first two quarters of the Great Depression. Moreover, the fall in real GDP during the second quarter of 2020 exceeded the largest one-quarter real GNP contraction during the Depression.' Between February and April 2020, industrial production experienced 'the largest two-month decline in the history of the index, which begins in 1919 … The unemployment rate increased sharply in the 2020 recession, from 3.5% in February to nearly 15% in April before falling back to 11.1% in June.'[21]

The picture was the same globally in 2020: world output fell by 3.1%, while there were much sharper drops in India (−7.3 per cent), Mexico (−8.3 per cent), and South Africa (−6.4 per cent), for example.[22] In Britain, output fell by 9.9 per cent in 2020 – the sharpest contraction since the Great Frost of 1709.[23] As Tooze puts it, '[i]in the historic record of modern capitalism, there has never been a moment in which close to 95% of the world's economies suffered a simultaneous contraction in per capita GDP, as they did in the first half of 2020'.[24]

Partly because of the counter-measures to be discussed in the next section, this recession was short-lived. But disruption to the labour market and to supply chains persisted after economies started to recover from the collapse caused by the initial lockdowns; and this helped to unleash an inflationary upsurge. James Meadway argues that the intersection of the external and internal limits to capital promise a future of greater economic instability. In particular, the widening of the 'metabolic rift' (Marx) between humans and the rest of nature is depriving capitalism of the degree of control over its physical environment that, as Andreas Malm shows in *Fossil Capital*, reliance on fossil fuels has given it over the past two hundred years. This is confirmed by the food and energy crises that developed in 2021–2: behind them lay the increasingly direct impact of climate change reflected, for example, in the droughts that gripped both China and Europe:

> A capitalism buffeted by successive environmental disasters starts to look rather like its early, pre-industrial form: not able to produce regularly and systematically, but suddenly subject to forces that remained always outside of its control. The problem of labour – which, annoyingly, remains the problem of managing people who, annoyingly, may have their own ideas about being managed – would be joined by (indeed, increasingly *is* being joined by) the problem of managing the environment.[25]

The rise of technocratic Keynesianism

The onset of the pandemic was marked by a more extreme version of the panic that hit financial markets in the autumn of 2008. The money markets froze up again, and investors were desperately liquidating assets in order to gain access to cash. This reflected the fragility of a world economy whose recovery since the global financial crisis had been based on a huge expansion of debt, chiefly by companies this time. By the end of 2020, corporate debt amounted to $83 trillion, 98 per cent of global GDP. Over a decade of ultra-cheap credit had allowed a rapid growth in the number of 'zombie' firms, whose profits didn't even cover their interest payments, and of the kind of firms that the Bank for

International Settlements calls 'fallen angels': firms that took advantage of ultra-low interest rates to issue bonds that funded risky takeovers. This corporate addiction to debt reflected the way in which bailouts and QE had prevented the clear-out of unprofitable capitals that is the historical function of economic recessions.[26]

This time even US Treasury bonds were hit. Treasuries are the main way in which the US state borrows; they act as measure of value and means of payment in a global monetary system no longer anchored in gold, but in the hegemonic state's ability to raise money.[27] Normally, during panics, the price of Treasuries rises, as they are the safest asset available. In March 2020 they fell, as fund managers desperate for dollars sold them off. The panic was halted only by the fact that the Fed, in coordination with the other leading central banks (once again, supported by extensive swap facilities), went even further than it had in 2008–9 to restore the markets to proper functioning, in particular through large-scale buying of corporate bonds.

The central banks' activism was matched by government fiscal policy. On 25 March 2020, two days after the Fed's most decisive intervention, the US Congress passed the Coronavirus Aid, Relief, and Economic Security (CARES) Act, allocating $2.2 trillion of additional spending, tax cuts, and the like, equivalent to 10 per cent of US GDP. Many governments elsewhere followed suit, including in the 'emerging market' economies of the global South; by January 2021, the International Monetary Fund estimated the total fiscal stimulus at $14 trillion.[28] This massive surge in state funding – for example through short-time working schemes and other job subsidies – served to counteract the contractionary effect on incomes and spending of the closure of large parts of the economy during lockdowns.

The move was financed through borrowing: in 2020, governments in the United States, Japan, and Europe issued $18 trillion worth of new debt.[29] This debt was largely bought by central banks, usually indirectly but sometimes more visibly. In early 2021, the *Financial Times* reported a survey's finding that 'investors believe' the Bank of England's 'quantitative easing programme is a thinly veiled attempt to finance the government's deficit to keep its borrowing costs down … investors are convinced the BoE bought an additional £450bn of gilts [UK government bonds] during the COVID-19 crisis in order to ease the government's huge programme of borrowing by keeping debt servicing costs at rock bottom.'[30]

What the Bank of England did openly and other central banks more discreetly amounts to monetary financing – that is, as van t' Klooster puts it, 'the issuance of money to finance government spending beyond the levels that can be funded by borrowing from the private sector'.[31] Historically not uncommon, this practice became taboo during the neoliberal era, when it was condemned for allowing inflationary increases in the money supply. It was prohibited by the 1992 Treaty of Maastricht establishing the European Economic and Monetary Union, which represented the high-water mark of institutionalized neoliberalism.[32] The treaty gave responsibility for issuing the European single currency to a politically unaccountable ECB, which is forbidden to buy bonds from member states and other EU institutions. But the ECB's disastrously inept and dogmatic handling of the global financial crisis and its evolution into the eurozone crisis of 2010–15 led to a tacit shift after Mario Draghi became president of the ECB in 2012, particularly given the adoption of quantitative easing in 2015. As van t' Klooster notes, '[w]ith the introduction of the Pandemic Emergency Purchase Programme (PEPP), the ECB became much more explicit with regard to the objective of monetary financing. Announced in March 2020 as a €750bn asset purchase programme, its envelope increased to €1850bn by December 2020.'[33]

Tooze asks whether 'the monetization of giant stimulus spending was the belated and long overdue triumph of radical Keynesianism, a return to the logic of functional finance first spelled out in World War II'.[34] He elaborates on the thought associated with the contemporary school of modern monetary theory, which holds that governments are free, within very broad limits, to set the level of spending they choose and to create the money they need in order to achieve it: 'State finances are not limited like those of a household. If a monetary sovereign treats the question of how to organize financing as anything more than a technical matter, that is itself a political choice. As John Maynard Keynes once reminded his readers in the midst of World War II: "Anything we can actually do we can afford."'[35]

Keynesianism's heyday during and after the Second World War came against the background of mobilization for total war (continued in a more limited form in the era of the permanent arms economy) and of consolidation of liberal democracy in the western capitalist bloc thanks to full employment and the entrenchment of the welfare state after 1945.[36] The context of the present shift in economic policy is very different, as I shall explore more fully in the next section. Van t' Klooster argues that we are witnessing the emergence of a 'new regime of Technocratic Keynesianism', which 'is driven by, and assigns more power to, technocratic actors at central banks and independent regulatory agencies. Their role between the private and the public sphere provides such monetary technocrats with considerable freedom from the traditional constraints of liberal constitutionalism.'[37]

Fathimath Mushtaq argues, along somewhat similar lines, that '[u]nconventional central banking, understood as the use of central balance sheets to shape and stabilize financial markets, is increasingly becoming conventional'. She suggests that these practices have developed over recent decades in response to successive crises. Thus, emerging market central banks in the wake of the Asian financial crisis of 1997–8 have sought to ensure their businesses' access to essential dollar liquidity by using their own balance sheets to manage foreign exchange reserves (Mushtaq's research includes a case study of the Bank of India). This kind of intervention parallels the way in which, in both 2008 and 2020, the Fed and other 'core' central banks went beyond their traditional role as lenders of last resort, backstopping the banking system at the moment when markets lose confidence, and became market *makers* by purchasing illiquid financial assets. This 'new normal' is that of 'a crisis-prone system that can only function on central banks absorbing risks'. Thus 'central bank operations stabilize a financial system increasingly prone to liquidity shocks by mobilizing public resources in the service of private financial accumulation'.[38] Here again, then, Walter Benjamin's '"state of emergency" ... is not the exception but the rule'.[39]

These analyses underline one of the most striking features of the economic crisis unleashed by the COVID-19 pandemic, namely that its management was topped and tailed by the central banks. Using the methods described by Mushtaq, they restored calm to the money markets when these froze in March 2020. They went on to create the additional money that governments needed to spend to counteract the recession produced by the lockdowns and, directly or indirectly, to lend it to them. But this spectacular performance was dissimulated, van t' Klooster stresses, by 'the crucial role of *strategic ambiguity*. To ensure both legal permissibility and political feasibility, policymakers strategically justify their policies in terms of the older liberal market paradigm, while also putting forward novel justifications ... By suggesting continuity while also successfully addressing new problems, monetary technocrats minimize legislative involvement and avoid politicization.'[40]

Daniela Gabor argues that 'central banks have quietly put in place a *shadow monetary financing* regime since the global financial crisis'. She suggests that the function of this shift is not fiscal – to finance government spending (which she sees as 'a side-effect, not a policy target') – as much as it is to support the money markets, which, as we saw in the first section of this chapter, are central to the operation of contemporary global capitalism. The vast repo (repurchase) market that specializes in short-term loans depends on the collateral provided by borrowers, typically in the form of sovereign government bonds (usually US Treasuries and German Bunds). According to Gabor, 'central bank purchases reflect the new macro-financial role that government bonds play in this collateral-intensive financial system organized around securities, derivatives, and wholesale money markets. As Alberto Giovannini – the main architect of the Eurozone's macro-financial architecture – put it, the state has become a collateral factory for modern financial systems.'[41] Central banks' bulk purchases of government bonds at times of stress help to keep the price of this collateral stable.

Apart from the contortions that central bank governors have undergone to deny that they are engaging in monetary financing, van t' Klooster points to how central banks have justified their shift back to the pre-neoliberal practice of guiding the allocation of credit by banks. In the ECB, this is increasingly legitimized by the objective of 'greening the financial system', an objective justified by 'the potential threat of environmental and climate-related risk to financial stability'.[42] Thus future stress tests will include the impact of extreme weather events. The protective embrace of the central banks extends now to preserving markets not just from their internal dysfunctions but from the external effects of the investments they finance.

The end of neoliberalism?

'You can't buck the market', Margaret Thatcher famously declared. But in 2008 and, again, in 2020 the market bucked so much that the state had to step in to steady it. (Strictly speaking, the ECB isn't part of any state, but is an institution of the EU, constitutionally still primarily a confederation of states. But ultimately it is dependent on the capabilities and political will of the most powerful member states.) Where does this leave neoliberalism, of which Thatcher was one of the main creators? Its demise has been much announced in recent years, mainly in different academic quarters, with widespread discussion of the shape of 'post-neoliberalism'.[43] Does the emergence of technocratic Keynesianism, amid the onset of the age of catastrophe, mark an important step towards the demise of neoliberalism?

Since neoliberalism is a complex phenomenon, the answer is, necessarily, also complicated. One can identify three dimensions of neoliberalism – as ideology, reassertion of capitalist class power, and economic policy regime. The first dimension is that of neoliberal ideology. As numerous commentators have noted, central to this ideology is a conception of freedom.[44] Thus Milton Friedman's best-known book is called *Capitalism and Freedom*. We are dealing here with a particular conception of freedom – that famously dubbed 'negative freedom' by Isaiah Berlin and apparently invented by Thomas Hobbes during the English Revolution: 'LIBERTY, or FREEDOM, signifieth (properly) the absence of Opposition; (by Opposition, I mean external Impediments of motion)'.[45]

The importance, for neoliberals, of this conception of liberty as freedom from interference has been very evident during the pandemic. The right wing in the US Republican Party and in the British Conservative Party, for example, has invoked it to justify its opposition to lockdowns and social distancing. In September 2020 the British prime minister, Boris Johnson, explained that COVID-19 infection rates were higher in the United Kingdom than in Germany and Italy because 'there is an important difference between our country and many other countries around the world. That is that our country is a freedom-loving country ... And it is very difficult to ask the British population uniformly to obey guidelines in the way that is necessary.'[46] Johnson seemed to have forgotten that perhaps the most influential articulation of liberalism, by John Stuart Mill in *On Liberty*, affirms '[t]hat the only purpose for which power can be rightfully exercised over any member of a civilized community, against his [*sic*] will, is to prevent harm to others'.[47]

Infecting others with a deadly virus seems like a pretty straightforward example of serious harm that warrants the use of state power to prevent it. There are, in any case, other conceptions of freedom available, for example the classical republican conception, which equates liberty with the absence of domination. Hobbes's redefinition was intended to supplant this conception of liberty, which was tied to the idea of popular sovereignty and learned through the reading of ancient Greek and Roman texts, thanks to which 'men from their childhood have gotten a habit (under a false shew of Liberty) of favouring tumults, and of licentiously controlling the actions of their Sovereigns; and again of controlling those controllers, with the effusion of so much blood'.[48]

There is, of course, much more to neoliberal ideology than the ideal of negative freedom. It is mistakenly associated with the idea of a minimal state. In a valuable corrective, Quinn Slobodian writes:

The core of twentieth-century neoliberal theorizing involves what they called the meta-economic or extra-economic conditions for safeguarding capitalism on the scale of the whole world ... the neoliberal project focused on designing the institutions – not to liberate markets but to encase them, to inoculate capitalism against the threat of democracy, to create a framework to contain often irrational human behaviour, and to reorder the world after empire as a space of competing states in which borders fulfil a necessary function.[49]

To understand what converted these ideas from the property of small circles of intellectuals in the mid-twentieth century – for example Friedrich von Hayek, the German ordo-liberals, and the postwar Mont Pelerin Society – into the dominant form of capitalist ideology towards the end of the same century, we have to look to the second dimension distinguished earlier. David Harvey argues that neoliberalism is best understood as 'a *political* project to re-establish the conditions for capital accumulation and restore the power of economic elites'.[50] With the collapse of the long boom during the 1970s, the Keynesian economic policy regime was unable effectively to address stagflation, that is, the combination of mass unemployment and a rising inflation rate that emerged in this period.

It was then that neoliberalism found a growing audience in ruling-class circles, initially chiefly in the United States and Britain. Friedman's 'monetarist' critique of Keynesianism diagnosed stagflation as the consequence of futile government efforts to reduce unemployment below its natural rate through increased public expenditure.[51] But this was folded into a much broader critique of what Samuel Brittan pinpoints as the 'economic contradictions of democracy': party competition encouraged voters to develop 'excessive expectations', which politicians sought to assuage through the inflationary policies targeted by Friedman.[52] Neoliberals also targeted the efforts of postcolonial states, in the 1960s and 1970s, to construct a new international economic order that would enhance the South's bargaining power with the North and allow these states to pursue economic development autonomously. This project was condemned for erecting new obstacles to the growth of the global market.[53]

Neoliberalism therefore required a third dimension: the installation of a new economic policy regime. Keynesianism, which encouraged policymakers to use fiscal and monetary tools to manage effective demand so that full employment could be maintained and economic growth maximized, was replaced by a policy regime where economic actors were subordinated to market disciplines and democratic mechanisms were marginalized. The new regime was pioneered in Chile after the military coup of September 1973 had crushed the workers' movement; thus it demonstrated the inner connection between market discipline and extra-economic coercion. But Chile was initially an outlier. It was the failure of the US administrations of Gerald Ford (1974–7) and Jimmy Carter (1977–81) to overcome stagflation through what had come to be seen as traditional Keynesian deficit spending that precipitated the shift to a new policy regime.[54]

The political turning point came in 1979, first with the election of the Thatcher government in Britain and then with Carter's appointment of Paul Volcker as chairman of the US Federal Reserve Board. Both sought to restore market discipline – Thatcher, by using high interest rates, a strong pound, and public spending cuts to eliminate unprofitable firms and the resulting mass unemployment to weaken organized labour; Volcker, by shifting Fed policy to restrict the growth of the money supply, thereby forcing up interest rates, the dollar, and unemployment. This was the context in which Thatcher and her Republican counterpart Ronald Reagan mounted brutal offensives against trade unions. Their success was symbolized by the decisive defeat of the year-long British miners' strike in 1984–5.

The 'Volcker shock' of 6 October 1979 represented the first and most decisive stage in the globalization of neoliberalism. With Mexico's bankruptcy in August 1982, high interest rates and a rising dollar precipitated the Third World debt crisis. Governments in the global South that turned to the International Monetary Fund and the World Bank – the international financial institutions (IFIs) – for help found that the price was the abandonment of statist developmental policies – a major target of the neoliberal offensive from the start – and their replacement by a forced diet of austerity, privatization, and economic liberalization. The IFIs were reconfigured to act as enforcers of the neoliberal economic policy regime. This shift greatly facilitated the spread of manufacturing production to parts of the South, as global supply chains developed to take advantage of technological innovations such as containerization and digitalization and lower labour costs outside the advanced capitalist 'core'. It also helped to sustain the Great Acceleration, which is now inflicting climate chaos.

The neoliberal economic policy regime, which came as close as it ever did to being genuinely global after the collapse of the state capitalist regimes in the Soviet Union and Central and Eastern Europe in 1989–91, was, however, in no sense the realization of a coherent ideological blueprint developed by Friedman or Hayek. As Harvey puts it, '[t]he capitalist world stumbled towards neoliberalization as the answer through a series of gyrations and chaotic experiments that only really converged as a new orthodoxy with what became known as the Washington Consensus in the 1990s'.[55] Indeed the early, 'heroic' era of neoliberalism can be seen as a crisis-driven learning process that reached what proved to be only a temporary resting point in the 1990s. As the cure to stagflation, Friedman recommended 'steady but moderate growth in the quantity of money'.[56] Nigel Lawson, a key architect of Thatcher's economic policy, described this policy as restoring 'the constraint which operated quasi-automatically for a country on the gold standard, as Britain was for most of the pre-Keynesian period'.[57]

The trouble was that controlling the money supply proved impossible. The Thatcher government found itself constantly changing the definition of money that it sought to target, confirming the law formulated by the economist Charles Goodhart: 'Any observed statistical regularity will tend to collapse once pressure is placed upon it for control purposes'.[58] How to overcome this central policy failure, which became entangled with the problem of Britain's relationship with the European Union, increasingly divided the government, leading to Lawson's resignation as Chancellor of the Exchequer in October 1989 and Thatcher's fall barely a year later. The key monetarist assumption that, as Lawson put it, 'government is able to determine the quantity of money' proved to be false.[59] Money is largely created by private transactions in the credit system; banks create money when they issue loans and allow overdrafts. As Keynes knew, what matters is not so much the supply of money as the demand for it. In other words, workers and capitalists borrow to finance, respectively, consumption and investment. The state underwrites this process of money creation but doesn't control it.

The solution proved to be what Edward Luttwak – presciently, in 1996 – called 'central bankism':

> Like all religions, it has both a supreme god – hard money – and a devil, inflation ... Like many religions, central bankism has its high priests, constantly striving to assert their independence from secular parliaments, politicians and public opinion. Although, like any other public officials, they receive their salaries from the tax-payer, central bankers claim the right to ignore the public will by invoking their duty to a higher authority – the sacrosanctity of hard money. Central bankers in office – invariably for terms of Papal length, often

prematurely renewed in fear of the fears of financial markets – are surrounded by an aura of sovereign power very properly denied to government ministers or even prime ministers and presidents, mere mortals voted in and out of office by the ignorant masses, or reshuffled at even shorter intervals.[60]

The key objective of neoliberal economic policymaking, keeping inflation low and steady, was thus now to be achieved, not through the futile targeting of monetary aggregates, but by transferring control over monetary policy from elected politicians to unelected and politically unaccountable central bankers. This was already the practice in two of the main western economies. The Federal Reserve System was established just before the First World War as a state apparatus that could manage the banking system in the interests of the large corporations that increasingly dominated the US economy, while keeping politicians at arm's length.[61] The West German Bundesbank, created after the Second World War, became a key institution that pursued a strategy of maintaining the competitiveness of German firms by keeping inflation low and the exchange rate strong, and thereby promoting technological innovation and industrial restructuring.[62] Both central banks were subject to considerable pressure from governments concerned in particular to prevent restrictive policies that could damage their re-election prospects; but the Bundesbank was especially effective in fighting these pressures off.

'Central bankism' represented a generalization of this practice. It was pioneered by the radical neoliberal Labour government in New Zealand, which in 1989 tied the governor of the Reserve Bank's salary to the fulfilment of a contract with the minister of finance to meet an inflation target of 0–2%.[63] The New Labour government in Britain transferred control over monetary policy to the Bank of England soon after its election in May 1997. Other European central banks were given independence during the preparations for economic and monetary union, which involved the creation of the ECB – in many ways the apogee of this process. Judged by the low-inflation objective, this institutional innovation was a success (according to Duncan Foley, inflation targeting 'might more accurately be described as "surplus value targeting"').[64] Price increases hovered around the normal 2 per cent target for nearly 30 years – if anything, they tended to dip below it, reflecting the deflationary pressures caused by successive financial crises, notably the bursting of the Japanese 'bubble economy' in the early 1990s and the global financial crisis some 15 years later. But the role played by the central banks in managing the latter underlines the power shift that has taken place.

Like nuclear weapons, the techniques of aggregate demand management associated with the Keynesian era can't be uninvented. But now they are primarily deployed not by finance ministers responsible to parliaments and voters, but by central bank governors who are institutionally protected from any kind of democratic accountability. Van t' Klooster's use of the label 'technocratic Keynesianism' to describe the policy shift since the global financial crisis alludes to how this power is legitimized: by reference to the technical expertise and political neutrality of the central bankers. In terms of the evolution of neoliberalism, this is a shift from rules – the formal targeting of monetary aggregates that failed in the 1980s – to actors. More precisely, macroeconomic management is now entrusted to financial experts and their exercise of discretion.

Given the importance of the decisions that central bankers take, especially now, in the era of 'unconventional central banking', it is pure ideological fantasy to portray them as disinterested technical experts. Their actions affect directly the levels and distribution of income, output, and employment. These are inherently political matters, and therefore they attract the attention of state managers, elected and unelected, and of society more broadly. Paradoxically, it is the ECB, supposedly the purest incarnation of neoliberal ideology, that illustrates this most clearly, notably in Draghi's performance as president between 2011 and 2019.[65] Deeply implicated in the neoliberal turn in Europe, he nevertheless nudged the Bank's practices in the direction of technocratic Keynesianism, constantly wheeling and dealing, concentrating his efforts especially on reassuring the German political elite, and cutting the necessary deals with their presiding deity, Chancellor Angela Merkel. It is therefore of little surprise that, after retiring from the ECB, he should cash in politically on the prestige gained through this performance, by becoming the Italian prime minister – a role that may be capped ultimately by a further ascent to the presidency.

Tooze therefore is right to stress how the rise of 'functional finance' unfolded within the parameters set by neoliberalism:

> If central banks since 2008 have massively expanded their remit, it was out of necessity, to contain the instability of the financial system. But that was politically possible – indeed, it could be done with no fanfare whatsoever – because the battles of the 1970s and 1980s had been won ... Democracy was no longer the menace that it had been

in neoliberalism's years of struggle. Within the sphere of economic policy, that expressed itself in the startling realization that there was no risk of inflation. For all the centrist hand-wringing about 'populism', class antagonism was enfeebled, wage pressure was minimal, strikes non-existent.[66]

But if technocratic Keynesianism presupposed the achievements and institutions of neoliberalism, this could not conceal the extent of the ideological and policy shift. In 2008–9 and, on a much greater scale, in 2020–1, the levels of output, employment, and income were decisively influenced by states – and not simply in the advanced capitalist world, but also in the emerging market economies of the South.[67] The dependence of money markets on a 'derisking state' (Gabor) for the provision and protection of collateral reflects the needs of a highly financialized capitalism; but it is a world away from the neoliberal fantasy of self-regulating markets.[68]

Friedman's critique of Keynesianism rests on the concept of the natural rate of unemployment – that is, the rate of unemployment determined by 'real' factors such as productivity and wages. In the heyday of 'functional finance' during the Second World War, the Marxist economist Michał Kalecki explained why big business is attached to doctrines of this kind:

> Under a *laissez-faire* system the level of employment depends to a great extent on the so-called state of confidence. If this deteriorates, private investment declines, which results in a fall of output and employment (both directly and through the secondary effect of the fall in incomes upon consumption and investment). This gives the capitalists a powerful indirect control over Government policy: everything which may shake the state of confidence must be carefully avoided because it would cause an economic crisis. But once the Government learns the trick of increasing employment by its own purchases, this powerful controlling device loses its effectiveness. Hence budget deficits necessary to carry out Government intervention must be regarded as perilous. The social function of the doctrine of 'sound finance' is to make the level of employment dependent on the state of confidence.[69]

Moreover, 'under a regime of permanent full employment, the "sack" would cease to play its role as a disciplinary measure. The social position of the boss would be undermined and the self-assurance and class-consciousness of the working class would grow. Strikes for wage increases and improvements in conditions of work would create political tension.'[70] During the 1980s, mass unemployment indeed played a decisive role in breaking the self-confidence, organization, and militancy that key groups of workers (car-workers, dockers, miners) had built up during the long boom. Since this 'heroic' moment, what kept workers disorganized and on the back foot has been more continuous market pressures, and in particular the threat of shifting manufacturing capacity to Asia, Mexico, or Central and Eastern Europe – alongside the fear of capital flight designed to discipline any government that deviates from the neoliberal norm. The rapid shift to austerity in Europe and the United States after the global financial crisis was a determined attempt to restore this norm after the emergency measures taken to prevent another Great Depression. But it was never fully successful: the governments that drove austerity, for example under Merkel in Germany and the Conservative–Liberal coalition in Britain, continued to rely on what the British Chancellor of the Exchequer of the time, George Osborne, called the 'monetary activism' of the central banks to prevent the cuts in public spending from precipitating another recession.

But the pandemic saw a much more sustained return to the 'politicized economy'.[71] Perhaps the most interesting development came with Joe Biden's administration in the United States. Biden, a veteran Democratic Party politician, was generally seen as the continuity candidate when he ran for president in 2020. 'Continuity' here means with the previous Democratic administrations of Bill Clinton (1993–2001) and Barack Obama (2009–17). They used Washington's muscle to promote neoliberalism globally and to maintain US hegemony. And certainly Biden's cabinet was packed full of veterans of these administrations, including many hawks who thought that Obama was too reluctant to take military action. Biden indeed pursued business as usual, notably in the confrontation with Russia. But he also deviated from the Clinton–Obama template, pulling the US troops out of Afghanistan when resistance from the Pentagon stopped Obama, or indeed Donald Trump, from taking this step.

But the most significant shift was in economic strategy. Biden followed up his initial $1.9 trillion American Rescue Plan – extra spending financed by borrowing, by announcing in the spring of 2021 a $2 trillion American Jobs Plan designed to upgrade and overhaul the decaying infrastructure and a $1.8 trillion American Families Plan that aimed to improve welfare provision.

The commentator James Medlock tweeted in January 2021 that 'The era of "the era of big government is over" is over' (the original quotation comes from Clinton's 1996 State of the Union Address).[72] Brian Deese, director of Biden's National Economic Council, points to three changes since Obama took office in 2009 that had led to this shift.

The first is climate change, which ostensibly is driving the infrastructure programme (though the watered-down version that eventually limped through Congress involved generous handouts to the fossil fuel corporations). Second, Deese says, 'our economy is becoming more unequal'.[73] Neither Clinton nor Obama gave the impression of caring much about how neoliberal policies have widened inequality. This shift probably reflects in part the impact of Bernie Sanders, of left-wing Congresswomen such as Alexandria Ocasio-Cortez, and of their young supporters – that is, their success in pulling even mainstream Democrats such as Biden leftwards. But it is also a response to the polarization of US society under Trump and the Black Lives Matter revolt. According to the White House, the Jobs Plan 'prioritizes addressing long-standing and persistent racial injustice. The plan targets 40 percent of the benefits of climate and clean infrastructure investments to disadvantaged communities.'[74]

Third, according to Deese,

> China is in a very different place than it was a decade ago. We are in a different place vis-à-vis our international competitors. And my openness to more targeted efforts to try to build domestic industrial strength ... has increased, because I think we are not operating on a level playing field.
>
> There's not a market-based solution to try to address some of the big weaknesses that we're seeing open up in our economy when we're dealing with competitors like China that are not operating on market-based terms.[75]

This makes it clear that Biden's aim is to use state intervention to revamp US imperialism in the face of China, which Deese describes as 'the ascendant economic and military power in the world'.[76] The White House says that the infrastructure plan 'will unify and mobilize the country to meet the great challenges of our time: the climate crisis and the ambitions of an autocratic China'.[77] Nevertheless, Cédric Durand underlines the significance of the shift: 'the scale of the Administration's public spending is deliberately designed to generate a high-pressure economy, which necessarily involves an element of inflationary risk. It is on this point that 2021 can be considered a 1979 coup in reverse ... This seems to be Biden's strategy: increasing employment, reducing inequality and fostering productivity growth, via high-pressure economic policy.'[78]

Biden's and Deese's economic ambitions quickly ran aground in a deeply polarized Congress where the balance between the two parties had tilted only narrowly in the Democrats' favour in 2020–1. Their difficulties were exacerbated by a dramatic shift in the economic context, namely a resurgence in inflation, which by 2022 was hitting the highest rates for 40 years in the major economies and roiling the financial markets. This development hardly amounted to a vindication of austerian critiques of QE, let alone of Republican opposition to Biden's economic policies. Inflation had remained subdued through the 2010s. The huge infusions of central bank money into the financial system boosted not the general price level, but the prices of financial assets, and hence the wealth of the rich (see Figure 3 in Chapter 2).

The take-off in inflation rates in 2020–2 was largely a consequence of two factors. The first was the disruptions to labour markets and supply chains caused by the continuing pandemic and exacerbated by a lockdown-induced shift in consumer demand from services to goods. The second was a rise in energy prices that (a) was caused by increased competition for the supply of natural gas, as governments, in their first feeble steps towards a 'green transition', encouraged a switch away from reliance on coal and petrol; and (b) was intensified by the Putin regime's exploitation of Russia's pole position as an energy supplier.[79] The outbreak of the war in Ukraine, which further disrupted the production and circulation of energy, food, and raw materials, gave another fillip to inflation.

The inflationary surge recalled the central bankers to their original vocation as 'high priests' of 'hard money' (in Luttwak's words). Their main preoccupation was that the resulting rise in the cost of living would produce a 'wage–price spiral' as workers reacted by demanding compensating pay increases and employers pushed up prices further in response. When the Bank of England became the first major central bank to impose monetary tightening by raising interest rates and rowing back on QE in February 2022, the *Financial Times* explained: 'Most troubling for the BoE was information from its regional agents showing companies expect pay settlements to rise to 4.8% in 2022 amid a hot labour market, while a central bank survey found businesses saying they would raise prices by a similar amount.'[80] In an interview with the BBC, Bank of England Governor Andrew Bailey spelled out the harsh class logic of his policy shift: 'Mr Bailey said that while it would be "painful" for workers to accept that prices would rise faster than their wages, he added that some "moderation of wage rises" was needed to prevent inflation becoming entrenched.'[81]

The post-Keynesian economist Nicholas Kaldor once wrote: 'all inflationary processes that proceed in time, that is to say which do not peter out of their own accord, are cost-induced inflations: they reflect the failure of society to distribute its real income in a manner that is acceptable to the great majority of its inhabitants.'[82] Bailey's strategy of forcing down real wages to protect profits amply confirms this judgement. Criticizing the 'class warriors of the Bank of England', Martin Sandbu of the *Financial Times* puts it well: 'the crux of the matter is really distributional. Who bears the cost, in terms of their real income, of a negative terms-of-trade shock – wage earners or business owners?'[83] There is considerable evidence that what was developing was in fact a profit–price spiral. In Britain, for example, one study points to the role in the current inflation of companies that benefit from higher energy prices ('windfall profits') or from market power that allows them to increase profits by raising prices ('excess profits').[84]

Nevertheless, the central bankers stuck to their guns. Interestingly, the economic disruption caused by the Russian invasion of Ukraine and the western response did not prompt a retreat. The Fed started to raise interest rates in March 2022, the first in a succession of increases (sharper, as inflation proved stubborn), and promised that it would soon start cutting its $9 trillion balance sheet 'at a rapid pace' – 'quantitative tightening' replacing QE.[85] Donald Rissmiller of Strategas Research Partners commented: 'The Fed is now likely in a "tighten until something breaks" mode. The key question remains whether it's inflation or growth that breaks first.'[86] The combination of rising interest rates and inflation and an increased debt burden thanks to the strengthening dollar is likely to strike the poorer parts of the world, still reeling as they are from the effects of the pandemic, like a hammer blow. The end – perhaps temporary – of the cheap money era and the further instability this brought were underlined in Britain in October 2022, when the financial markets destroyed the short-lived ultra-Thatcherite government of Liz Truss after it announced a massive package of debt-funded tax cuts. This display of market power brought to office the fiscal conservative Rishi Sunak.

Behind the fear of a wage–price spiral lie class memories of the stagflation of the 1970s, when well-organized workers indeed sought to protect their living standards by demanding big pay rises. Perhaps there is also a concern that the disruption of labour supplies as a result of the pandemic may increase workers' bargaining power. After all, the terrible collapse in mediaeval Europe's population as a result of the Black Death tilted the balance in favour of tenants and labourers. Ole Benedictow writes: 'Consequently, and in the long term, rents and fines fell strongly, and both urban and agricultural real wages rose correspondingly. This was "the golden era of the wage worker", as W. Abel called it. It was also the "golden era" of poor people in the countryside.' [87]

Two Fed economists have recently drawn on Kalecki to argue that 'the "missing inflation" puzzle [after the global financial crisis] is due to a collapse of workers' bargaining power' in the neoliberal era.[88] It is possible that the pandemic might mark the beginning of a shift in power back to labour – there has been an uptick in strikes in the United States, partly encouraged by the presence of a more sympathetic administration in Washington, and also in Britain, where trade unionists confront a hard-right Tory government. But this is too early to tell. Joseph Choonara warns that the so-called great resignation – workers taking advantage of economic recovery to quit their jobs, especially in the 'hospitality' sector, which is notorious for its poor pay and conditions – is likely to be short-lived: 'If recovery continues, the whip of economic necessity will likely force workers who have dropped out of the workplace, particularly younger ones, to return ... a long-term shift in the position of labour is unlikely without a higher degree of struggle by workers. Market mechanisms cannot substitute for this.'[89]

But the central bankers' reaction to the resurgence of inflation underlines the limits of the institutional shift away from neoliberalism. This is hardly surprising. The New Deal in the United States – the most powerful single impulse behind the formation of the Keynesian economic policy regime – was driven on, not just by Franklin Roosevelt's dramatic election victories and battles in Congress and with the Supreme Court, but by the wave of mass strikes and plant occupations that unionized basic industry during the second half of the 1930s and rolled on till after the Second World War.[90] A comparable upsurge from below, rather than the initiatives from above that we have seen, will be needed to break the back of neoliberalism and open the way to a different future.

4

Hegemonic Decline and Geopolitical Antagonism

A geopolitical rift in globalization

Today the rivalry between the United States and China is the dominant feature of world politics. Even the conflict between Russia and NATO that sparked the Ukraine War must be seen in the context of this antagonism. Before Donald Trump became president of the United States, it was still a trend – more a possibility than an actuality. Trump made it real by launching a trade war with Beijing in March 2018. But it is his successor, Joe Biden, who has confirmed the centrality of the conflict, essentially by continuing and even radicalizing Trump's policies towards China. Indeed, whereas Trump vacillated, slapping tariffs on Chinese imports yet seeking to ingratiate himself to President Xi Jinping, Biden has made the antagonism between Washington and Beijing the central plank of his administration's policies. Thus, presenting his American Jobs Plan in March 2021, he said:

> I truly believe we're in a moment where history is going to look back on this time as a fundamental choice that had to be made between democracies and autocracies.
>
> You know, there's a lot of autocrats in the world who think the reason why they're going to win is democracies can't reach consensus any longer; autocracies do.
>
> That's what competition between America and China and the rest of the world is all about. It's a basic question: Can democracies still deliver for their people?[1]

After the announcement of the AUKUS (Australia, United Kingdom, United States) deal in September 2021, under which the United States and Britain are to help Australia to build nuclear submarines that can operate close to the coasts of Asia, Edward Luce of the *Financial Times* wrote an article headlined 'For Biden – and America – It's Basically China from now on'.[2] Secretary of State Anthony Blinken confirmed this in May 2022:

> Even as President Putin's war continues, we will remain focused on the most serious long-term challenge to the international order – and that's posed by the People's Republic of China.
>
> China is the only country with both the intent to reshape the international order and, increasingly, the economic, diplomatic, military, and technological power to do it. Beijing's vision would move us away from the universal values that have sustained so much of the world's progress over the past 75 years.[3]

Despite the bitter divisions between Democrats and Republicans in US domestic politics, there is a consensus between the two parties about containing China. Turning round the famous slogan coined by Bill Clinton's campaign manager James Carville ('It's the economy, stupid!'), another *Financial Times* columnist, Rana Foroohar, writes: 'It's geopolitics, stupid' … It turns out that the world *isn't* flat, after all and the general public feels the bumps.'[4]

Here, then, we confront the reality of imperialism today: the interweaving of economic competition and interstate rivalries. Geopolitical antagonisms cut across the transnational production networks that helped to create the illusion, prevalent before the global financial crisis and articulated by the *New York Times* columnist Thomas Friedman in a ridiculous book, that, economically at least, the world is flat.[5] The Russo-Ukrainian War is indeed the definitive refutation of the theory put forward by ideologues of globalization – but also by the autonomist Marxists Michael Hardt and Toni Negri – that global economic integration would render geopolitical competition obsolete.[6]

The Europe-wide hunt for the wealth of Russian oligarchs has served to confirm how much the latter, with their Mayfair mansions, their football clubs, their yachts, their private jets, their family offices, their children at British public schools, have been part of the global superrich. Commenting on western states' targeting of the Russian central bank, the *Financial Times* observed: 'The weaponization of finance has profound implications for the future of international politics and economics. Many of the basic assumptions about the post-cold war era are being turned on their head. Globalization was once sold as a barrier to conflict, a web of dependencies that would bring former foes ever closer together. Instead, it has become a new battleground.'[7]

The problems facing chip manufacturers as a result of the disruption caused by the COVID-19 pandemic were exacerbated by the war in Ukraine: Ukraine supplies 50 per cent of the world's neon gas and 40 per cent of krypton gas; these gases are used in the production of semiconductors.[8] But a confrontation between the United States and China could have an even worse impact on chip supplies, and hence on global production and consumption. The Taiwan Semiconductor Manufacturing Company (TSMC) is the most important producer of advanced chips in the world, responsible for almost 90 per cent of the most advanced nodes in production.[9] Most of TSMC's manufacturing plants are concentrated in Taiwan itself, which Beijing reserves the right to invade if it deems this action necessary in order to reunite the island with the Chinese mainland.

Imperialism after the Cold War

Biden's focus on China shows that the antagonism can't be blamed on Trump. Both Washington and Beijing present it as an ideological conflict – western freedom versus Chinese authoritarianism and Chinese state-guided 'common prosperity' versus neoliberal anarchy and decline. Ideology undoubtedly plays a role, but the conflict only makes sense starting from the Marxist theory of imperialism. As I argued in Chapter 1, the generalization of capitalist imperialism in the late nineteenth century marked the intersection of economic and geopolitical competition. But imperialism, like capitalism itself, changes over time.[10]

It has had two previous phases. The first was the era of classical imperialism (1870–1945); its dominant feature was the colonial partition of the world by rival Great Powers that precipitated the first age of catastrophe. The second phase, superpower imperialism (1945–91), was the era of the Cold War, when two blocs of states, headed respectively by the United States and the Soviet Union, competed geopolitically and ideologically. The Soviet Union's key weakness was that it was a much smaller and less productive economy than the United States. Western capitalism dominated the world market, which had been reconstituted under US leadership after 1945. The state capitalist regimes eventually broke under the double burden of the arms race with the West and of the foreign debt they had accumulated in their final decades.[11] Mazen Labban suggests that the Soviet Union's increasingly important role, from the 1960s onwards, as an energy supplier to the West helped to transform 'the Soviet Union from a relatively advanced industrial economy, potentially equal in its industrial capacity to the industrialized West, into a resource-exporting, peripheral dependency'.[12]

The third phase of imperialism, which opened with the end of the Cold War in 1989–91, is defined by the efforts of the United States to maintain its hegemony and to make it genuinely global. One can differentiate four distinct subperiods here. The first, which corresponds roughly to the 1990s, was characterized by what international relations experts call 'unipolarity'.[13] The United States sought to consolidate its hegemony by actively promoting economic globalization, on the assumption that open markets would favour its banks and corporations; the crushing defeat of Saddam Hussein's Iraq in 1991 demonstrated the military supremacy of the Pentagon, which was maintained at a level that could deal with any challenge from Russia and China.[14] Bill Clinton's administration (1993–2001) presided over what proved to be the apogee of US global power; Washington's dominance was legitimized by the ideology of liberal internationalism, according to which liberal capitalist states have an interest in cooperating among themselves and in isolating, assimilating, and, if necessary, attacking 'authoritarian' states that represent inherent threats to them.[15] China's admission to the World Trade Organization (WTO) in 2001 was understood in Washington as a concession granted from a position of strength and as a means of educating Beijing into its responsibilities as an increasingly important member of the liberal capitalist order.

This comparatively brief subperiod highlighted the character of US imperialism. Washington's refusal to recognize the validity of regional 'spheres of influence' (for example the one claimed by Russia) reflected US policymakers' treatment of the entire globe as *their* sphere of influence, even though they conceptualized it as the 'rules-based international order' regulated by international institutions that they had either created (the United Nations, the International Monetary Fund (IMF), the World Bank, and the WTO) or promoted (above all, NATO and the European Union).[16]

The 9/11 attacks on New York and Washington brought an abrupt end to this unipolar moment, marking the opening of a new subperiod dominated by the 'war on terror'. The administration of George W. Bush (2001–9) sought to reassert US dominance and reinforce Washington's control over access to Middle East oil by invading and occupying Iraq in March 2003. This proved a disastrous mistake: the occupations of Afghanistan and Iraq led to the most serious military defeats the United States has ever suffered, at the hands of armed Islamist insurgencies.[17] The huge defeat the United States suffered in Vietnam in 1975 made only a limited breach in the international system. Aided by the effective alliance it had struck with China against the Soviet Union, Washington was able to confine the communist victories to Indochina. In subsequent decades East and South-East Asia became the venue for the most dynamic expansion of capitalism in the system's history, which, at least in the short term, reinforced US hegemony.

By contrast, the Iraq debacle destabilized the Middle East, shifting the regional balance of power in favour of the Islamic republican regime in Iran, setting the scene for the revolutions in Tunisia, Egypt, Libya, and Syria in 2011, and unleashing the Islamic State group. The disarray was increased by the outbreak of the global financial crisis of 2007–9. Even though, as we saw in Chapter 3, the United States played a decisive role in managing the crisis, the evident failure of the economic policy regime reinforced the sense of what even the neoconservative Robert Kagan called 'America's crisis of legitimacy'.[18] The WTO's stalemated 'Doha round' of negotiations on trade liberalization (launched in the aftermath of 9/11) underlined the shift in the global power balance, as emerging market economies such as China, India, and Brazil refused to go along with the proposals of the United States and of the European Union.

Subperiod 3 – the decade or so that started with Barack Obama's accession to the presidency in January 2009 – seems, in retrospect, to have been transitional. Domestically, Obama continued the crisis management measures started by the Bush administration while striving to restore neoliberal normality. Internationally, he sought to reduce US military commitments in the Greater Middle East (though he continued to wage war against radical Islamists through the use of special forces and drone assassinations.)[19] The main exception was the 2011 NATO intervention in Libya, which sought to take advantage of the rising against Muammar al-Gaddafi to install a pro-western regime, but in fact precipitated the country into an unending and devastating civil war.[20] By stepping back in the Middle East, Obama hoped to facilitate a 'pivot to Asia' that would allow Washington to concentrate on containing China, whose economic ascent had been only briefly interrupted by the global financial crisis, in marked contrast with the 'secular stagnation' into which the United States and the European Union had sunk. This strategic shift was hindered by turbulence in a Middle East destabilized by war and revolution and by the efforts of Vladimir Putin's Russia to take advantage of the United States' distraction by seizing Crimea and intervening in the Syrian Civil War.[21]

For all the noise he made, Donald Trump in many respects continued Obama's foreign policy. Thus he resisted pressure from the national security establishment (dismissed by Obama's adviser Ben Rhodes as 'the Blob')[22] to escalate what he called the 'forever wars' in the Greater Middle East, though he maintained the US military presence in the region and ordered the assassination of the Iranian Revolutionary Guard commander Qassem Soleimani in January 2020. As Andrew Bacevich sardonically puts it, '[l]ike the war on drugs or the war on poverty, the War for the Greater Middle East has become a permanent fixture in American life and is accepted as such.[23] The most important change Trump made was to ditch Obama's multilateral strategy for economically isolating China through the Trans-Pacific Partnership for a unilateral confrontation over trade. One way of understanding Biden's China policy is that it combines the approaches pursued by both his predecessors – brigading US allies together against China and directly challenging Beijing as well.

Sources of the antagonism between the United States and China

In any case, we can say that the COVID-19 pandemic marked the opening of a fourth subperiod in the evolution of contemporary imperialism: as we saw in Chapter 2, international cooperation to combat the virus was undermined by the rivalry between Washington and Beijing. This conflict is widely dubbed a new cold war. But there is a very striking difference. The Soviet Union and its client states were closed economies, largely isolated from the world market. By contrast, China's rise to the position of second biggest economy in the world depended on its opening up to global markets, a move orchestrated by the Communist Party leader Deng Xiaoping from 1978 onwards. Today it is the biggest producer and exporter of manufactured goods and the biggest importer of oil; in 2020 it became the biggest recipient of foreign direct investment, though it slipped back into second place in 2021, as foreign direct investment in the United States more than doubled, thanks to the economic recovery from the impact of COVID-19.[24] The rest of the world's dependence on production in China has been dramatized by the effects of the disruptions to supply chains during the pandemic.

Why the antagonism between the United States and China, then? First, the Chinese economy remains at its core state-directed, despite its integration in the world market and in international capital flows. The financial system is controlled (not very well) by the central bank and the four state banks. State-owned enterprises continue to dominate production, and even private firms are caught up in the Communist Party of China's (CPC) system of patronage. This works both ways: private capital can colonize the party-state bureaucracy, but Xi's anti-corruption campaign has seen billionaires executed. The Chinese government has started blocking big private platform firms such as Alibaba, which sought share launches in New York, out of fear that their integration in global financial markets would undermine the CPC's political control of the economy and would give western regulators access to sensitive data.

According to the *Financial Times*, increasingly centralized state guidance of Chinese stock markets is pushing both local and foreign investors towards funding investment 'in either the kinds of high-end manufacturers and AI companies needed to protect China from the impact of US sanctions or the renewable energy and electric vehicle companies the leadership considers central to the future of the global economy.'[25] China is thus much less permeable to western capital than most major economies. This does not make it any less capitalist: the Chinese state and the capitalists based within its borders, whether private or (as Chris Harman puts it) political, are subject to the same logic of competitive accumulation as their western rivals.[26] Indeed, this logic underlies the antagonism between Washington and Beijing.

Second, the CPC leadership is pursuing its own imperialist agenda. China remains outside the system of alliances that the United States has constructed since the Second World War in order to bind the other major capitalist states to it. The Chinese leadership doesn't necessarily aim at replacing the United States as the hegemonic capitalist state globally, at least not in the short term. But it does want to push the United States out of the Indo-Pacific region, which it has dominated since defeating Japan in the Second World War. Given that this region is now the main hub of global capitalism, representing about 40 per cent of global GDP, such a retreat would certainly reduce the power and the status of the United States drastically, and there is no doubt that its ruling class would not tolerate peacefully such a demotion.[27]

Beijing also intends to complete the reunification of China after the country's parcellization at the hands of outside powers during the nineteenth and early twentieth centuries. This means, above all, reincorporating Taiwan, which was annexed and colonized by Japan at the end of the nineteenth century and became the base of the defeated Guomindang regime after the victory of the Chinese Revolution in 1949. Ever since, Taiwan's security has been underwritten by the United States. China is also busy consolidating its control of the hotly contested South China Sea. It is using different forms of pressure to push states to align with it and to punish states that stick with Washington; for example, it imposed informal economic sanctions on South Korea and Australia. Beijing's claims to Indian territory – which led to the death of a number of both countries' soldiers in a fight in a disputed border zone in June 2020 – helped to push the other Asian giant towards the United States.

Some Marxists deny that contemporary China is an imperialist state. The most sophisticated argument has been developed by Guglielmo Carchedi and Michael Roberts. They define imperialist states as states whose capitalists benefit from the global redistribution of surplus value from technologically backward to technologically advanced firms through the formation of a worldwide rate of profit. They contend that

> none of the so-called large 'emerging economies' are making net gains in trade or investments – indeed they are net losers to the imperialist bloc – and that includes China. Indeed, the imperialist bloc extracts more surplus value out of China than out of many other peripheral economies. The reason is that China is a huge trading nation; and it is also technologically backward compared to the imperialist bloc. So given international market prices, it loses some of the surplus value created by its workers through trade to the more advanced economies.[28]

Despite the insights that Carchedi and Roberts's analysis offers, their definition of imperialism is too narrowly economic and excludes the interaction between capital accumulation and geopolitical competition. The rising imperialist states of the early twentieth century – the United States, Germany, and Japan – were similar to China today in that their power was based on a rapid industrialization of their domestic economies. But, as exporters of capital, they lagged far behind Britain and France, the main financial players, which benefitted from extensive networks of colonies and semi-colonies; and the newcomers depended on them for help with financing investment in their domestic economies. According to Herbert Feis's classic study, by 1914 foreign investment represented 'substantially over' 25 per cent of Britain's national income, about 16 per cent of France's, and 6 per cent of Germany's.[29] Nevertheless, industrialization allowed Germany and Japan in particular to build up sufficiently large military capabilities to grab a 'place in the sun', to use Kaiser Wilhelm II's expression. (As for US capitalists, they benefitted from the colonization of a vast continent and expansion southwards into Latin America and westwards across the Pacific.) Today Xi Jinping is using China's economic muscle to support its territorial expansion.

The paradox is that western capital is still eager to participate more deeply in the Chinese economy. The big Wall Street banks have been desperate to consolidate their position in the Chinese financial market in order to get access to the vast pool of savings that has been built up there. Rana Foroohar recently asked: 'Am I the only one amazed by the juxtaposition of China testing hypersonic weapons and NATO's new mission to fend off the Middle Kingdom, with Goldman Sachs joining JPMorgan as the second independent bank to be allowed to operate freely in China without a local partner?'[30] Moreover, as we will see in more detail in what follows, the patterns of capital accumulation in the United States and China are interdependent. In this sense China's relationship with the United States is more similar to the Anglo-German antagonism before 1914 than to the Cold War conflict between East and West. Britain was Germany's biggest export market, while German firms tended to finance their investments through bills of exchange raised on the City of London. This didn't prevent the two countries from going to war.[31]

Germany challenged Britain both economically and geopolitically. So too does China vis-à-vis the United States. Xi's 'Made in China 2025' programme, which aims at technologically upgrading the economy, is a direct threat to the United States' traditional lead in hi-tech industries. The two states are now locked in a geoeconomic struggle, in which (as we saw in Chapter 2) adaptation to climate change is one of the main fields of competition. The disruption to global supply chains caused by the pandemic, and in particular the Chinese government's policy of shutting down regions affected by COVID-19 infections, have intensified western concerns about global capitalism's dependence on factories in China. Meanwhile the People's Liberation Army is rapidly improving its military capabilities – and especially its ability to strike at the US Navy off the coasts of Asia. But the arms race is much broader. In October 2021 the *Financial Times* reported that China has tested a hypersonic missile that might be able to bypass US antiballistic missile defences. General Mark A. Milley, chairman of the US Joint Chiefs of Staff, described this development as 'very close' to a 'Sputnik moment'.[32] In April 2022 AUKUS was extended to cooperation in producing and countering hypersonic weapons. This contest is a recipe for collision between the two biggest capitalist economies in history.

The setbacks US imperialism has suffered this century – the global financial crisis, defeat in Iraq and Afghanistan, the Trump presidency that culminated in the lethal chaos surrounding the pandemic, the bungled pull-out from Kabul in August 2021– have encouraged the Chinese elite to assume that the United States is in irreversible decline. Thus, according to Zheng Yongnian of the Chinese University of Hong Kong,

> the US looks like the Soviet Union from the outside, and looks like China's late Qing Dynasty from the inside ... In the late Qing Dynasty, many elites in China still thought the empire a 'celestial empire' and 'centre of civilization' while regarding the Westerners as barbarians despite its backwardness and failure in the two Opium Wars ... This is strikingly similar to the conditions of American elites and intellectuals who rarely reflect themselves. The vast majority of Americans still consider themselves to be the centre of the world ... From the outside, the US is much like the Soviet Union back then with the core problem of over-expansion with limited capability of doing so. The over-expansion that started from the Obama administration has turned China and Russia to the US' enemies.
>
> China, on the other hand, is more like the US back then ... China is open and confident. It is good at learning from history as it has done so. The US, however, is too young. It doesn't have a long history that could be served as its mirror. The US will continue to make serious mistakes as a result.[33]

After the upheavals of the past century or so, it would be foolish to rule out the possibility that the United States will suffer the fate of late imperial China or of the Soviet Union, particularly in the light of the internal strains that will be explored in chapters 5 and 6. But, as a power, the United States is very far from being finished. It remains very much the leading capitalist state. Its share of global output may be declining (albeit comparatively slowly), but it has four big assets.[34]

The first asset is Wall Street. Thanks to their role in orchestrating a response to the global financial crisis, the US Treasury and the Federal Reserve are, if anything, more central to the management of the international financial system than previously. This enhances Washington's power geopolitically, for example by allowing it to impose sanctions on the states it opposes – a marked feature of US statecraft in recent years that has been taken to a new level in the response to Russia's invasion of Ukraine.[35] Second, big tech gives US capitalism the lead in an astonishingly profitable sector. The United States has ten out of the twenty most valuable technology companies, Apple, Microsoft, Amazon, Alphabet (owner of Google), Facebook, Nvidia, and Intel among them. China has three.[36] Biden's decision in October 2022 to deny China access to advanced chips made with US equipment is thus a serious blow to Xi's hi-tech ambitions. The third great US asset is, of course, the Pentagon. In 2021, US defence spending was greater than the combined military budgets of China, India, Britain, Russia, France, Germany, Saudi Arabia, Japan, South Korea, Italy, Australia, and Spain.[37] Moreover, the Pentagon is reconfiguring its capabilities in order to deal more effectively with the challenge from China.[38]

Finally, one of the great strengths of Washington's statecraft is the system of alliances it has built up since the 1940s. AUKUS is a new pact; but a much broader brigading together is going on, especially among states in the Indo-Pacific region, the aim being to encircle China. There are the Quad (the United States, Japan, India, Australia), the Five Eyes intelligence pact (the United States, Britain, Canada, Australia, New Zealand), and the Five Powers Defence Arrangement (Britain, Australia, Malaysia, Singapore, and New Zealand). Many of these alliances are based in the 'Anglosphere' – the United States, Britain, and Britain's former colonies. Washington's mobilization against China came at a good time for Boris Johnson in his search for a role for 'global Britain' after Brexit. The voyage of the task force headed by the new British aircraft carrier *Queen Elizabeth II* in 2021 involved US participation and offered provocations to both Russia and China. British imperialism, with its relatively large military capabilities and close integration with the US military–industrial complex, is reasserting its traditional role as Washington's most loyal strategic partner.

The United States is also deploying its existing alliances. The most important of these is NATO, which expanded into Central and Eastern Europe in tandem with the European Union, in the first years of the third millennium. Its original role in militarily containing the Soviet Union remains active – witness the mobilization of support for

Ukraine against Russia in 2021–2 and the efforts to expand further, into the Baltic. But NATO is also shifting towards helping Washington to counter China. At its Madrid summit in June 2022, NATO adopted a new 'strategic concept', which identifies Russia as 'the most significant and direct threat to Allies' security and to peace and stability in the Euro-Atlantic area', but also warns that China's 'stated ambitions and coercive policies challenge our interests, security and values' and that the 'deepening strategic partnership' between Beijing and Moscow and 'their mutually reinforcing attempts to undercut the rules-based international order run counter to our values and interests'.[39]

Debt-driven accumulation on both sides of the Pacific

Zheng's failure to consider these strengths reflects the self-confidence that Chinese people understandably feel after the extraordinary ascent China has experienced over the past 40 years. But all the signs are that the economic model on which this achievement has been built is running aground. In a very important and compellingly argued book, *Trade Wars Are Class Wars*, Matthew C. Klein and Michael Pettis argue that the extraordinarily high levels of investment required to make China the largest producer and exporter of manufactured goods presuppose repression of consumption, as reflected in the failure of wages to rise in line with increases in output. The authors estimate that 'workers at nonfinancial corporations in China are paid only 40% of the value they produce. In most other countries, by contrast, the labour share of corporate value added is closer to 70%.'[40] This strategy allowed China to run up chronic balance of payments surpluses; increasingly cheap manufactured goods and capital flowed from China across the Pacific, to sustain a US economy that is itself more and more driven by the accumulation of financial assets.

As Pettis puts it,

> Today's trade war is not really a conflict between the United States and China as countries, nor is it even a broader conflict between deficit countries and surplus countries. Rather, it is a conflict between economic sectors. Bankers and owners of capital in both the surplus and the deficit countries have benefited from suppressed wages, rising profits, and increased mobility of international capital. Workers in the surplus countries paid for the imbalances in the form of lower incomes and depreciated currencies. Workers in the deficit countries paid for the imbalances in the form of higher unemployment and rising debt.

Reversing inequality and other distortions in income distribution in both the surplus and the deficit countries is therefore the only durable way to end the trade war.[41]

Meanwhile, both the United States and China have found their current paths of growth increasingly hard to sustain. We saw in the previous chapter how the Biden administration has sought to initiate a state-directed restructuring of US capitalism. Beijing was able to limit the impact of the global financial crisis and the resulting collapse in the demand for its exports by instructing the banks to increase lending by around $600 billion and thereby to sustain investment and economic growth. This helped further to shift the global distribution of economic power to the advantage of China, which benefitted from an increasing redirection of international trade networks towards it. But it also reinforced the tendency to move 'from high investment to over-investment', as Klein and Pettis describe it.[42]

The ratio of debt to GDP in China rose from below 150 per cent in 2006 to over 250 per cent at the start of the pandemic. Unlike in other big economies such as the United States and Japan, where government borrowing is the largest contributor to indebtedness, in China non-financial corporations' debts have reached 160 per cent of national income.[43] Increasingly in the 2010s, the driver of growth came to be the real estate sector, where companies closely linked to local governments, which are heavily dependent on land sales as a source of revenue, launched vast debt-financed housebuilding programmes. According to the *Financial Times*, 'China's property sector is estimated to account for about 30 per cent of total economic output. In 2020 local governments raised Rmb8.4tn from land sales, accounting for about a third of their total revenues.'[44] Beijing's Belt and Road Initiative (BRI) was intended to reduce China's dependence on the Straits of Malacca, connecting the Pacific and Indian oceans as the main route for its imports and exports, and hence to limit its vulnerability to US naval power. But it also serves to offset this crisis of overaccumulation by offering new projects for Chinese firms.[45]

In the past few years the Chinese government has sought to rein in this debt-driven overaccumulation. In a keynote article published in 2021, Xi himself repeated earlier calls 'to shift the focus to improving the quality and returns of economic growth, to promoting sustained and healthy economic development, and to pursuing genuine rather than inflated GDP growth' – the Chinese original is more vivid here: 'growth with water' – 'and achieving high-quality, efficient, and sustainable development'.[46] Beijing's revival of the slogan 'common prosperity', originally coined by Deng Xiaoping, represents an acknowledgement of the environmental destruction and economic inequality wrought by its growth model. The slogan aspires to reorient the economy around technical innovation and the domestic market.

Thus, in response to the outbreak of the COVID-19 pandemic, China stood out from the rush to technocratic Keynesianism elsewhere (see chapter 3), with a significantly smaller fiscal stimulus than in 2008–9 and very little direct support to households.[47] In August 2020, in line with the same policy, Beijing imposed the 'three red lines': hard limits on property developers' debt-to-asset, debt-to-equity, and cash-to-short-term-debt ratios. Companies responded by issuing off-balance-sheet commercial paper (debt that the firms' suppliers often are forced to accept) to get around these restrictions, in what the *Financial Times* called 'a classic example of how, for every central government regulatory action in China, there is often a market-driven reaction that helps the companies targeted to work around it'.[48]

But by the end of 2021 the second biggest real estate developer, China Evergrande Group, was close to defaulting on 'accumulated liabilities of about Rmb2tn, equivalent to 2 per cent of gross domestic product, which are owed to creditors ranging from individuals who bought high-yielding investment products from the group to the country's largest construction companies and banks'.[49] Real estate has become so central to the Chinese economy that Beijing was under pressure to rescue, if not Evergrande itself and the likes of it, at least their creditors and suppliers, at the price of retreating from its policy of reducing its reliance on debt-driven growth.[50] Indeed, in grappling with the problems of an economy that was slowing thanks to the lockdowns imposed for the sake of combating the spread of Omicron, the government doubled down on the debt-financed high-investment–high-export model; China's industrial subsidies are the highest in the world.[51]

So the rivalry between the United States and China is no simple confrontation between a weary Titan such as Edwardian Britain, no longer able to support economically its hegemonic position, and a buoyant rising power, open and confident. Both rivals have pursued mutually dependent debt-driven accumulation strategies whose limits are now very visible. These economic difficulties could of course encourage the political leaderships on both sides of the Pacific to beat the nationalist drum in order to focus discontent outwards. This is, in essence, what Trump did, with great political success. Thus, as in the 1930s, economic crisis can fuel geopolitical antagonisms.

Regional power struggles

Capitalist imperialism can't be equated simply with empire in the transhistorical sense of a powerful state imposing its will on its neighbours. It is a *system* of capitalist domination and inter-capitalist competition. Capitalist imperialism is necessarily plural, because it is regulated by the logic of competitive accumulation. The process of uneven and combined development inherent in capitalism creates a global hierarchy of states that reflect the unequal distribution of economic and military power. At the top lies a small group of imperialist states whose economic and financial weight and capabilities of power projection allow them to compete globally. Today these are mainly the United States (still far ahead of the rest), China, Britain, Japan, Germany, France, and Russia.[52] The next rung in the hierarchy is occupied by 'sub-imperialisms': the dynamic of economic and geopolitical competition constitutive of imperialism manifests itself at the level of specific regions, where the most powerful states seek to assert their interests against one another and against their weaker neighbours.[53] Today the smaller imperialisms and regional sub-imperialisms are all manoeuvring for advantage amid the overdetermining conflict between the two big powers, the United States and China.

Russia under Vladimir Putin is the most important player after them. In terms of relative power, it is much weaker than the Soviet Union and has an economy the size of Italy's. Nevertheless, in a very perceptive analysis, Adam Tooze notes that, 'though it is tempting to dismiss Putin's regime as a hangover from another era, or the harbinger of a new wave of authoritarianism, it has the weight that it does and commands our attention because global growth and global integration have enabled the Kremlin to accumulate considerable power'.[54] Russia vies with the United States and Saudi Arabia for the position of top producer of crude oil and is the second largest producer (after the United States) and biggest exporter of natural gas.[55] The revenues from its energy exports have allowed Russia to maintain its position as a leading military power.

After he assumed the presidency in 1999 and enforced order on the rampant oligarchs who dominated Russia's privatized economy, Putin played his cards astutely, at least until launching the invasion of Ukraine in 2022. He used the energy revenues not merely to rebuild the military but to buy a degree of domestic social peace. He was able to reassert Moscow's primacy in its near abroad, punishing pro-western neighbouring governments by waging a short war in Georgia in 2008 and by seizing Crimea in 2014 and conducting a low-intensity war in southeastern Ukraine thereafter. The more recent, full-scale invasion of Ukraine reflected Putin's determination to maintain this primacy (see next section). He also took advantage of Obama's and Trump's cautious policies in the Middle East to rebuild his influence in a region where the Soviet Union played a major role during the Cold War. Russia has become a power broker in both Syria and Libya and has extended its influence in sub-Saharan Africa – another region where the former Soviet Union had been able to exert significant influence, notably through its support for movements against European colonialism and against apartheid in South Africa.

According to a 2019 report in the *Financial Times*,

> While lacking the financial firepower of China or the longstanding trade relations of former colonial powers, Russia has sought to use its military exports, security apparatus and state-controlled natural resource companies to gain footholds across the continent.
>
> Across Africa, Moscow has deployed teams of military instructors to train elite presidential guards, sent arms shipments and assisted shaky autocrats with election strategies. It has also promised to build nuclear power plants and develop oil wells and diamond mines.[56]

The Russian intervention in the Middle East is part of a broader struggle for regional hegemony unleashed by the United States' defeat in Iraq and the Arab risings. Iran, Saudi Arabia, and Turkey have been the biggest players, feeding the wars in Syria and Libya. Meanwhile, the Gulf states – the main capitalist hub in the region – have been developing closer links with China, which is the biggest market for their oil and gas and an increasingly important supplier of advanced technologies. Also, Beijing doesn't ask awkward questions about human rights, or about Saudi Arabia's barbarous war in Yemen. 'There's a trust deficit with America which is growing by the day', according to Abdulkhaleq Abdulla of Emirates University. 'The trend is more of China, less of America on all fronts, not just economically but politically, militarily and strategically in the years to come. There's nothing America can do about it.'[57] China and its traditional ally Pakistan are also likely to be the dominant influence on Afghanistan under the restored Taliban regime.

Turkey's shift, under Recep Tayyip Erdoğan, from a loyal NATO ally to an increasingly assertive regional power provides a good example of how fluid interstate relationships have become. Erdoğan intervened in the Syrian War (partly to bring down the Bashar al-Assad regime, partly to contain the US-backed Kurdish statelet in north-western Syria), offended Arab rivals such as Saudi Arabia and Egypt by tipping the military balance in Libya in favour of the Tripoli government, and in 2020 tweaked Putin's nose in the Caucasus by helping Azerbaijan to win its latest war with Armenia over the Nagorno-Karabakh enclave. The Russo-Ukrainian War gave Erdoğan fresh opportunities, thanks to Turkey's control of the Straits, which connect the Mediterranean and the Black Sea, and thanks to his threat to block Finland's and Sweden's applications to join NATO.

The Greater Middle East is the venue for the most intense regional rivalries, but we can see the same logic of imperial and sub-imperial competition at work elsewhere. Mozambique is a particularly sad case. One of the poorest countries in the world, it has become a magnet for outside interests since the world's fourth largest liquefied natural gas (LNG) field was discovered in the Rovuma Basin off northern Mozambique in 2010. Total, ExxonMobil, ENI, Galp, and the China National Petroleum Corporation have been actively investing in extracting the LNG. Patrick Bond points out that the 'climate dangers to Mozambique's extremely vulnerable coastline, inland infrastructure and agricultural land' have been 'completely ignored', despite the fact that the LNG is 'made up mainly of methane, whose climate-destructive potency via extraction, processing, storage, transport and combustion is more than 80 times worse than CO_2 (the main cause of climate catastrophe), in the coming (critical) two decades and 25 times worse over the coming century'. Mozambique is already 'the world's fourth worst-affected country' by climate change – witness the 2019 floods I mentioned in the Introduction.[58]

Meanwhile, since 2017, an insurgency mounted by the radical Islamist movement al-Shabaab, which has sympathies with Islamic State, has developed in Capo Delgado, a province in the far north of Mozambique. More than 3,700 have been killed and 800,000 displaced. The brutal and corrupt Mozambican army has been bolstered by outside military intervention, notably from the Southern African Development Community (dominated by South Africa), Rwanda, and the Russian mercenary Wagner Group.[59] Mozambique isn't the first African country whose natural resources have attracted predators in recent years. Between 1998 and 2003, the Democratic Republic of Congo (DRC), source of such vital raw materials for advanced technologies as coltan, was the victim of a terrible war in which no less than nine African armies intervened. According to the International Rescue

Committee, more than 5.4 million people died as a result of the war and its aftermath, mainly from disease.[60] In mid-2022 a new conflict developed from rivalries between the DRC and the neighbouring states of Rwanda and Uganda, over the lucrative trade in Congo's resources.

Before the war in Ukraine broke out, the European Union might have seemed a world away from such horrors, a zone of advanced capitalism that prides itself on progress achieved through interstate cooperation, which is based on norms rather than force (though this is belied by European powers' rivalry in Libya and by France's failed military intervention in Mali). The European Union is a cartel of states with differing interests and, like states in other regions, they too feel contradictory pulls from the United States, China, and Russia. Germany in particular benefits hugely from its trade with and investments in China and, like the rest of Europe, relies on Russia as its main supplier of natural gas. European dependence on Russian oil and gas dates back to the Cold War era, as the Middle East became a less reliable supplier after the 1956 Suez crisis and US reserves declined.[61] But Europe also remains heavily dependent on the United States as the guarantor of its security against Russia.

France, the biggest military power in the European Union now that Britain has left, is feeling the pinch, finding itself under pressure from Islamists, Turkey, and Russia in its old neocolonial preserves in north and west Africa; at the same time it is humiliated by the AUKUS submarine deal, which supplanted an earlier French contract with Australia. These setbacks are important for a state whose relative economic position within the European Union has deteriorated by comparison with Germany's and that has become reliant on its military–industrial complex and power-projection capabilities, especially in its former African colonies.[62] The French president, Emmanuel Macron, calls regularly for the European Union to develop 'strategic autonomy'. But the Russian invasion of Ukraine pushed Germany strongly back towards NATO. Moreover, the Central and Eastern European states, which now have more reason than ever to look to Washington for protection against their old master in Russia, would strongly oppose any weakening of NATO (which the United States is meanwhile pulling into the confrontation with China).

Access to energy supplies further aggravates interstate competition. According to Simon Bromley, oil has been a 'strategic commodity' for the United States since the Second World War: 'US control over world oil became a key resource in the overall management of its global leadership after 1945, particularly given the greater dependence of the other main centres of Western capitalism – Western Europe and Japan – on imported oil.'[63] Washington's domination of the Middle East has therefore been a crucial underpinning of its hegemony. Accordingly, against the background of the United States itself becoming dependent on imported oil, President Jimmy Carter reacted to the Iranian Revolution and the Soviet occupation of Afghanistan by promulgating, in January 1980, what came to be known as the Carter Doctrine, which threatened to use force against any attempt to take control of the Gulf.[64] The strategic significance of Middle East energy was enhanced by China's becoming an oil importer during the 1990s. As David Harvey points out, keeping control of the 'global oil spigot' has been a key motivation for the US 'forever wars' in the Greater Middle East.[65]

But there have been two important changes over the past decade or so. First, as we saw in Chapter 2, climate change has prompted increasing geoeconomic competition around developing the technologies necessary to support the move to a decarbonized economy. But, paradoxically, the broader efforts at a 'green transition' have encouraged greater reliance on one fossil fuel, natural gas, because its consumption emits less CO_2 than that of coal. China, whose government has ambitious decarbonizing plans, has therefore become a growing gas importer, as have other big Asian economies such as Japan and South Korea. Second, thanks to the fracking revolution (itself largely financed through the flood of cheap credit made possible by the Fed's quantitative easing programmes since 2009), energy imports into the United States started to decline in 2005, and by 2019 this country had become a net energy exporter.[66] This major economic transformation facilitated the partial retreat from the Greater Middle East after the United States' failure in Iraq.

In her important new book *Disorder*, Helen Thompson highlights the impact of these changes on the rivalry between the United States, China, and Russia:

> Where oil and gas are concerned, the United States has acquired the capacity for more energy autonomy than at any time since the 1960s, and extreme American financial leverage complements this power. This renewed American strength became an agent of geopolitical havoc in the Middle East. It also made China's dependency on foreign oil pivotal in oil markets and gave Russia a serious rival in exporting gas to Europe. This American–Russian competition has pressed against the post-Cold War fault lines around Ukraine and the longer one around Turkey. Since China is both the world's largest carbon emitter and already has large-scale advantages in renewable

energy as well as the metals on which it depends, green energy is now a second source of geopolitical instability running concurrently with that generated by fossil fuel energy.[67]

The war in Ukraine and a polarizing international system

The Ukrainian crisis illustrates in concentrated form the tensions developing at both global and European levels. One of Putin's most consistent objectives has been to halt the eastern expansion of NATO before it begins to encircle Russia. NATO's expansion was pursued by the administrations of Clinton and George W. Bush, in violation of promises made to the last Soviet president, Mikhail Gorbachev, when he agreed to German reunification within NATO after the fall of the Berlin Wall in November 1989. The US Secretary of State James Baker told him on 9 February 1990: 'If we maintain a presence in a Germany that is a part of NATO, there would be no extension of NATO's jurisdiction for forces of NATO one inch to the east.'[68] Gorbachev had proposed that a reunited Germany should be neutral and denuclearized. According to M. E. Sarotte, here is what the diplomat Robert Blackwill told Brent Scrowcroft, National Security adviser to George H. W. Bush (president 1989–93), in a memorandum of 7 February 1990 entitled 'The Beginning of the Great Game': 'For Washington, however, this outcome was completely unacceptable because it "would forfeit the prime assets" – the troops and weapons – "that have made the United States a postwar European power."'[69]

This 'great game' led between 1999 and 2004 to the expansion of NATO, together with the EU, into Central and Eastern Europe. The aim was to entrench and extend the United States' position as a European power; moreover, as Strobe Talbott, Clinton's deputy secretary of state and the policy's chief architect, put it in September 1994, 'NATO expansion will ... be punishment, or "neo-containment", of the bad Bear'. Like the invasion of Iraq a few years later, the policy reflected the hubris that reigned in Washington even as its short-lived 'unipolar moment' started to fade. The result was, Sarotte suggests, 'a post-Cold War order that looked much like its Cold War predecessor, but with a more easterly European dividing line'.[70] Putin's counter-moves, designed to block NATO membership for Georgia and Ukraine, began with the brief 2008 war with Georgia, one of the accumulating signs of the limits to US power.[71] It was followed by his decision in 2014 to seize Crimea and back pro-Russian separatist forces in south-eastern Ukraine.

The strategic significance of Ukraine since it became independent in 1991 is very clearly set out by Zbigniew Brzezinski, Carter's National Security adviser, in a book originally published in 1997 and devoted to consolidating US global primacy after the Cold War. He was one of the main advocates of the eastward expansion of both NATO and the EU, describing Europe as 'the Eurasian bridgehead for American power and the potential springboard for the democratic global system's expansion into Eurasia':

> Ukraine, a new and important space on the Eurasian chessboard, is a geopolitical pivot because its very existence as an independent country helps to transform Russia. Without Ukraine, Russia ceases to be a Eurasian empire … However, if Moscow regains control over Ukraine, with its 52 million people and major resources as well as its access to the Black Sea, Russia automatically again regains the wherewithal to become a powerful imperial state, spanning Europe and Asia.[72]

Brzezinski, while seeking to exploit Ukrainian independence in order to entrench and extend US hegemony in western Eurasia, acknowledges the deep unhappiness of the Russian policy elite with the project, and highlights 'a difficult dilemma regarding tactical balance and strategic purpose' facing Washington, 'especially as the EU and NATO expand. Should Russia be considered a candidate for eventual membership in either structure? And what then about Ukraine? The costs of the exclusion of Russia could be high – creating a self-fulfilling prophecy in the Russian mindset – but the results of dilution of either the EU or NATO could also be quite destabilizing.'[73]

We can now see just how high the 'costs of the exclusion of Russia' are likely to be – though this doesn't in the slightest excuse the brutal invasion of Ukraine that Putin ordered on 24 February 2022. His initial military build-up may have been intended to extract security concessions from Washington, above all a commitment not to allow Ukraine to join NATO. But there was also a powerful ideological surplus at work that involved both Putin's ethno-nationalist fantasy about the historical bonds between Russia and Ukraine and his resentment of the United States. Although he sought to keep the world guessing, his strategic aim was clear: to reverse the apparently decisive tilt westwards that Ukraine took in as a result of the 'Maidan Revolution' of February 2014, after nearly a quarter century of geopolitical vacillation, economic decline, and domestic political chaos.[74]

The Biden administration responded to Putin's demands by negotiating while refusing to make concessions around the principle of Ukraine's right to join NATO; it also talked up the danger of war and mounted its own military build-up in Central and Eastern Europe. (This policy found strong echoes in London from the Johnson government, which was eager to find distractions from the exposure of the prime minister's multiple violations of his own COVID-19 restrictions.) The result was the most dangerous process of escalation of tensions between Washington and Moscow since the Cold War. In US historical mythology the Cuban Missile Crisis of October 1962 was an 'eyeball-to-eyeball' confrontation; but neither side seemed willing to blink this time – Biden because the chaotic abandonment of Kabul in August 2021 sparked an immediate fall in his polling, Putin because he was determined to force the United States to recognize Russia as more than a 'regional power' (as Obama once arrogantly dismissed it).[75]

But Washington's hard line was almost certainly taken also with Beijing in mind. As Gideon Rachman of the *Financial Times* puts it,

> The Ukraine crisis is also about 'world order' because it has clear global implications. The US knows that if Russia attacks Ukraine and establishes its own 'sphere of influence', a precedent will be set for China. During the Xi era, China has built military bases all over contested areas of the South China Sea. Beijing's threats to invade Taiwan ... have also become more overt and frequent. If Putin succeeds in invading Ukraine, the temptation for Xi to attack Taiwan will rise, as will the domestic pressure on the Chinese leader from excitable nationalists, sensing the end of the American era.[76]

The interaction between the United States–China antagonism and the contest between Russia and NATO has had the effect of drawing Beijing and Moscow closer together. There was nothing inevitable about this. The two states compete for influence in Central Asia, and Russian policymakers have been nervous about China's ability economically to assimilate their Far East territories (which were acquired through a process of imperial expansion in the nineteenth and early twentieth centuries, partly at China's expense). Moreover, Beijing has long been cautious about getting involved in geopolitical crises that don't directly affect its interests.

But the conflicts that both had with the United States have led to increasing economic and security cooperation between the two powers.

During the build-up to war, Xi repeatedly and publicly backed Putin in his opposition to NATO expansion and signed a 'no limits' strategic partnership on 4 February 2022, just before the invasion. Once war broke out, however, Beijing was plainly embarrassed by Russia's violation of Ukraine's national sovereignty, and Chinese businesses were fearful of being hit by the western economic campaign against Russia. Nevertheless, Hu Jiyun of the nationalist *Global Times* spelled out why Beijing should not abandon Moscow:

> For the moment, China and Russia are taking turns in bearing the heaviest weight in terms of resisting US hegemony …The China–Russia comprehensive strategic partnership of coordination in the new era is special. The ties have no limit, which deters the US. With Russia as a partner, if the US carries out maximum strategic coercion against China, China won't be afraid of the US' energy blockade, and our food supply will be secure. So will other raw materials. It will be harder for the US to make up its mind in engaging in a strategic showdown with China.[77]

To a degree, then, the long-standing conflict between Russia and the United States is being subsumed under the United States–China rivalry. Nevertheless, the Russo-Ukrainian War means that Biden, like Obama before him when confronted with Russia's seizure of Crimea in 2014, has been forced to shift the United States' strategic focus away from the challenge posed by China in the Indo-Pacific and back on Europe, the main stake in the Cold War. Just as, in the 1930s, Britain was distracted from the increasing threat from Nazi Germany by Italian self-assertion in the Mediterranean and by Japanese expansion into China, so the United States today has to spread its attention over geographically diverse points of conflict.

This book was completed deep in the fog of war, during the months after the Russian invasion. Therefore it is hard to say here anything definitive about this new catastrophe. Moreover, despite the great suffering this war is causing and the far worse suffering that it might cause, I write in the spirit of Spinoza, who said that he had 'taken great care not to deride, bewail or execrate human actions, but to understand them'.[78] But I will say that the widespread shock expressed at the fact that a war is happening in Europe not only erases the horrors that accompanied the break-up of Yugoslavia in the 1990s but forgets that the European state system was forged through a *longue durée* of war making, conquest, and political centralization that developed in intimate connection with the process of capital accumulation.[79]

That process continues today on a global scale; the fact that Europeans have been largely insulated from interstate violence since the paroxysm they unleashed on the world between 1939 and 1945 is no guarantee that they will remain so. The western powers' condemnations of Russia's unjust and brutal invasion of Ukraine sit ill with their own record of military intervention in the Greater Middle East. The spectacle of Condoleezza Rice, National Security adviser and secretary of state under George W. Bush and one of the chief architects of the Iraq War, solemnly agreeing on Fox News that 'invading a sovereign nation' is 'certainly against every principle of international law and international order' is beyond satire.[80] Only the abolition of an imperialist system driven by economic and geopolitical competition can make the world and humankind safe from predators like Putin and Bush.

Alas, the war in Ukraine is likely to drive in the opposite direction, to judge by its immediate effects. In the first place, the invasion has pushed the United States and Europe together. Most notable was the reorientation of the new German social democratic–Green–liberal coalition government, which sought to resolve the structural dilemma caused by its reliance on the United States for security and on Russia for energy. Chancellor Olaf Scholz, proclaiming a *Zeitenwende* (turning point) in the Bundestag on 27 February 2022, abandoned the Nord Stream 2 gas pipeline with Russia, pledged to spend an additional €100 billion (financed through borrowing) on upgrading the decrepit Bundeswehr, and announced plans to develop the infrastructure required to import liquefied natural gas, presumably from the United States and the Middle East. It remains to be seen, however, whether Berlin is capable of sustaining the political will to reorient German capitalism drastically, given the structural power of its export industries and their historical interdependence with Russia and China.[81]

Second, while the United States and its allies promised that they would not join the war in Ukraine militarily, the scale of their support for Ukraine amounted to NATO's waging a war by proxy against Russia. The *New York Times* describes 'the tenuous balance the Biden administration has tried to maintain as it seeks to help Ukraine lock Russia in a quagmire without inciting a broader conflict with a nuclear-armed adversary or cutting off potential paths to de-escalation'.[82] Leon Panetta, director of Central Intelligence under Obama, put it more bluntly: 'It's a proxy war with Russia whether we say so or not.'[83] Its aim, according to Lloyd Austin, Biden's defense secretary, was to get a 'Russia weakened to the point where it can't do things like invade Ukraine'.[84]

Western military cooperation with Ukraine had been developing since the upheavals of 2014. The former commanding general of US Army Europe reports that 'an ongoing operational programme called "Fearless Guardian"' to train the Ukrainian armed forces was started by the US 173rd Airborne Brigade in April 2015. 'The program was progressive, training everything from individual soldier skills to battalion-level operations, all based on lessons learned from the eastern and southern Ukrainian combat zones. In December 2015, US Army Europe formally established Joint Multinational Training Group – Ukraine (JMTG-U) where a multi-national team of Americans, Poles, Canadians, Lithuanians, and Brits began training Ukrainian battalions as combined arms teams.'[85]

Having provided nearly $1 billion worth of military aid to Ukraine in the year leading up to the invasion, the Biden administration pledged a further $3.4 billion in the following weeks, and at the end of April requested from Congress an additional $33 billion in aid (which the Senate raised to $40 billion). The weapons supplied or in the pipeline included more than 1,400 Stinger anti-aircraft systems, 4,600 Javelin anti-armour systems, 72 155mm howitzers with 144,000 rounds, M142 HIMAR multiple rocket launchers, more than 120 drones, 300 grenade launchers, 5,000 rifles, 600 machine guns, 600 shotguns, over 40 million small arms, grenade, mortar, and artillery rounds, and 25,000 helmets and sets of body armour. Britain supplied 10,000 NLAWS and Javelin anti-tank missiles, Starstreak air-defence systems, anti-ship missiles, and 120 armoured vehicles, while the EU pledged an unprecedented €900 million in lethal aid. 'Every day, eight to 10 cargo flights, most of them operated by the United States, land near the country's western borders, carrying hundreds of millions of dollars worth of increasingly heavy weaponry, US officials' told the *Financial Times*.[86] The NATO summit in June 2022 pledged to increase forces on high alert from 40,000 to over 300,000, while Biden announced increased military deployments in Europe, raising US troop numbers in the region from 80,000 before the Ukraine crisis to 120,000.[87]

Third, the western powers led by the United States used their dominance of the financial system to hit Russia hard. The most important measures were to exclude some Russian banks from the SWIFT inter-bank communication system and to deny the Central Bank of Russia access to its $640 billion foreign exchange reserves. Biden boasted: 'these economic sanctions are a new kind of economic statecraft with the power to inflict damage that rivals military might'.[88] Although the United States has frequently resorted to financial sanctions in recent years, James Meadway is no doubt right that the European Central Bank (ECB) was also drawing on its experience of policing the eurozone, most notably when it shut down the Greek banking system in July 2015, in reaction to a referendum vote to reject the austerity imposed from Brussels and Frankfurt: 'The same ECB technique ... has now moved from threat to application against a hostile country, presently at war with a close ally of those applying sanctions. The warhead of the weapon is the same, but the context is radically different, and radically more dangerous as a result: Putin's lurch from dark hints to the mobilization of Russia's nuclear forces shows both how effective the weapon is, but also the grave consequences of actually using it.'[89]

The Ukraine crisis has therefore starkly confronted two different kinds of power: financial in the West and nuclear in Russia (although the United States has plenty of nukes of its own, too). But the economic break shouldn't be overstated. The sanctions carefully excluded the energy sector, which reflects Europe's dependence on Russian gas; switching to LNG imported from outside Europe will take years. This crucial exception undermines the attempt to block the Central Bank of Russia to use its reserves to support the rouble. As Lev Menand points out in a tweet, '[b]ecause the EU is still buying energy from Russia through Russian banks using dollars and euros, the Russian exporters and banks [can] turn around and sell those dollars and euros for roubles, substituting for the central bank'.[90] Indeed a combination of strict capital controls and high energy prices soon made the rouble the best performing currency. Russia's oil export volumes held up despite the western embargo, India's imports of Urals crude jumping from zero to 1 million barrels a day in the first half of 2022.[91]

As Thompson incisively puts it,

> Whatever Russia's military weaknesses, the strength of Ukrainian resistance, and the medium-term consequences of losing Western capital and technology in the energy sector, Moscow is winning the resource war. Since Russia is a Eurasian energy exporter, its resource power cannot be seriously dented by energy sanctions imposed only by Western governments. As Gazprom is demonstrating by cutting gas supplies to European countries, energy is Russia's weapon. Since the measures against the Russian central bank have not worked as a compensatory coercive force, Ukraine's independence can only be defended by an enormous weapons supply, the provision of which must

always grapple with the risk of escalation into general war in a world of mutually assured destruction.[92]

Is the international system now experiencing the kind of polarization into two rival blocs of states that was characteristic of the Cold War? The close linkages between both China and Russia and the rest of the world economy cut across any such division. Rather than a struggle between the 'liberal world order' and alien 'autocracies', this is a conflict *within* global capitalism, just as the two world wars of the twentieth century were. There is, as yet, little evidence that the pandemic, which had a much smaller impact on world trade than the global financial crisis, has led to a 'reshoring' of production. The *Financial Times* Trade Secrets column reported in late 2021: 'The growth of global value chains slowed after 2008 and has remained anaemic since the "slowbalization" after the early 2000s "hyperglobalization" … While the events of last year did put severe strain on value chains, the Asian [Development] bank concludes that the 2020 number was largely in line with the post-2010 trend … There just isn't a lot of evidence that supply chains are being shortened, or even radically restructured.'[93]

Moreover, one very interesting aspect of the Ukraine crisis has been the refusal of states closely linked to the United States on other issues to take sides. This is true, for example, of India, Saudi Arabia, and the UAE. Strategic cooperation between Moscow and New Delhi goes back to the Cold War era. In the case of the Gulf autocracies, neutrality reflects a combination of disaffection with what they regard as Washington's failure to back them up sufficiently against the Arab revolutions and Iran and the need to deal with Russia as an important player in the region since 2015 and as a partner in the OPEC+ energy cartel; thus Riyadh ignored Biden's plea to increase oil output in response the outbreak of the war in Ukraine. According to Abdulkhaleq Abdulla, 'Russia, like China and others, are [*sic*] trying to fill the vacuum left by America. And Russia is well positioned to play a bigger role. They are winning. Putin has calculated it very well.'[94] This remains to be seen, but it's clear the Russo-Ukrainian War may look very different in other parts of the world from how it does in Washington and Brussels – in part because of the West's own sorry record of using its military power to impose its will globally.

At the United Nations General Assembly on 2 March 2022, 141 member states voted for a resolution to condemn the invasion. Only four – Belarus, Eritrea, Syria, and North Korea – joined Russia in voting against. But another 35 abstained in the vote. They included China, Cuba, India, Iran, Iraq, Pakistan, and South Africa. A host of other African countries either abstained or didn't vote at all. Moreover, only a handful of states joined in the sanctions against Russia. David Adler of the Progressive International points out: 'The US, the UK, Canada, South Korea, Switzerland, Japan, Australia, New Zealand, Taiwan, Singapore, the EU: beyond this fortified coalition, very few nations have chosen to take part in the economic warfare set against the Putin government.'[95]

Nevertheless, the more the two main antagonists seek to reduce their economic dependence on each other and push other states to take sides, the greater the risk of polarization. Willy-nilly, Russia has little choice but to strengthen its economic links with China, at least as long as the Putin regime survives. China would benefit from having privileged access to Russia's energy and from buying up assets hit by western sanctions at bargain basement prices. The partnership could also give Beijing greater access to Russian military technology – though in the longer run China, which has much greater manufacturing capacity than Russia and three times its defence spending, may overtake its partner as an arms producer.[96] Propping up Russia may also help Beijing in its efforts to develop an alternative to the US-dominated financial system. Other states might be tempted to cooperate in order to reduce their own vulnerability to US sanctions. Indeed, according Meadway, thanks to Washington's increasing use of the dollar as a political weapon, 'regional currency blocs are forming, each guarded by a jealous and suspicious hegemon: the dollar, the euro and the renminbi.'[97]

A recent study carried out on behalf of the IMF documents what it calls the 'stealth erosion of dollar dominance', pointing to a drop in the share of central banks' reserves held in the US currency, from 71 per cent in 1999 to 59 per cent in 2021. This drop is to the advantage of the renminbi, but even more to that of other, 'non-traditional' reserve currencies aligned with the United States such as the Canadian, Australian, and Singapore dollars, the South Korean won, and the Swedish krona.[98] In the short term, as Tooze puts it, 'Russia and China find themselves in a euro–dollar trap', given that the two currencies account for more 80 per cent of global reserves. He suggests: 'What we are seeing is the formation of polarities rather than blocs. There are clear geopolitical antagonisms, but on the main axis, in Asia, this does not add up to consolidated blocs. The striking thing so far about the ripple effect from Russia is that though a new Cold War front may emerge in Europe, it is unlikely that will translate to East Asia.'[99]

Geopolitically, however, there is the risk of self-fulfilling prophecy. Right-wing Republican denunciations of 'Communist China' by the likes of Mike Pompeo, former secretary of state under Trump, feed paranoia on both sides. And there are enough genuine points of friction, notably over rival US and Chinese ambitions in the Indo-Pacific, that could lead to confrontation. The world is becoming a much more dangerous place, as Putin's decision to activate Russian nuclear forces in response to western sanctions indicates. And, although we are still some way from another Cold War partition of the globe, the existing polarization is sufficient to find political and ideological expression.

The Trump presidency was widely seen as marking a crisis of the liberal capitalist international order. Colin Kahl and Thomas Wright, in their study of the COVID-19 pandemic, draw a striking comparison with the last age of catastrophe:

> Many of the factors that made the world so volatile, crisis-prone, and dangerous during the inter-war period – mounting inequality, widespread civil strife, rising populism and xenophobia, growing economic nationalism and pressures to deglobalize, resurgent authoritarianism, backsliding democracy, escalating great-power rivalry, American retreat, brittle international institutions, and a free world in disarray – were *already* re-emerging in our own time during the years before the coronavirus pandemic struck. And ... COVID-19 and the shockwaves flowing from it have made all these problems worse.[100]

Thus 'the post-World War II international order was careening toward a cliff, and the COVID-19 pandemic pushed it over the edge'.[101] Kahl is now under-secretary of defense for policy in the Biden administration, so this judgement carries some official weight. A crisis of this order necessarily rebounds onto its legitimizing ideology, liberal internationalism, which is dominant in both Washington and Brussels. But this ideology has been under heavy intellectual pressure ever since it was used to justify the disastrous invasion of Iraq in 2003.[102] Two of its chief academic defenders, David Deudney and John Ikenberry, recently hit back, amalgamating an incongruous 'coalition' of critics of US foreign policy from the libertarian right, academic realism, and the anti-imperialist left.

The quality of this polemic can be judged from this attack on the left:

> Left-revisionists also harbour a resolute hostility to capitalism and market economics that separates them from the modern liberal

embrace of a modified market capitalism, cast not just as a necessary evil for the generation of wealth but as an essential part of the freedom programme. They commonly link their antipathy to capitalism with various types of communalism and collectivism, which compromise individual freedom. They fail to realize that popular democracy and revolutionary movements are often the enemies of limited government constitutionalism and the protection of minority rights. And they fail to recognize that the hard-fought struggles against the greater evils of fascism and communism required toleration of lesser evils, such as situational support for anti-communist dictatorships.[103]

Disentangling all the questions that are begged here would take too long (though it is interesting to see the greatest critic of US foreign policy, Noam Chomsky, reduced to a footnote – perhaps because it is hard to portray a lifelong anarchist as an enemy of individual freedom). But the evasions of the final sentence I quoted are worth pausing on. Deudney and Ikenberry conveniently forget the role played by the Soviet Union in the defeat of Nazi Germany, as well as the effective alliance between the United States and another Stalinist state, China, during the later phase of the Cold War. And was the 'support for anti-communist dictatorships' – presumably a reference to Washington's backing of the bloody military coups in Indonesia and Chile (inter alia) – so 'situational'? The family autocracy that is Saudi Arabia remains a key US ally in the Middle East, despite the erratic and murderous policies of Crown Prince Mohammed bin Salman, as does the brutal military dictatorship of Field Marshal Abdel Fattah el-Sisi in Egypt. Beyond these elisions, the champions of democracy against autocracy ignore the powerful authoritarian trends in contemporary liberal capitalist states that we noted in Chapter 2.

Nevertheless, Deudney and Ikenberry's characterization of the current international situation as one where 'the global balance of power between liberal democracy and autocracy is unfavourably shifting' is widely shared among western elites.[104] And the Biden administration, after what liberals hope was the Trump interruption, is doubling down on liberal internationalism, for example by returning to the idea of a 'league of democracies' floated by the neoconservative Robert Kagan when he advised the Republican Senator John McCain in his unsuccessful run for the presidency in 2008.[105] 'Autocracy' has indeed become the standard way of labelling regimes that refuse to align themselves with the western liberal bloc. This framing is a form of ideological mystification, and not only because it slides over the autocracies in the western camp and liberal democracy's own authoritarian tendencies. Its function is to delegitimize the interests of the West's rivals by implying that such interests arise from their undemocratic character and that any conflicts could be peacefully overcome if liberal capitalist economic and political structures were universalized.

In response to the Russian invasion of Ukraine, Biden escalated this rhetoric, notably in a speech in Warsaw, on 26 March 2022, where he warned that sanctions would force the Russian economy out of 'the top 20 in the world' and called for Putin's removal. Biden announced a new chapter in 'the great battle for freedom: a battle between democracy and autocracy, between liberty and repression, between a rules-based order and one governed by brute force' – but warned: 'This battle will not be won in days or months either. We need to steel ourselves for the long fight ahead.'[106] Like the increasingly frequent invocations of the 'free world', this seems like a conscious reactivation of western Cold War discourse.[107]

The Russian and Chinese states that are the chief geopolitical targets of contemporary liberal ideology are significantly different sociopolitical forms. China remains a Stalinist one-party state, where the CPC monopolizes political power and exerts, as we have seen, considerable control over the economy. Xi's personal dominance has been reflected in the CPC's affirmation of 'Xi Jinping Thought', but its author has made it clear that its roots lie firmly in the version of Marxism–Leninism developed by Mao Zedong in the struggle against China's subordination to outside powers. Thus Xi says in a key speech: 'It is Marxism–Leninism and Mao Zedong Thought that guided the Chinese people out of the darkness of that long night and established a New China; it is through socialism with Chinese characteristics that China has developed so quickly.'[108]

Putin, by contrast, presided, before the Ukraine crisis and the resulting break with the West, over a nominally pluralist (though very tightly managed) political system and a neoliberal economic policy regime. The governing ideology is strongly anti-Marxist, rejecting the October 1917 Revolution and harking back to the Great Russian nationalism of the late tsarist era and its roots in Orthodox Christianity. Both regimes are autocracies, but of very different kinds. China undoubtedly has much greater ideological appeal globally, above all because of the attraction that its developmental model has exerted, particularly on the rest of the postcolonial world.

What is true is that the rise of the far right has interacted with the increasing polarization of the interstate system. This topic needs to be handled with some care, because allegations of Russian manipulation of western public opinion have become an alibi for the domestic failures of the neoliberal 'extreme centre'. Nevertheless, Trump, an outspoken critic of the liberal international order, although constrained by the national security 'Blob' to impose additional sanctions on Russia, and despite slapping tariffs on Chinese imports, sought to ingratiate himself with Putin and Xi. He also strongly supported Brexit and maintains close links with one of its main architects, Nigel Farage.

The most right-wing government in the European Union, under Viktor Orbán in Hungary, relatively discreetly took Moscow's side in the conflict over Ukraine until the Russian invasion, when he shifted to a neutral stance. Elsewhere in the European Union, Putin's main political instrument, United Russia, struck cooperation agreements with the Austrian Freedom Party and the Lega in Italy.[109] Rodrigo Duterte, perhaps the most vicious of the current wave of far right leaders, while president of the Philippines, tilted away from the United States and towards China, despite a long-standing territorial dispute in the South China Sea. But, as ever, geopolitical interests and domestic political loyalties don't necessarily line up straightforwardly. In the Ukraine crisis, Poland, another rightist-dominated EU member state, was firmly in the NATO camp against the historical enemy in Moscow. Nevertheless, this crisis saw many on the far right lining up with Putin – for example, both Marine Le Pen and Éric Zemmour took his side against Emmanuel Macron during the French presidential elections, while Trump declared that it was 'genius' for Putin effectively to annex the two separatist enclaves in eastern Ukraine, though the outright invasion led them to back-pedal.[110]

Probably more important than any specific alignments is the vaguer sense that China's rise signals above all that western liberalism is on the wane, as its chief state sponsor faces a formidable economic and geopolitical challenge. Fukuyama's 'end of history', when liberal capitalism defined the horizons of the future, is definitively at an end. This creates a space in which a host of alternatives could gain support. Why, then, has it been mainly the far right that has filled the vacuum? We'll find out in the next chapter.

5

Revolt and Reaction

Strategies of containment

Since the late 1990s, the increasingly destructive nature of neoliberal capitalism has generated what Joseph Choonara describes as three cycles of revolt, all coming from the left: first, the Zapatista revolt in Mexico and other anti-neoliberal risings in the South, above all in Bolivia, as well as the international movement for another globalization and the opposition to the war against Iraq (1994–2005); second, the Arab uprisings, the occupation of the squares in Greece and in the Spanish state, and Occupy Wall Street (2011); and, third, a new cycle of revolt from spring 2019 on – uprisings in Algeria and Sudan and mass protests in Hong Kong, Chile, Ecuador, Colombia, Lebanon, Haiti, Guinea, Kazakhstan, Iraq, Iran, France and Catalonia.[1] This cycle survived the onset of the pandemic thanks to the Black Lives Matter risings in the United States and the solidarity they received around the world in the summer of 2020 (see Chapter 6).

But these movements are counterpointed to, and have to a significant degree been overshadowed by, the rise of the far right – especially in the North. It has been the likes of Donald Trump and Marine Le Pen who have projected the discontent of neoliberal capitalism onto Black and Muslim scapegoats. In this chapter I seek to understand the nature of the contemporary far right, to explain why its adherents are now tending to set the political agenda, and to assess the danger that they represent. I focus especially on the United States, since I agree with Cas Mudde, one leading academic authority on the subject, that 'the far-right threat to US democracy is more acute and significant than in most other countries'.[2]

The neoliberal version of capitalism is breaking down amid a multi-dimensional crisis that is simultaneously economic, (geo)political, and biological. The result is a crisis of hegemony, the decay of the dominant forms of bourgeois rule.[3] Antonio Gramsci famously characterized such a crisis thus:

> If the ruling class has lost its consensus, i.e. is no longer 'leading' [*dirigente*], but only 'dominant', exercising coercive force alone, this means precisely that the great masses have become detached from their traditional ideologies, and no longer believe what they used to believe previously, etc. The crisis consists precisely in the fact that the old is dying and the new cannot be born; in this interregnum a great variety of morbid symptoms [*fenomeni morbosi*] appear.[4]

Chantal Mouffe puts it somewhat differently when she argues that 'our present conjuncture' is best described as 'a "populist moment"', which 'signals the crisis of the neoliberal hegemonic formation' opened by the global financial crisis of 2007–9.[5] But there hasn't been any breakthrough to the left, let alone anything remotely comparable to the revolutionary upheavals at the end of the First World War that provided the context for Gramsci's reflections. The closest we came to witnessing comparable events was the Egyptian Revolution of 25 January 2011, in which political opposition to the dictatorial regime of Hosni Mubarak fused with the discontent caused by the economic and social impact of neoliberalism and the global financial crisis, sparking a rising that started with the youth but drew in a working class with long traditions of struggle.[6] But the Egyptian Revolution was crushed by a military coup launched on 3 July 2013 by Field Marshal Abdel Fattah el-Sisi, who in the aftermath imposed an even more brutal and repressive dictatorship than Mubarak's.

In the developed capitalist world, the most advanced struggles were probably those waged in Greece against EU-imposed austerity in 2010–12. These struggles led to electoral victory for the Coalition of the Radical Left (Syriza) in January 2015, only for Prime Minister Alexis Tsipras to capitulate to Brussels and Berlin six months later.[7] The inspiring upsurges in the reformist left led by Bernie Sanders in the United States and by Jeremy Corbyn in Britain went down to electoral defeat in 2019–20. Ireland remains an important exception, as the radical left-wing People Before Profit advances on both sides of the border – a very important development, given how Brexit, by keeping Northern Ireland in the European Single Market, has been destabilizing the partition of the island imposed by Britain in 1921–2.[8] And in the 2022 French legislative elections, Jean-Luc Mélenchon succeeded in reuniting and revitalizing the left, although this must be set alongside the electoral progress made by the far right.

This is the context in which Mouffe's 'populist moment' has been dominated by the far right. The latter's influence has grown spectacularly in the past few years, thanks to the accumulated resentments of the neoliberal period, which have been intensified by the economic suffering and dislocation caused by the global financial crisis.[9] The far right's advance, however, must be seen in a global context formed at the intersection of the economic and geopolitical crises. The challenge to dominant neoliberal capitalism has involved not only the cycles of revolt distinguished by Choonara but also resistance to US hegemony through the guerrilla wars against the occupation of Afghanistan and Iraq. Counter-revolution – in the shape of efforts to crush or rechannel the Arab risings – has led to the prolonged and destructive wars in Syria and Libya. The wars in the Greater Middle East in turn helped to increase the flow of refugees across the Mediterranean and into Europe. We can see similar processes at work in the Americas as well. A combination of factors – poverty, climate change, political, criminal, and gender violence – have produced growing population displacements within Latin America as well as outflows of migrants and refugees to the United States and Europe. Berta Joubert-Ceci traces these phenomena back to what she calls 'the neoliberal war on underdeveloped countries'.[10]

The political and ideological effects were highlighted in the European 'refugee crisis' of 2015 – so styled by European elites that, in 2022, readily welcomed millions of white Ukrainians in their flight from the Russian invasion but responded to the flight of Afghans, Africans, and Arabs by raising more barriers. Against the background of the large-scale failure of mainstream social–democratic parties and trade unions to resist austerity, the racial polarization produced by this 'crisis' worked to the advantage of the far right, particularly since the radical left proved only intermittently able to mount a robust welcome to migrants and refugees or to address the broader impact of the global financial crisis.[11] Mudde argues: 'It is the socio-cultural translation of socio-economic concerns that explains most support for far-right politics. Egged on by nativist narratives in the political and public debates (e.g. "immigrants are taking your jobs and your benefits"), many far-right voters link immigration to economic problems.'[12]

Or, as Agnieszka Graff and Elzbieta Korolczuk succinctly but arrestingly put it, 'the success of contemporary right-wing populism is owed largely to its ability to moralize issues and concerns that the left would like to frame in economic terms.'[13] Here it is useful to return to the problematic of totalization explored in the Introduction. Discussing the Marxism of Georg Lukács in his classic *History and Class Consciousness* (1923), Fredric Jameson argues that 'Lukács's method of ideological critique – like the Hegelian dialectic itself and its Sartrean variant, in the methodological imperative of totalization proposed in the *Critique [of Dialectical Reason]* – is an essentially critical and negative, demystifying operation'. Lukács thus develops 'a creative and original variant on Marx's theory of ideology, which is not, as widely thought, one of false consciousness, but rather one of structural limitation and ideological closure'.[14]

From this perspective, ideologies represent 'strategies of containment'. They simultaneously reveal and repress – in Jameson's words and, further back, Althusser's – 'History or the Real as an "absent cause"': 'History is what hurts, it is what refuses desire and sets limits to individual as well as collective praxis, which its "ruses" turn into grisly and ironic reversals of their overt intentions. But this History can be apprehended only through its effects, and never directly as some reified force.'[15] Critique operates by exposing the limits of specific ideological discourses that fail sufficiently to respect the 'imperative of totalization', above all by not bringing fully into play the logic of capital as a mode of production. The ideology of the far right provides an excellent example of this kind of strategy of containment.

Donald Trump's Inaugural Address on 20 January 2017 is an exemplary far right text.[16] The speech identifies an addressee, the American people, which is also a political subject, and Trump as its privileged interlocutor, picked out by his presidential oath. It diagnoses the deplorable condition of this people – 'American carnage' – which is characterized primarily in socioeconomic terms, though 'the crime and the drugs and the gangs' Trump invokes is a metonym for 'race' for those who want to hear it. The cause is identified – the subordination of the interests of the US nation to those of other nations: 'For many decades, we've enriched foreign industry at the expense of American industry, subsidized the armies of other countries while allowing for the very sad depletion of our military. We've defended other nations' borders while refusing to defend our own and spent trillions and trillions of dollars overseas while America's infrastructure has fallen into disrepair and decay.' The culprit is also named: 'Washington', 'the establishment'. The speech vindicates the anger of 'righteous people and a righteous public', (largely) produced by the effects of real processes on living standards and jobs – processes such as the neoliberal restructuring of capitalism, itself intensified by the Long Depression since 2007–8; but it displaces that anger from its source in the capitalist mode of production, shifting it onto the Washington elite in this case – but, as we know from other Trump speeches, also onto people of colour.

In counterposing 'the establishment' and 'the people', Trump's discourse is a good example of populism – in the restricted sense that is of some use. One index of the western ruling classes' refusal to understand the political upheavals of the past decade is a propensity, shared by their media and academic auxiliaries, to spray the word 'populism' around: it has become a catch-all, an umbrella term used to dismiss and by the same move lump together all the challenges to the neoliberal status quo.[17] Used more restrictedly, however, populism is helpful in identifying an ideological strategy employed by a range of parties of the racist right.[18]

UKIP and, later, the Brexit Party (now Reform UK) under the leadership of Nigel Farage offer a paradigm case: Farage claims to represent a 'British nation' whose interests have been denied by an elite wedded to the European Union. This is typical of what Ernesto Laclau calls the 'logic of equivalence' at work in populism: the 'people' is constructed as a totality, through antagonism with an 'excluded element' – in this case, the pro-EU elite but also the migrants from the rest of Europe with whom, according to Farage, this elite has flooded the country.[19] Parties of the populist right are undoubtedly racist: indeed, Nigel Farage's success lay in his ability to marry Euroscepticism to anti-migrant racism and then use this toxic cocktail to drag the mainstream parties further to the right. In the process, UKIP and its counterparts elsewhere sucked up and converted into votes some of the anger generated by the economic suffering that neoliberalism and the state of crisis have inflicted.

The movements that have developed to contest the necessity of anti-COVID lockdowns and to oppose vaccination, and especially government-required vaccine mandates, are striking evidence of the dynamism of the far right and of its ability to latch onto new issues. In an interesting study centred on Germany and covering the first year of the pandemic, William Callison and Quinn Slobodian write:

Led in many cases by angry freelancers and the self-employed, amplified by entrepreneurs of speculative and *totalizing* prophecies, these movements are less what José Ortega y Gasset called 'the revolt of the masses' and more 'the revolt of the *Mittelstand*' – small- and medium-sized businesses. In comparison to the populism that dominated discussion in 2017, they are less tethered to mediagenic leaders and parties, slipperier on the traditional political spectrum, and less fixated on the assumption of state power ... [They] tend to contest conventional monikers of left and right (while generally arcing toward far-right beliefs), to express ambivalence if not cynicism toward parliamentary politics, and to blend convictions about holism and even spirituality with a dogged discourse of individual liberties.[20]

But it is the pandemic, along with how states have managed it, that is the focus of this movement, to which the more institutionalized politicians of the far right have lent their support. The wave of mass protests inspired by these ideas throughout liberal capitalist societies has provided a far right counterpoint to the Black Lives Matter rising of 2020. In January–February 2022, the Freedom Convoy – a convoy of around five hundred truckers and other anti-lockdown protesters opposed to the Canadian government's requirement that lorry drivers who crossed the border with the United States be vaccinated – succeeded in paralysing the centre of Ottawa and, by blocking the vital Detroit-Windsor crossing, disrupting the highly integrated North American auto industry. In the United States the protesters won the support of the likes of Trump, Senator Ted Cruz of Texas, and the grandstanding Tesla boss Elon Musk. Justin Trudeau, the Canadian prime minister, reacted by invoking powers under the Emergencies Act – for example the power to freeze, without a court order, bank accounts used to finance the blockade.

The confrontation illustrates how managing the pandemic has allowed states to resort to greater repression. But it also underlines that the right and the far right have dominated the opposition to this management. By contrast, the radical left has found it hard to get an effective handle on the politics of the pandemic. This is no doubt because of the complexities of the issue, which requires campaigning for more effective safety measures and for ensuring protection for the lives, jobs, wages, and conditions of workers as well as opposing the expansion of repressive powers – in other words, simultaneously asking for *more state and less state*. On the other hand, the far right has hammered away at a simple, ultra-libertarian message, and done so with a significant degree of success.

Contours of the far right

The far right has thus succeeded in directing the anger generated by the ills of the neoliberal era, at least in certain sections of the population, on the one hand, onto a cosmopolitan elite and, on the other, onto migrants and refugees. By rhetorically championing jobs and welfare against globalization, 'the right ate the left's lunch', as Walden Bello puts it.[21] Whether conservative or social–democratic, the neoliberal 'extreme centre' (in Tariq Ali's terminology) has found itself squeezed electorally.[22]

But this has not been in any sense a simple repetition of what happened between the world wars. First, in the North the far right has been less directly counter-*revolutionary*, less a response to the advance of the left than it was in the 1920s and 1930s. The last great global upturn in workers' struggles, in the late 1960s and early 1970s, stimulated the neoliberal effort to shift the balance of class forces back in capital's favour. What we are witnessing today is the disintegration of the neoliberal order without (yet) a strong enough drive of workers' struggles from below to offer a progressive alternative, capable of capturing the imagination of the masses. This has allowed the far right to capitalize on the discontent and anger created by the multiple dysfunctions in the status quo.

When we widen our focus globally, the picture changes somewhat. The rhythms of revolt and reaction vary in the North and in the South. This reflects in part the different pace at which neoliberalism was introduced. We see, for example in Asia, the rise of a phenomenon that Priya Chacko and Kanishka Jayasuriya call 'authoritarian statism', taking this concept from Nicos Poulantzas, for whom it means 'intensified state control over every sphere of socio-economic life *combined with* radical decline of the institutions of political democracy and with draconian and multiform curtailment of so-called "formal" liberties'.[23]

According to Chacko and Jayasuriya, in Asia this shift does not represent the breakdown of the neoliberal regime; rather it demonstrates how introducing such a regime has a disruptive impact on the specific political forms through which ruling parties secured the consent of the mass of the population. Neoliberal restructuring – for example of the clientelistic networks through which state resources were used to subsidize employment and consumption – leads to 'political disincorporation': 'In the wake of the fracturing of dominant modes of political incorporation, political elites have struggled to create forms of legitimacy for capitalist social relations. The mobilization of cultural nationalism and anti-pluralist politics by both societal actors and political leaders must be understood in this context.'[24]

As Chacko and Jayasuriya point out, the Bharatiya Janata Party in India is a good example of this process. This is an electorally extraordinarily successful Hindu chauvinist party that has at its core the fascist Rashtriya Swayamsevak Sangh (RSS; National Volunteer Organization). Although the founders of the RSS were explicit in their admiration for Hitler, the party has been able to exploit the disintegration of the base of the historic nationalist Congress Party – and has done so thanks to the neoliberal policies that the Congress Party itself pioneered. Then there is the 'fascist original' (Bello), Rodrigo Duterte, who won the presidency of the Philippines with an anti-crime programme and, riding a wave of popular revulsion against decades of failed neoliberalism, incited the murder of thousands of drug users. But there are also examples outside Asia – above all in Brazil, where Jair Bolsonaro was able to capitalize on the disintegration of the Workers' Party under the double blow of the global financial crisis and exposure of the party's involvement in corruption, which is endemic in the country's political elite.[25] Bolsonaro's very narrow defeat at the hands of the Workers' Party former president, Lula, in October 2022 was a tribute to his astonishing success in mobilizing Brazil's middle classes, with the help of the evangelical churches.

Sisi's coup in Egypt also conforms to this pattern. It was preceded by an enormous demonstration of the middle classes against the Muslim Brotherhood president, Mohamed Morsi, on 30 June 2013. The demonstration was partly mobilized by leaders who had been allied with the radical left – notably the Nasserist Hamdeen Sabahi, the main left candidate in the 2012 presidential election, and the independent trade unionist Kamal Abu Aita. Sisi didn't just use military power to overthrow Morsi but framed the conflict as one between secularism and Islamism, a trap into which much of the left fell.[26]

But we see the red river of revolt running in the South, too, and much more strongly. The Arab risings are the most striking example – a revolutionary process that continues despite defeat in Egypt and Syria, the more recent upheavals being in Algeria and Sudan. But consider the case of Bolivia and what it has witnessed in the past twenty years: two mass risings that brought down neoliberal presidents, in 2003 and 2005; the election, in 2006, of a left-wing government based on the indigenous working poor and headed by Evo Morales, from the

Movement for Socialism; a right-wing coup in October 2019; and the presidential victory of Luis Arce, from the Movement for Socialism, one year later. Here there is a very direct interplay of revolution and counter-revolution. As for the rest of Latin America, we have recently seen radical leftist victories in presidential elections in Chile, Colombia, and Peru.

Meanwhile, in India, the farmers' movement of 2020–1 took militant direct action on a huge scale. Forging a coalition that embraced big farmers and landless labourers, higher castes and Dalits, and in which women played a relatively prominent role, they confronted not just riot police but the fascist thugs of Modi's RSS, and forced his government to repeal deregulating legislation favourable to agribusiness.

Second, there is a significant shift in the ideology of reaction. Today the key element of far right ideologies is Islamophobia, in other words anti-Muslim racism. In an important article, Ed Pertwee identifies

> a transnational field of anti-Muslim political action known as the 'counter-jihad' ... The variety of white nationalism cultivated within the counter-jihad was, at the time it first emerged, a novel one. For the Hitlerian philosophy of history as Darwinian struggle between different biological 'races', in which the Jew was cast as the antitype of the Aryan, it substituted a culturalist melodrama of agonistic struggle between radically incommensurable 'civilizations', in which 'Islam' was cast as the youthful and virile antitype to the moribund husk of the 'Judeo-Christian West'. The influence of these ideas on far-right groups in Europe, North America and Australasia, and especially on Trumpian Republicanism, is difficult to overstate.[27]

Here we see the connection between the contemporary far right and imperialism. For of course Islamophobia acquired its deep hold on western societies as a result of the United States' reaction to the Iranian Revolution and the 'war on terror' launched by George W. Bush and Tony Blair in their failed attempt to entrench US domination over the Greater Middle East. The far right version is a radicalization of state and media targeting of Muslims as the 'enemy within'. The racist stereotyping of Muslims is a response to the armed resistance and mass risings that have weakened the grip of western imperialism in the Middle East and North Africa. Sections of the far right have even shifted from their traditional support for women's subordination within the family, as a way of highlighting the alleged incompatibility between Islam and 'western values'.[28]

Pertwee, however, argues that contemporary far right discourses bear strong affinities with the 'revolutionary conservative' ideologies of inter-war fascism, and in particular with the romantic nostalgia for a mythologized past highlighted by Ernst Bloch (see Chapter 1). They share a 'common, counterrevolutionary temporal structure, wherein a mythic past is mobilized to legitimate projects of cultural purification in the present ... Today, this counterrevolutionary temporal structure is inscribed in the Trumpian slogan "make America great again".'[29]

Moreover, there are continuities in the content of far right ideologies. First, hostility to the left remains an important element, if only because the cultural breakdown of western societies that has supposedly allowed their Islamization is typically traced back to the 1960s. Trump's denunciations of the Democrats as socialists and his attacks on critical race theory are symptomatic of a persistent anti-Marxism. In Latin America, traditional anti-communism fuses with what one might call, following Pierre Bourdieu, class racism directed at poor people of indigenous and slave origins, particularly in the movements against left-wing governments in Bolivia and Venezuela, but also in the activities of the Bolsonaro presidency in Brazil. Second, anti-Semitism remains important especially for the fascists, because of its role in continuing to provide the basis for a pseudo-critique of capitalism that locates the source of the problem not in the system, but in the corrupting effects of 'cosmopolitan Jewish finance capital'. The name of the liberal hedge fund billionaire George Soros has almost supplanted that of the Rothschilds as a metonym for this mythological representation of capitalism. Remarkably, far right anti-Semitism coexists with support for Israel, which is seen as a bulwark against the Muslim hordes that supposedly threaten western civilization. Hostility to the left and anti-Semitism fuse in the discourse of 'cultural Marxism'.

We can find a contemporary version of fascist fake anti-capitalism in this defence of the family offered by Giorgia Meloni, leader of the far right Fratelli d'Italia and now, terrifyingly, Italian prime minister, at the 2019 World Congress of Families in Verona:

> [The enemies of the family] would like us to no longer have an identity and just become slaves, the perfect consumers. And so national identity, religious identity, gender identity and family identity are under attack. I must not be able to define myself as Italian, Christian, woman, mother – no, I must be citizen x, gender x, parent 1, parent 2, I must be a number. Because when I am only a number, when I no longer have an identity, when I no longer have roots, then I'll be the

perfect slave at the mercy of huge financial speculation. The perfect consumer.[30]

The third distinctive feature of the contemporary far right is the predominance of racist–populist electoral parties with a dangerous and substantial fascist element. In Europe the context is very different from that of the 1920s and 1930s, when authoritarian regimes developed largely as an extension of the dominance of traditional agrarian elites. The US-directed reconstruction of Western Europe after 1945 gave liberal capitalism a much more stable base, crucially thanks to the development of Fordist mass production and advanced welfare regimes reinforced by the process of European integration, which was also promoted by Washington.[31] The state capitalist regimes installed by the Red Army on the other side of the Iron Curtain, in Central and Eastern Europe, swept away the old landed classes.[32] The incorporation of these states into the western neoliberal capitalist order after the revolutions of 1989 involved their adoption of liberal–democratic constitutions and incorporation into NATO and the European Union (once again, under US patronage). The embarrassment that the authoritarian drift of Poland and Hungary is causing Brussels is an indication that outright dictatorship is not (yet) tolerable.

So the contemporary far right tends to consist of populist outsiders who have been able to elbow their way into the electoral big leagues thanks to the debility of mainstream parties – for example the Lega in Italy, the Alternative für Deutschland (AfD) in Germany, UKIP and now Reform UK in Britain, and the Danish People's Party. There are even cases of traditional conservative parties showing signs of morphing into far right formations: this is true of the Tories under Boris Johnson, the Austrian People's Party under Sebastian Kurz, Les Républicains in France, and the Moderates in Sweden. Thus we witness, as Mudde observes, 'the mainstreaming of the far right ... In more and more countries, populist radical right parties and politicians are considered *koalitionsfähig* (acceptable for coalitions) by mainstream right, and sometimes even left, parties. Moreover, populist radical right (and even some extreme right) ideas are openly debated in mainstream circles, while populist radical right policies are adopted, albeit generally in (slightly) more moderate form, by mainstream parties.'[33]

In Europe, the far right tends to specialize in a mixture of Euroscepticism and anti-migrant racism. This combination of racist scapegoating and anti-elite rhetoric (whether directed against the European Union or, more broadly, against 'cosmopolitan' elites) makes it correct to describe the main tendency of the contemporary far right, Trump included, as racist–populist, and in this sense different from inter-war authoritarian conservativism. But, as in the 1920s and the 1930s, the contemporary far right represents a spectrum. There are fascist political nuclei that have been able to repackage themselves as electorally successful parties. They, too, focus on racist–populist themes, but seek radical authoritarian solutions. The most important of these are the Rassemblement national (RN, formerly Front national) in France, the Freedom Party in Austria, the Sweden Democrats, and the Fratelli d'Italia.

France demonstrates the role that the far right can play in disorganizing and polarizing the existing party system, in this case in one of the leading liberal capitalist states, a nuclear power to boot. The two presidential contests between the RN leader, Marine le Pen, and the neoliberal authoritarian Emmanuel Macron, in 2017 and 2022, have demolished the mainstream centre-left and centre-right parties (the Parti socialiste and Les Républicains), leaving, as Mudde puts it, 'only two strong political forces in France, the far right ... and Macron. One is an ideological bloc, with a strong organization, another one single person.'[34] The June 2022 legislative elections marked a breakthrough for the RN, which won the third largest bloc of deputies, ahead of the centre right. This was followed in September by further electoral breakthroughs for the Sweden Democrats and for the Fratelli that led in Italy to a government of the right headed by Meloni.

Fourth, while the contemporary far right benefits from disaffection with neoliberalism, it lacks a distinctive economic programme. The RN, for example, plays constantly on the ills caused by globalization, as Trump has done. But no far right group or regime offers a coherent economic alternative to neoliberalism. Indeed, one strand – notably in the AfD and UKIP/Brexit Party – combines Euroscepticism and economic ultra-liberalism. Trump strayed from the neoliberal playbook in weaponizing tariffs, especially against China, but otherwise his economic policies were standard post-Reagan Republican fare, offering goodies to business in the shape of tax breaks and deregulation. The Lega, once vocally anti-EU, supported a government of 'national unity' headed by Mario Draghi, the former president of the ECB.

This is striking, because the global financial crisis that has given the far right greater political leverage represented, just like the Great Depression of the 1930s, the failure of economic liberalism. But, while the Mussolini and the Hitler regimes moved fairly sharply in the direction of state capitalism, the contemporary far right offers no comparable break with the neoliberal economic policy regime. The Indian Marxists Utsa and Prahbat Patnaik have something interesting to say about this:

> There was a brief period between the end of the Depression and the start of the war... during which the fascists succeeded in placing their economies in a better position than the liberal capitalist ones.
>
> In contemporary conditions, however, larger state spending, no matter for what purpose, which would have to be financed either by taxes on the rich or by a fiscal deficit to be able to enlarge activity, would be frowned upon by globalized finance, which would oppose both these means of financing. And since no fascist movement anywhere is proposing controls over cross-border financial flows, this opposition would be decisive in preventing any expansion in domestic aggregate demand through state spending.[35]

The Patnaiks may be underestimating the economic room for manoeuvre for contemporary capitalist states. After all, the pandemic has seen states go further than they had done in response to the global financial crisis, hugely increasing government spending and borrowing, and central banks engaging in 'monetary financing', that is, buying government bonds to cover the extra expenditure (see Chapter 3). But the Patnaiks' observation that the greater internationalization of capital today limits the ability of far right governments to pursue alternative economic policies to neoliberalism is important. Indeed, the acceptance of this constraint, in the 1990s, by social–democratic parties that embraced neoliberalism – the so-called Third Way of Bill Clinton, Tony Blair, and Gerhard Schröder – helped to create the opening for the far right in the first place.

As this overview indicates, the boundaries between mainstream conservative, populist–racist, and outright fascist formations are very blurred. This fluidity is unavoidable, particularly in a rapidly moving situation where – for example – bit players such as Bolsonaro and Trump suddenly hit the big time. The picture is further complicated by the role played by grassroots far right networks that campaign and coordinate via social media and apps such as Telegram. This complexity prompts even as perceptive an analyst as Enzo Traverso to argue that what we are dealing with is 'post-fascism'. He claims that 'the racism of the far right ... has significantly blurred its original fascist matrix. In this sense, ideology is no longer a problem for the far right. All in all, its relationship with fascism is rather like social democracy's relationship with socialism' – something that it has in practice abandoned in order to embrace neoliberalism.[36]

Traverso is right to the extent that some contemporary far right leaders, notably Marine le Pen, have presented themselves as modernizers of their parties in ways that are at least superficially comparable to Blair's construction of New Labour. But Traverso seriously underestimates especially the importance of the distinctive kind of anti-Muslim racism diagnosed by Pertwee in contemporary far right ideology. The point, in any case, is not so much what label to attach to specific formations, but rather to understand the contemporary far right as a dynamic force field that is changing rapidly. Fascism exerts a gravitational pull within this field, not primarily because of the historical legacy of different formations but because radicalization to the right is a real political option in the present: we see this, for example, in the factional struggle between the 'national–conservative' and the 'national–revolutionary' wings of the AfD. The dominance of electoral politics in the contemporary far right acts, moreover, as an obscuring factor, since it exerts pressure on leaders to dissociate themselves from the barbarism of Hitler and Mussolini. But, just as in the inter-war period, there is an interplay between elite politics and grassroots movements that can favour the genuinely fascist elements. The United States offers perhaps the best illustration of the forces at work.

The United States: the weak link?

It seems extraordinary to describe the United States as the weak link in the advanced capitalist world, since, as we saw in Chapter 4, it remains *the* hegemonic state, having especially military and financial capabilities that are vastly greater than those of any other polity. But it is a thought we must take seriously after the far right storming of the Capitol on 6 January 2021. Three determinations seem to stand out:

- *The cumulative economic effects of neoliberalism and the global financial crisis.* The Trumpian rhetoric of 'make America great again' presents the United States as a victim of globalization. But this is not a description that the big US banks and corporations would recognize. They have hugely profited from the globalization of production and from the emergence of what Peter Gowan calls 'the Dollar–Wall Street regime' in finance.[37] Moreover, the five IT giants that constitute the FAANGs – Facebook, Amazon, Apple, Netflix, and

Google – represent the United States' ambition to dominate the future of capitalism, and are a major stake in Washington's conflicts with both Beijing and Brussels.

Nevertheless, Robert Brenner argues that the latest government bailout of markets in March 2020 shows that,

> with the US economy performing so very badly, ... the bipartisan political establishment and its leading policymakers have come to the stark conclusion, consciously or unconsciously, that the only way that they can assure the reproduction of the non-financial and financial corporations, their top managers and shareholders – and indeed top leaders of the major parties, closely connected with them – is to intervene politically in the asset markets and throughout the whole economy, so as to underwrite the upward redistribution of wealth to them by directly political means ... What we have had for a long epoch is worsening economic decline met by intensifying political predation.[38]

For wide sections of the US population, the experience of the past generation has been one of compressed wages, evaporation of large swathes of manufacturing employment, jobs, savings, and homes lost in the global financial crisis, and family members killed, disabled, or traumatized in the lost wars in the Greater Middle East. This divergence in experiences – as many upper white-collar employees share modestly in the prosperity enjoyed by big capital – has been weaponized by Trump and the Republican right. According to Thomas Piketty, Emmanuel Saez, and Gabriel Zucman,

> the bottom half of the income distribution in the United States has been completely shut off from economic growth since the 1970s. From 1980 to 2014, average national income per adult grew by 61 percent in the United States, yet the average pre-tax income of the bottom 50 percent of individual income earners stagnated at about $16,000 per adult after adjusting for inflation. In contrast, income skyrocketed at the top of the income distribution, rising 121 percent for the top 10 percent, 205 percent for the top 1 percent, and 636 percent for the top 0.001 percent.[39]

The Economist found that the best predictor of where Trump did better in 2016 than Mitt Romney, the Republican candidate in 2012, was county-level data on life expectancy and the prevalence of obesity, diabetes, heavy drinking and regular physical activity (or lack thereof) ... Some argue that deteriorating health outcomes are linked to deindustrialization: higher unemployment rates predict both lower life expectancy and support for Mr Trump, even after controlling for a bevy of demographic variables ... what the geographic numbers do show is that the specific subset of Mr Trump's voters that won him the election – those in counties where he outperformed Mr Romney by large margins – live in communities that are literally dying. Even if Mr Trump's policies are unlikely to alleviate their plight, it is not hard to understand why they voted for change.[40]

- *Dysfunctional political structures increasingly favouring the Republicans.* Capital, large and small, has benefitted from a constitution designed by its framers to protect property from majority rule, an executive president who, even in the era of universal suffrage, is chosen indirectly, by an Electoral College weighted in favour of the 50 states, an extremely powerful but highly unrepresentative upper chamber, the Senate, in which states have equal representation regardless of differences in population, and a Supreme Court of judges appointed for life whose power as constitutional arbiters has been enhanced by gridlock in Washington.[41]

Capital's prerogatives have been further buttressed by a first-past-the-post electoral system that restricts political competition to two profoundly pro-capitalist parties and by the Supreme Court-affirmed right of the corporate rich to flood compliant politicians with money. In recent decades the Republican Party, which has won only one presidential popular vote in the past thirty years, has ruthlessly used gerrymandering and voter suppression to entrench itself particularly at the state level and in Congress. All this has been very good for capital, which has colonized every level of the state, but the result is a political system largely impervious to popular movements for change in any direction. Meanwhile, the Democratic administrations of Bill Clinton (1993–2001) and Barack Obama (2009–17) operated as efficient managers of the neoliberal order, disappointing their more progressive supporters and helping the Republicans to capture both houses of Congress in 1994, the House again in 2010, and the Senate in 2014 and to block all legislative initiatives from the White House. Despite Joe Biden's more adventurous economic policies, there is a good chance that his administration will suffer the same fate.

- *The racial fracture*. All advanced capitalist states are structurally racist, but nowhere is racial oppression more central than in the United States. Slavery and settler colonialism are inscribed into the fetishized constitution: Article 1, Section 3 gives states federal representation on the basis of 'adding to the number of free Persons ... and excluding Indians not taxed, three fifths of all other Persons'.[42] The complex and tense balance between white slave planters and petty producers broke down as the United States expanded territorially and started its own Industrial Revolution in the first half of the nineteenth century. Lincoln won the ensuing Civil War of 1861–5 by adopting increasingly revolutionary means, as Marx predicted – above all, by issuing the Emancipation Proclamation and arming the former slaves. But the defeat of the attempt made by Black people and their white allies to reconstruct the slave South after the Union's victory in 1865 meant that the formal legal and political equality granted by the Fourteenth and Fifteenth Amendments was denied to African Americans, especially in the South, where they were subjected to the Jim Crow regime of racial segregation.[43]

The so-called Second Reconstruction imposed on the federal government by the Civil Rights movement of the 1950s and 1960s and the inner-city risings in the North that it helped to stimulate ended the Jim Crow regime and elevated a Black middle class that now has some serious political clout. But African Americans are still stuck at the bottom of the socioeconomic ladder and are the object of systemic state violence, be it in the form of police shootings or in that of mass incarcerations in the 'prison–industrial complex', described by Michelle Alexander as 'another racial caste system in the United States'.[44] It is too simple to call the contemporary United States a case of 'white supremacy', just as it would have been to join the short-lived celebrations of a 'postracial society' under Obama; but there are plenty of white suprema*cists*, whom embedded racist structures steer towards Blacks, Latinx, and Muslims as outlets for their discontent.[45]

Against this background, the Trump presidency represented a clear case of overdetermination, as defined by Althusser: the condensation of multiple contradictions into a transformative synthesis.[46] Starting with his run for the White House in 2015–16, Trump systematically sought to play on the sense of victimhood, the anger at Washington's corruption and gridlock, and the racism of sufficiently many US citizens to win in November 2016, to sustain himself during a chaotic term of office and to secure more than 74 million votes (the second highest total in US history) in November 2020.

Trump is no fascist but an adventurer, one who has parlayed his celebrity business dealings and media stardom into at least the appearance of great wealth and has used this image in order to reach a wider audience for his far right critique of how the United States has allegedly been screwed by globalization – and, more concretely, by its allies and by China.[47] His relationship with big capital has been far from straightforward. Jeffrey Sonnenfeld of the Yale School of Management reports: 'I would bring Donald Trump to our CEO summit years ago and the top tier CEOs would say "Don't bring him in here. We don't consider him a top CEO," he recalls. When he told the president this after his 2016 election victory, Mr Trump replied: "Well, they're all coming by to see me now."'[48] Even in the White House, however, he remained problematic for big capital. His most distinctive economic policies – trade wars with China and the European Union and the aspiration to repatriate the global supply chains developed in the neoliberal era – clashed directly with the interests of the main US transnational corporations and banks.

Trump's class base came from elsewhere, as Mike Davis explains in a brilliant sketch of the social geography of Trumpism:

> If Reagan came to power aligned with a historic anti-union offensive led by the Business Roundtable – a coalition of Fortune 500 corporations – Trump came to the White House thanks to the love of Jesus and a motley crew of what Sam Farber refers to as 'lumpen capitalists'. Although defence contractors, the energy industry and Big Pharma pay the dues to the White House as is always the case when Republicans are in power, the donor coalition that financed the revolt against Obama and after the defeat of [Ted] Cruz in the [2016] primaries, united behind Trump, is largely peripheral to the traditional sites of economic power. In addition to family dynasties, mainly based on oil wealth like the Kochs, who have been around since the days of Goldwater and the John Birch Society, Trump's key allies are post-industrial robber barons from hinterland places like Grand Rapids, Wichita, Little Rock and Tulsa, whose fortunes derive from real estate, private equity, casinos, and services ranging from private armies to chain usury.[49]

These 'lumpen billionaires' – as Davis also calls them – are dependent on the domestic market and, indeed, often on federal and state governments, as is shown by the telling example of Forrest Preston's Life Care Centers of America, the largest nursing home chain in the United States and the site of numerous COVID-19 deaths in the spring of 2020.[50] Confrontation with the manufacturing and trading giants of Asia and Europe probably didn't affect their interests too negatively; it may even have helped smaller industrial firms. Transnational big business, by contrast, went along with Trump because he cut taxes, promoted deregulation, and boosted a stock market bubble. As the *Financial Times* Lex column sourly put it after the assault on the Capitol,

> Mr Trump repeatedly staked his presidency on rising financial markets, tacitly inciting Wall Street and better-off Americans to ignore his creeping illiberalism because they were getting rich in the process. Business grew weary of his capriciousness on tariffs and trade with China.
>
> But Mr Trump largely gave Corporate America what it wanted. Emerging markets have typically had the same flavour: a political state that is untidy or corrupt but where commerce and capitalism still flourish.[51]

But in the longer term what was significant about Trump was not so much his ambivalent relationship with big capital as his transformation of right-wing politics in the United States, which started with 'his rapid take-over and ruthless cleansing of the GOP in 2017–18 … Trump's nuclear advantage was his astounding popularity at the base, a frenzy routinely stoked by evangelical leaders, Fox News and, of course, his endless tweets'.[52] Moreover, Trump gave national leadership, media attention, and political legitimacy to a plethora of far right groupuscules, from the 'patriot' militias that started to emerge in the 1990s to the QAnon conspiracy theorists. Peter Simi of Chapman University says: 'He's kind of an ink blot of sorts where a lot of these different segments of the far right – and into the mainstream – are able to project on to him their hopes and fears and anxieties and frustrations.'[53]

The relationship between Trump and the far right grassroots is an interactive one, in which he cultivated and mobilized them in his attempt to win a second term. Key signposts include Trump's responding to the clash between the Unite the Right rally and antifascists in Charlottesville, Virginia, in August 2017 by saying: 'there were very good people on both sides' (one of the antifascists was killed in that confrontation); his encouragement of far right groups who in the summer and autumn of 2020 protested against lockdowns and clashed (sometimes fatally) with Black Lives Matter protestors; his call to the fascist Proud Boys to 'stand back and stand by' in the presidential debate of 30 September 2020; and, last but not least, his speech to the Stop the Steal rally in Washington on 6 January 2021 that led to the storming of the Capitol. In all these interventions Trump was trying to help himself, not to create a new political regime, but he also helped the far right crystallize as a movement.

6 January 2021

How, then, does the assault on the Capitol fit into this picture? Liberal and leftist commentators were quick to denounce this action – as a result of which five people died – as a coup. Did it match Edward Luttwak's classic 'formal and functional definition of a coup' as 'the infiltration of a small but critical segment of the state apparatus, which is then used to displace the government from its control of the remainder'?[54] One obvious difference is that the assault of the Capitol was intended not 'to displace the government', but to keep Trump in office. The invaders of the Capitol were seeking to intimidate Congress into reversing the election result and keeping Trump in the White House. Naunihal Singh, another expert in coups, argues that their actions are best described as an 'attempted insurrection', because 'it is the involvement of state security forces' that defines a coup.[55]

There were elements of high farce about this 'insurrection'. The liberal historian Timothy Snyder commented: 'none appeared to have any very clear idea of how this was to work or what their presence would accomplish. It is hard to think of a comparable insurrectionary moment, when a building of great significance was seized, that involved so much milling around'.[56] But, as more video footage of the assault came out, the actual and potential violence involved became clearer. What those who chanted 'Hang Mike Pence!', Trump's vice president, because he was chairing the joint session of Congress to certify the election result, would have done if they had encountered Nancy Pelosi, the Democratic speaker of the House of Representatives, let alone the left-wing Congresswomen Alexandria Ocasio-Cortez and Ilhan Omar, doesn't bear thinking about. AOC has described how she hid in her office bathroom in fear of her life.[57] The FBI allege that one woman they arrested sent a video message to her children saying: 'We were looking for Nancy to shoot her in the friggin' brain, but we didn't find her.'[58]

Analysis of those who faced charges connected with the assault on the Capitol suggests that the 'insurrectionists' were drawn heavily from the struggling petty bourgeoisie. According to the *Washington Post*, 'nearly 60 percent ... showed signs of prior money troubles, including bankruptcies, notices of eviction or foreclosure, bad debts, or unpaid taxes over the past two decades'. Another 40 per cent were business owners or white-collar workers.[59] Prosecutions have revealed the planning for 6 January by far right groups such as the Proud Boys and the Oath Keepers.[60] The official inquiry conducted by the Democrat-controlled House of Representatives provided more evidence of a coordinated paramilitary assault on the Capitol that it alleged was orchestrated with Trump and some of his entourage and intended to force Pence into refusing to certify the election.[61]

The left-wing British writer Paul Mason draws a useful comparison with the events of 6 February 1934 in Paris.[62] Amid press agitation to replace the chaotic parliamentarism of the French Third Republic with an authoritarian regime, far right leagues organized a demonstration predominantly of former servicemen who sought to attack the Palais Bourbon, seat of the Chamber of Deputies, and the presidential Elysée Palace. They were protesting against a politico-financial scandal that surrounded the alleged suicide of the business adventurer Sacha Stavisky and against the formation of a government of the centre-left Cartel des gauches (Coalition of Lefts) – liberal–bourgeois Radicals supported by the Socialist Party – headed by Édouard Daladier, who had just sacked the right-wing chief of Paris police.

The protestors clashed violently with the police, who opened fire twice, killing fourteen people, and prevented the demonstrators from reaching their targets. But Daladier, despite having won two votes in the Chamber, resigned the next day. He was replaced by the former president, Gaston Doumergue, who formed a centre-right government that in effect reversed the outcome of the 1932 election, which the Cartel des gauches had won. Doumergue was one of many right-wing politicians who advocated the concentration of power in the hands of the executive.

So on 6 February 1934 the far right failed to reach its targets, but won a political victory. By contrast, on 6 January 2021 the far right got into the Capitol. But it failed politically, at least in the short term. Whatever mixture of complicity, conspiracy, or cockup proves to explain the extraordinary failure of the Capitol police and of the plethora of other security forces in Washington to protect Congress, the invaders were cleared out relatively quickly. There is no evidence of the leaders of the vast US national security state showing any sympathy with their cause. Indeed, according to two *Washington Post* journalists, General Mark Milley, chairman of the Joint Chiefs of Staff,

> saw Trump as a classic authoritarian leader with nothing to lose. He had earlier described to aides that he kept having a stomach-churning feeling that some of the worrisome early stages of 20th century fascism in Germany were replaying in 21st-century America. He saw parallels between Trump's rhetoric about election fraud and Adolf Hitler's insistence to his followers at the Nuremberg rallies that he was both a victim and their saviour.
> 'This [Trump's speech to the 6 January rally] is a Reichstag moment,' Milley told aides. 'The gospel of the Führer.'[63]

Milley later confirmed that he had twice rung his Chinese counterpart, General Li Zuocheng, in October 2020 and January 2021 to inform him that 'President Trump was not going to attack the Chinese just out of the blue'.[64] This underlines the weight, within the US state, of the national security apparatus – the 'Blob' – not surprisingly, given the role played by Washington's capabilities of power projection in underpinning its global hegemony. Michael Glennon, drawing on an idea of the nineteenth century liberal writer Walter Bagehot, argues thus:

> power in the United States lay initially in one set of institutions – the presidency, Congress, and the courts. These are America's 'dignified' institutions. Later, however, a second institution emerged to safeguard the nation's security. This, America's 'efficient' institution (actually ... more a network than an institution), consists of the several hundred executive officials who sit atop the military, intelligence, diplomatic, and law enforcement departments and agencies that have as their mission the protection of America's international and internal security... The United States has, in short, moved beyond a mere imperial presidency to a bifurcated system – a structure of double government – in which even the president exercises little substantive control over the overall direction of US national security policy.[65]

The primacy of the national security apparatus over the '"dignified" institutions' was dramatically expressed on 6 January, when his Secret Service security detail prevented Trump from joining the far right crowd in its march to the Capitol.[66] But, even if the 'Blob' eventually got its act together and restored order at the Capitol, the enormity of what happened on 6 January can't be ignored.⁶⁷ The United States remains the most powerful capitalist state in the world. Office had been transferred peacefully from president to president since the first one, George Washington, was elected in 1789. The inauguration of Washington's latest successor took place under the protection of 25,000 armed National Guards. Nothing like this had been seen since Abraham Lincoln's first inauguration in March 1861, amid threats of assassination, the secession of the slave states of the South, and the beginnings of the Civil War

It is important to stress here that, for the groups involved, the assault of the Capitol was a success, even if it didn't save the Trump presidency. The power of the federal government has been deployed against the 'insurrectionists', but the far right martyrs that the FBI and the courts will create can feed the mythology surrounding 6 January. Colin Clarke, a domestic terrorism expert at the Soufan Group, told the *Washington Post*: 'the fact that the Capitol Police allowed this to happen, you can call it a security breach, or intelligence failure, but these people do not look at this as a failure, they look at it as an overwhelming success, and one that will inspire others for years.'⁶⁸

The assault on the Capitol nevertheless led to a real rupture between Trump and the US ruling class. It's one thing to be a vulgar racist and a sexist bully, it's quite another to incite a far right mob to overturn the constitution; after all, it serves capital very well. Pence and McDonnell, who had used Trump to entrench the power of the Christian right – most notably by packing the federal judiciary with conservative judges, so that now there is a two-thirds right-wing majority on the Supreme Court – quickly dropped him, though they subsequently back-pedalled somewhat, in response to his popularity with the Republican base.

Even before the election, the US Chamber of Commerce, the Business Roundtable, and six other corporate lobby groups had called on 'all Americans to support the process set out in our federal and state laws and to remain confident in our country's long tradition of peaceful and fair elections'.⁶⁹After 6 January, the National Association of Manufacturers, 70 percent of whose 2020 campaign contributions went to Republicans, asked Pence 'seriously [to] consider working with the cabinet to invoke the 25th Amendment', which would have allowed him to take over as acting president if they declared Trump 'unable to discharge the powers and duties of his office'. 'There's not a major chief executive who's a Trump supporter now', Sonnenfeld told the *Financial Times*, as the bosses retreated from what one called their 'Faustian bargain with Trump'.⁷⁰

From the perspective of big capital, then, Biden's inauguration marked a welcome return to normality. But no one should kid themselves. Trump opened a Pandora's box, from which a serious national fascist movement could emerge. Snyder draws a perceptive distinction:

> Right now, the Republican Party is a coalition of two types of people: those who would game the system (most of the politicians, some of the voters) and those who dream of breaking it (a few of the politicians, many of the voters). In January 2021, this was visible as the difference between those Republicans who defended the present system on the grounds that it favoured them and those who tried to upend it.
>
> In the four decades since the election of Ronald Reagan, Republicans have overcome the tension between the gamers and the breakers by governing in opposition to government, or by calling elections a revolution (the Tea Party), or by claiming to oppose elites. The breakers, in this arrangement, provide cover for the gamers.[71]

The assault on the Capitol brought the gamers – headed by Pence and McDonnell – into open conflict with the breakers – not just Trump himself, but notably Ted Cruz and Josh Hawley, the two Republican senators who led the Congressional opposition to certifying the election results. Nevertheless, the party stuck together. Trump's electoral strength provided a strong incentive to maintain some kind of unity. In a notorious YouGov poll on 7 January 2021, 45 per cent of Republicans supported the attack on the Capitol.[72] Only 13 per cent of Republicans, compared to 92 per cent of Democrats and 52 per cent of independents, supported Trump's impeachment.[73]

Even after the storming of the Capitol, 8 out of 51 Republican senators and 139 out of 204 Republican members of the House of Representatives supported objections to the election count. Only 7 of 50 Republicans in the new Senate voted to convict Trump in the brief and half-hearted impeachment trial for inciting insurrection that was mounted against him. This was a tribute to the power his base still gave him. Once again, Snyder is perceptive:

> As Cruz and Hawley may learn, to tell the big lie [that the election was stolen] is to be owned by it. Just because you have sold your soul does not mean that you have driven a hard bargain. Hawley shies from no level of hypocrisy; the son of a banker, educated at Stanford University and Yale Law School, he denounces elites. Insofar as Cruz was thought

to have a principle, it was that of states' rights, which Trump's calls to action brazenly violated.[74]

In other words, Trump's Congressional champions were no doubt mainly motivated by their own political ambition, and in particular the size and commitment of his base appealed to them. But to satisfy that base they must imitate Trump's polarizing rhetoric. He is in any case still very much around. A little over a year after 6 January, Trump talked at a rally in Texas about running again in 2024 and, in case he won, of pardoning those convicted of offences related to the storming of the Capitol. These were no idle threats. Trump's political operations and allied political action committees had raised $143 million over the previous year. While 58 per cent of respondents told pollsters that they opposed a Trump re-election bid, 78 per cent of Republicans said they supported it.[75] Trump was also seeking to influence the selection of Republican candidates in Congressional and state races. 'If you went to people potentially running for office, whether it is Congress, senator or governor, they would cut off their hand and sell their first child to have a Trump endorsement', says the Republican operative Ford O'Connell.[76]

Whether or not Trump does achieve a comeback, the political and ideological struggles between the gamers and the breakers in the Republican Party can offer openings to genuinely fascist forces. So far such forces have failed to generate a credible national leadership. Sooner or later, however, they will tire of depending on the whims of an erratic and egotistical pseudo-billionaire (if Trump stays around), let alone on the more transparent opportunism of the likes of Hawley and Cruz, however much the fascists can continue to benefit from their mainstreaming of far right themes. Moreover, if the Biden administration fails, this will no doubt offer new opportunities for the entire far right. Paradoxically, the very fact that the two-party system survives intact in the United States (unlike for example in France) gives the far right direct access to political power, thanks to its growing influence in the Republican Party.

For example, the *Washington Post* reports: 'Wyoming's Republican Party has been slowly taken over by conservatives who identify more as Trump supporters than Republicans. The state party is now led by Frank Eathorne, a member of the Oath Keepers who stood on the Capitol's West Front during the insurrection, walkie-talkie in hand.' According to a former local Republican official, '[t]his [takeover] was planned over several years, very organized and very dedicated. And they had a long-term goal to take first the county parties, then the state party, then the legislature, and then all of the other elected positions.'[77]

The corporate revulsion at the assault on the Capitol underlines that the situation is not the same as it was in Italy in the early 1920s or in Germany ten years later. Big capital is in no way desperate enough to gamble on authoritarian solutions, let alone fascism, either in the United States or in Europe. Why should it, given the way the leaders of organized labour have acquiesced in the neoliberal offensive of the past generation and how feebly they responded to the devastating attacks on jobs, wages, conditions, safety – life itself – that have been launched since the outbreak of the pandemic?

There are two reasons for not reacting to this fact complacently. First, the situation can deteriorate still further, particularly in the United States. The severity of the multiple crises that confront capitalism today may encourage sections of the ruling class to mount an even more brutal assault on working people and to try to use a sufficiently powerful fascist movement to sustain this assault. We already witness the 'authoritarian hardening' of liberal capitalist states.[78] Second, there is the danger of a self-fulfilling prophecy: the far right may be able to destabilize the political system just enough for sections of the ruling class to start to welcome the fascists as a force capable of restoring order.

The quasi-implosions that US and British politics have suffered since 2016 illustrate how seemingly small changes in a complex system can unleash sudden and bewildering transformations. In Britain, Boris Johnson was able to use the political polarization caused by the June 2016 referendum vote to leave the European Union so as to seize the premiership, purge the Tory party of its pro-European wing, and win handsomely the general election of December 2019, on a platform that pledged 'to get Brexit done'; meanwhile he directed populist fire at 'elite' institutions such as the parliament and the Supreme Court (whose justices were branded 'Enemies of the People', in a notorious *Daily Mail* headline) and promised 'levelling up' to economically depressed and traditionally Labour-supporting but pro-Leave constituencies in the north of England. Johnson's subsequent efforts to maintain his position despite his government's disastrous handling of the pandemic and despite exposure of his and his staff's flouting of COVID-19 restrictions displayed a close study of Trump's playbook. The British Conservative Party, perhaps the most consistently successful political party since the emergence of mass politics in the nineteenth century, has become a textbook case of the mainstreaming of far right politics.

Civil war?

The internal strains go much deeper in the United States. Even before the assault on the Capitol, Mike Davis had concluded his analysis of the 2020 election: 'Deep structures of the past have been disinterred during Trump's presidency and given permission to throttle the future. Civil War? Some analogy is inevitable and should not be easily dismissed.'[79] Barbara Walter, a much more mainstream social scientist, has indeed made a strong case for not dismissing this danger in her recent book, which is titled *How Civil Wars Start*. She uses the methods of comparative politics, drawing on large datasets to elucidate this matter: 'It turns out that one of the best predictors of whether a country will experience a civil war is whether it is moving toward or away from democracy', occupying an unstable intermediate region dubbed 'anocracy'. Here states 'are neither full autocracies nor democracies but something in between … Citizens receive some elements of democratic rule – perhaps full voting rights – but they also live under leaders with extensive authoritarian powers and few checks and balances.'[80]

But it is Walter's application of these findings to the US case that has attracted attention. She argues that various institutional changes – for example the growth of gerrymandering and voter suppression, or Trump's taste for governing by executive order – mean that 'we have transitioned from a full democracy to anocracy in just five years'. Walter's reliance on quantitative indices to arrive at this conclusion and a degree of partisan bias on her part (she skates over Obama's reliance on executive orders to by-pass a Republican-dominated Congress) justify a degree of scepticism, particularly given the existence of the long-standing anti-democratic constitutional restrictions discussed earlier in this chapter and the power and autonomy of the national security apparatus. But her warning that civil war is possible in the United States is more persuasive when she develops a more concrete analysis, pointing to the extreme polarization between Democrats and Republicans, the way in which this conflict is increasingly racialized ('Two-thirds or more of Black, Latino, and Asian Americans consistently vote Democratic, while roughly 60% of white Americans vote Republican'), and the growth of far right paramilitary groups. All these are trends that didn't start with Trump but accelerated thanks to his presidency.[81]

Another landmark in this process of polarization came on 24 June 2022, when the right-wing majority in the US Supreme Court announced its decision to quash the 1973 *Roe vs Wade* judgement, which recognizes the constitutional right to abortion. This move was, in its own way, of a piece with the 6 January assault on the Capitol. In the first place, it showed the ruthlessness of the Republican right. This time gamers and breakers worked together to take over the Supreme Court. McConnell sabotaged Barack Obama's typically feeble attempt, towards the end of his presidency, to fill a vacancy in the court and helped Trump to appoint three ultra-conservative judges. When they were seeking confirmation from the Senate, all Trump's nominees lied solidly, swearing that they would respect 'precedent' – in other words would not overturn *Roe vs Wade*. And then the new right-wing bloc used its majority in the Court to deprive women of a right they had exercised for nearly fifty years.

Second, the decision itself is only the start of a much broader ideological offensive. Clarence Thomas, the longest serving judge, filed a concurring opinion in which he said that the court should 'reconsider' other precedents that, like *Roe vs Wade*, rely on the principle, which he rejects, of substantive due process. He named three cases, which upheld the right to contraception, the right to sex with someone of the same sex, and the right to same-sex marriages, and proposed 'overruling these demonstrably erroneous decisions'.[82] Thomas, whose wife was under investigation for her support for the far right assault on the US Capitol on 6 January 2021, was announcing a counter-revolution, a massive invasion of individuals' personal liberties.

'What Clarence Thomas wants to do is radical, not conservative', Michael Klarman of the Harvard Law School says.[83] Between the 1950s and the 1970s, notably during the period when Earl Warren was Chief Justice (1953–69), the Supreme Court made a series of judgements that extended individual liberties. Like the cases supporting Black people's demands for civil rights, *Roe vs Wade* was an attempt to accommodate the pressures from the huge mass movements for emancipation that were sweeping not just the United States but the world. These victories survived into the neoliberal era. From the 1980s onwards, governments championed economic liberalism, which removed obstacles to capital's making profits. But they also respected, and sometimes extended, what is sometimes called social liberalism – that is, individual freedom in people's private lives. Big corporations and banks were happy to pay lip service to the values of equality and diversity, even as they were widening real economic inequality.

The Republican right wants to reverse the limited steps towards a genuinely emancipated society that were made thanks to the movements of the 1960s and 1970s. Liberal opinion in the United States lionized Mike Pence because he refused to do Trump's will on 6 January and overturn Joe Biden's election. The Supreme Court decision left it up to states to decide whether to allow or proscribe abortion. But Pence, a pillar of the Christian right, immediately called for a national ban on abortion. The Democrats' relative passivity wasn't simply a reflection of the difficulties that Biden, like Clinton and Obama before him, faced with a deeply polarized Congress. The party leadership is committed to maintaining the pre-Trump status quo, the synthesis of economic and social liberalism; in the White House, Democratic presidents focus on short-term crisis management. The Republicans have, by contrast, what Gramsci would recognize as a hegemonic project of conquering both civil society and the state. The Democratic strategist Jim Kessler puts it well: 'Republicans have had a 50-year plan to win the long game and Democrats have mostly worked to win the next cycle.'[84]

Third, the suppression of *Roe vs Wade* is likely to accelerate the political fragmentation of the United States, as Democrats seek to transform the states they control into 'sanctuary states' – states that safeguard, and indeed extend, abortion provision – whereas Republican-dominated legislatures strive to ban abortion pills, stop their citizens from travelling to other states to receive abortions, and prosecute members of the medical staff who treat them. Many were quick to recall the barbarities of the antebellum era, when the politically dominant South pressurized Northern states to capture and return fugitive slaves. According to Wendy Parmet, the director of Northeastern University's Center for Health Policy and Law, '[w]e haven't seen this kind of battle about … the reach of the jurisdiction of one state over another in a very long time. Nothing of this magnitude have we seen since the Civil War.'[85]

This is, of course, relevant to Walter's argument. Although she talks about 'a second civil war', she does not mean that a repetition of the gigantic struggle of 1861–5 is likely – a struggle between semi-industrialized mass armies that anticipated the total wars of the twentieth century. The US military is too powerful and the far right's popular base is too scattered throughout the country for such a geographical polarization to be feasible. Much more probable, Walter argues, is that, 'if the demands of far-right groups in America are ignored', they could launch 'a war of attrition', targeting public buildings, liberal politicians and their supporters, and federal government officials, 'until those in power offered the terrorists the concessions they wanted, or voters replaced existing politicians with ones who were more sympathetic to the extremists' cause'.[86]

The objective of such a strategy would be to carve out 'a set of white ethno-states in the rural heartland'. There are features specific to the political structure of the United States that could favour this kind of guerrilla campaign, which would then bypass the main weakness of the far right there, namely its failure to develop as yet a coherent national political articulation:

> In a country flush with guns, legal militias, and open-carry laws, politicians and citizens have good reason to be afraid. This is even more true in rural areas, where the reach of the federal government is weaker, and where overlapping jurisdictions between the federal, state, and local governments leave citizens uncertain about who is really in charge. One of America's unique attributes is its decentralized federal structure, but this also leaves it vulnerable to rogue elements taking control of a region – even gaining the support of local law enforcement. State-level militias are legal in twenty-two states, and during the pandemic, they frequently positioned themselves as defenders of small businesses that insisted on staying open despite government-mandated shutdowns.[87]

Such a war would in all likelihood involve pogroms and mass expulsions; it would perhaps lead to full-scale campaigns of 'ethnic cleansing' targeted at large numbers of people of colour and people whom the far right brands as 'leftists'. There is little doubt that the federal government would seek to prevent this kind of fragmentation, but its coercive power has limits. The wars in Afghanistan and Iraq showed that, while the US military has overwhelming tactical superiority in conventional combat, it failed to defeat decentralized guerrilla campaigns that were using many of the methods described by Walter. Some US military thinkers have been quite open about the fact that waging this kind of war on home ground would be even more difficult, given the divided loyalties that at least some federal soldiers would have – a very different situation from the comparatively 'clean' ideological divide over the Union and slavery during the Civil War.[88]

This kind of violent implosion may seem much less probable in Europe, where the far right has made considerable inroads by operating within the existing liberal–democratic system. But we should bear in mind the disruptions that climate change will bring to societies that now seem very well ordered. The rents in the social and economic fabric caused by extreme weather events will create openings for far right groups to attempt to seize power, at least at the regional or local level, and to implement programmes much more extreme that those currently espoused by the leadership of the racist–populist parties. John Locke famously wrote, early in the capitalist era: 'in the beginning all the World was *America*.'[89] And so it may become again, at the end of that era.

6

Pulling the Emergency Cord

Seeking resources of hope

'Marx said that revolutions were the locomotive of world history. But perhaps it is quite otherwise. Perhaps revolutions are attempts by the passengers on this train – the human race – to activate the emergency brake.'[1] Walter Benjamin came up with this arresting image in a draft for his essay 'On the Concept of History', written in 1939–40. His close contemporary and fellow victim of fascism, Antonio Gramsci, also grappled with the same problem, notably in a passage in his *Prison Notebooks*, which is almost as famous as the one I quoted in the previous chapter:

> A crisis occurs, sometimes lasting for decades. This exceptional duration means that incurable structural contradictions have revealed themselves (reached maturity) [*nella struttura si sono rivelate (sono venute a maturità) contraddizioni insanabili*], and that, despite this, the political forces which are struggling positively to preserve and defend the existing structure itself are making every effort to cure them, within certain limits, and to overcome them. These incessant and persistent efforts (since no social formation will ever admit that it has been superseded) form the terrain of the 'conjunctural' [*occasionale*], and it is upon this terrain that the antagonistic forces organize. These forces seek to demonstrate (a demonstration that in the last analysis succeeds and is 'true' only if it becomes a new reality, if the antagonistic forces triumph, but in the immediate is developed in a series

of ideological, religious, philosophical, political, juridical polemics, etc., whose concreteness can be assessed to the extent that they are convincing and displace the pre-existing array of social forces) that the necessary and sufficient conditions already exist to make possible, and hence imperative, the accomplishment of certain historical tasks (imperative, because any falling short before a historical duty increases the necessary disorder and prepares more serious catastrophes).[2]

This passage comes from a crucial note written in 1933–4, 'Analysis of Situations: Relations of Forces', where Gramsci sets out his method of politico-historical analysis; he seeks to integrate in the same progressive movement the 'structural contradictions' in the economic base and the struggle of the contending 'social forces' that unfolds in what he calls the 'superstructures'. It was only on rereading these lines recently that I rediscovered the final reference to 'catastrophes'. Gramsci was living, in his fascist prison, his own version of such a catastrophe. The preceding chapters have been devoted to exploring the different but interconnected dimensions of our own age of catastrophe.

Gramsci is not inverting the economic fatalism that his rereading of Marxism as a 'philosophy of praxis' aims to demolish. He does not think that catastrophe is inevitable any more than he thinks that the victory of socialism is inevitable. It all depends on whether the 'antagonistic forces' become 'a new reality' by developing a hegemonic project that is able to 'displace the pre-existing array of social forces' and win control over civil and political society. In his own way, Benjamin expresses the same thought: the revolution that we need is not the inevitable outcome of historical progress, but a desperate effort 'to blast open the continuum of history' before it is too late.[3] But revolutions need a subject to make them, a collective actor: Benjamin says that it is 'the human race' that pulls the emergency cord. From what social material and through what political processes is this subject constituted?

Thanks to his experience as a leader of the Third International in the years after the Russian Revolution of October 1917, Gramsci had a clear idea of the nature of the 'antagonistic forces' – crucially, the workers' movement and the Communist Party, out of which could be forged a collective subject capable of winning hegemony. Today, on the other hand, the antagonistic forces have no such sharply delineated contours. The first age of catastrophe was dominated by intense class struggles, and the fascists' bids for power were made possible by the defeats suffered by workers and the left. There is plenty of class struggle today as well but, in the 'advanced' economies at least, it is all too often one-sided, as capital succeeds in extracting ever more from wage labour. The organized working class, still a far from negligible social force by historical standards, is dominated by currents that have internalized the defeats suffered by trade unions at the height of the neoliberal offensive. The 'horizontalist' alternative, which flourished during the movement for another globalization at the start of the millennium and then enjoyed an afterlife in the Occupy protests of 2011, has largely faded from the scene.

In this chapter I approach this question of agency. I do so initially by looking at two terrains of current political and ideological contention – gender and 'race' – to see what resources of hope (to borrow a phrase of Raymond Williams's) they offer. Let me emphasize that this exploration is definitely *not* a version of the attempt, pioneered by Herbert Marcuse and cast in stone in sociological theories of the new social movements, to identify alternatives to the working-class struggle. On the contrary, I am examining how the contestation of gender and 'race' in contemporary ideologico-political conflicts might contribute to the formation of a new working-class subject of emancipation. I hope that this will become clear in the second part of the chapter, where I offer some thoughts about programme and strategy.[4]

Terrains of struggle, I: gender

Pat Buchanan, the right-wing conservative who ran unsuccessfully for the presidency against George H. W. Bush, made a speech at the Republican National Convention in August 1992: 'There is a religious war going on in our country for the soul of America. It is a cultural war, as critical to the kind of nation we will one day be as was the Cold War itself.'[5] Arguably this 'culture war' has been one of the far right's greatest successes: here its promoters have pursued, but also extended, an agenda of struggle that Buchanan set out in this speech and in which he focused on defending the family against progressive campaigns for 'unrestricted abortion on demand' and lesbian and gay rights. Today this struggle has become global and embraces gender more broadly.

As Agnieszka Graff and Elzbieta Korolczuk write in their outstanding study of the 'anti-gender' movement,

> Gender is no distraction from real politics; it resides at the heart of politics today, both as a set of specific policy issues and as the nexus of a symbolic struggle, a space where differences are negotiated and

defined. Not a marginal controversy, no mere 'cultural' issue, gender has become a site of powerful and sometimes violent conflict. The anti-gender campaigns feed on religious sentiments, and employ moralizing discourse, but their spread can only be properly understood in the context of the rise of right-wing political forces seeking ideological and affective means for gaining hegemony.[6]

Gender has become more broadly a politically contested concept – contested in a way that doesn't simply mobilize the right but also divides the left and feminists, as a polyvalent struggle has developed over the meaning of feminism. What has brought this conflict into focus is the emergence of a powerful movement for trans liberation and for the right it has affirmed for individuals to choose their own gender. The obvious response would be to welcome this movement as an extension of previous struggles, for example against the oppression of women, Black people, lesbians and gays, and disabled people and for a deepening sense of the universality of emancipation. Instead, the demand for trans liberation has been bitterly resisted by some feminists, with the support of elements of the radical left, and this has triggered embittered confrontations – on social media, in universities, and in trade unions.[7]

Feminist opponents of trans liberation – 'trans-critical' feminists, for short (and it's important to emphasize that very many other feminists disagree with them) – take a stand on the concept of woman as an essentially biological category: they strongly affirm it. Behind their insistence on doing so lies the distinction between sex and gender drawn at the beginnings of the women's liberation movement in the 1960s and 1970s, whereby the first is assigned to the realm of nature and the second to that of culture. The thought that motivated this theoretical strategy was that such a distinction was needed if one wanted to denaturalize women's subordinate social position and demonstrate that this position was the historically specific and contingent product of a male-dominated society, not something biologically inscribed in the nature of women and men.

But the nature–culture distinction is conceptually slippery, as Judith Butler has shown in a brilliant and prophetic dismantling of the opposition between sex and gender. There she highlighted in particular the way in which these categories tend to be conceptualized as binary, and hence as mirroring each other: 'When the constructed status of gender is theorized as radically independent of sex, gender itself becomes a free-floating artifice, with the consequence that *man* and *masculine* might just as easily signify a female body as a male one, and *woman* and *feminine* a male body as easily as a female one.' Analogously, when one begins to interrogate sex, it too loses the physical determinacy it apparently possessed, and a genealogy emerges 'that might expose the binary options as a variable construction ... If the immutable character of sex is contested, perhaps this construct called "sex" is as culturally constructed as gender; indeed, perhaps it was always already gender, with the consequence that the distinction between sex and gender turns out to be no distinction at all.'[8]

No wonder Butler was burned in effigy in October 2017 by ultra-conservative protesters, who opposed a conference she co-organized in São Paulo, Brazil.[9] For what trans-critical feminists and the right-wing anti-gender movement have in common is a conception of biology as the stable foundation of sexual difference. But biology is unlikely to offer them the secure ideological guarantee they seek. Quite independently of the difficulties of distinguishing between sex and gender, the biological and the social have proved hard to disentangle.[10] This doesn't mean that the biological disappears – COVID-19 has given us cause to remember its effectivity. As trans-critical feminists endlessly remind us, some humans are born with wombs and others without. But Richard Lewontin, Steven Rose, and Leon Kamin point out that '[t]he biological and the social are neither separable, nor antithetical, nor alternatives, but complementary. All causes of the behaviour of organisms ... are simultaneously both social and biological, as they are all amenable to analysis at many levels. All human phenomena are social and biological just as they are simultaneously chemical and physical.'[11]

Human societies have biological determinants, but what they and the people composing them make of these determinants is, historically, highly variable; and it varies in how they live their gender and how they enjoy sex as much as in other respects, as Peter Drucker shows in his rich historical account of different 'same-sex regimes'.[12] Recognizing the socially constructed character of sex and gender in no way implies a flight into postmodernism, as some trans-critical feminists assert. The processes through which sex and gender are formed and transformed are materially rooted in how the forces and relations of production shape specific social formations. Modern heteronormative family structures are central to how labour power is reproduced under capitalism, providing it with a workforce fractured by gender and by the multiple forms of oppression to which these structures give rise. As Butler has pointed out, '[i]f one continues to take the mode of production as the defining structure of political economy, then surely it would make no sense for feminists to dismiss the hard-won insight that sexuality must be understood as part of that mode of production'.[13]

If trans-critical feminists at least use the progressive language they inherited from the women's liberation movement in its heyday, the anti-gender movement bases its assault on a highly traditionalist conception of the heteronormative family. There is what Graff and Korolczuk call an 'opportunistic synergy' between 'ultraconservative religious actors' centred on the Catholic Church and the far right; and this synergy takes expression in transnational alliances such as the World Congress of Families and the Political Network for Values. Thus Pope Francis, who is often seen as a progressive figure, repeatedly plays on a key theme of anti-genderism: the supposed imposition of 'gender ideology' on the rest of the world by the liberal West. For example he said in Kraków in 2016 (Poland is one of the main centres of the 'anti-gender' movement): 'In Europe, America, Latin America, Africa, and in some countries of Asia, there are genuine forms of ideological colonization taking place. And one of these – I will call it clearly by its name – is [the ideology of] "gender". Today children – children! – are taught in school that everyone can choose his or her sex.'[14]

The speech that Matteo Salvini, leader of the Lega and Italian deputy prime minister at the time, made at the opening of the World Congress of Families in Verona in 2019 shows how the far right links the defence of the traditional family to its Islamophobic ideology:

> The feminists that speak of women's rights are the first to pretend to not see what is the first, only and major, real danger in 2019 for rights, social achievements, freedom to work, study, speak, study, dress as you like – and it's not the World Family Congress – it's Islamic extremism, a culture where the woman's value is less than zero ... The woman gets covered with a burka, the woman doesn't have the right to leave the house, the woman shouldn't wear a mini-skirt, and if she dresses too western, thinks too western or becomes too western, (they) beat her up.[15]

Salvini's emphasis here is typical of an important strand in contemporary far right discourse that does not reduce women's role to the roles encapsulated by the traditional conservative slogan *Kinder, Küche, Kirche* ('children, cooking, church'), but portrays Muslims as a threat to gender equality. Judith Orr notes how Marine Le Pen plays on this theme:

She portrays French culture in particular and Western values in general as symbolic of women's equality ... She regularly raises the alleged threat that immigration poses to women ... 'I am scared that the migrant crisis signals the beginning of the end of women's rights' ... the target of her rhetoric is unmistakable: 'In France we respect women, we don't beat them, we don't ask them to hide themselves behind a veil as if they were impure. We drink wine when we want, we can criticize religion and speak freely.'[16]

Butler comments:

For this reactionary movement, the term 'gender' attracts, condenses, and electrifies a diverse set of social and economic anxieties produced by increasing economic precarity under neoliberal regimes, intensifying social inequality, and pandemic shutdown ... When gender is thus figured as a foreign invasion, these groups clearly reveal that they are in the business of nation-building. The nation for which they are fighting is built upon white supremacy, the heteronormative family, and a resistance to all critical questioning of norms that have clearly restricted the freedoms and imperilled the lives of so many people.[17]

Thus, in Graff's and Korolczuk's words, 'anti-genderism is a right-wing critique of neoliberalism'. Fortunately it has not gone unanswered – we witnessed, for example, Black Monday, the women's strike on 3 October 2016 that forced the far right Polish government to abandon its plans to strengthen anti-abortion legislation; the international women's demonstrations that greeted Donald Trump's inauguration on 20 January 2017; and the five-million-strong 'feminist strike' in the Spanish state on 8 March 2018, International Women's Day. According to Graff and Korolczuk, 'the new wave of feminist activism that erupted around 2016 in countries such as Argentina, Italy, Poland, Spain and the US was a reaction to the rise of ultraconservative and right-wing populism discussed in this book: anti-genderism in its various manifestations as well as the misogyny of political leaders. The mass protests in these countries were in fact efforts to stop the progression of the right.' Nevertheless, '[a]bandoning the established liberal discursive frames of human rights, these movements built their power ... on emotions, both personal and collective. In effect, a new collective subject was constituted in the public sphere: angry women with a strong political identity.'[18] The US Supreme Court decision to overturn *Roe vs Wade* is going to bring plenty more angry women onto the streets.

Graff and Korolczuk see these movements as beginnings of the kind of 'left populism' advocated by Chantal Mouffe, one that mobilizes on a progressive basis against neoliberal elites.[19] But they correctly stress that explicit opposition to capitalism or neoliberalism (or both) has been marginal to these new women's protests. Indeed, the huge demonstrations in the United States against Trump's inauguration were politically dominated by the mainstream Democratic Party and, to a degree, by its defeated presidential candidate, Hillary Clinton, a pillar of the neoliberal order whose discontents the far right are seeking to channel. Latin America, where there have been huge movements against gender violence and for abortion rights in recent years, offers a contrast:

> Women are also leading struggles for justice and equality, including within larger protest movements. Chile is the perfect example of this confluence. There, the demonstrations that began in October 2019 against the rise in public transport fees turned into a wave of indignation against the economic model that has prevailed since the Pinochet dictatorship in the late 20th century.
>
> The protests were met with violent repression, including sexual abuse against women by *Carabineros* (police force). In that context, in December of that year, the feminist collective Las Tesis launched *Un violader in tu camino* ('A rapist in your path'), a song performance against macho violence that has become a worldwide feminist anthem.[20]

Unless the new feminism follows this example and more broadly develops a critique of neoliberal capitalism, it will be vulnerable to the far right's ability, so well explored by Graff and Korolczuk with respect to 'gender ideology', to play on the anger that the economic dislocations of past decades has caused. But of course this cuts both ways. The anti-capitalist left has to ensure that it consistently pursues the kind of total emancipation that seeks to sweep away not just economic exploitation but the myriad forms of oppression to which humans are subject. The trans movement is significant here, not merely because of the justice of its demands, but because of the radical energy provided by a new generation of young activists who challenge heteronormative family structures in their depths, where individual subjects are formed.[21]

Terrains of struggle, II: the racial fracture

'Race' too has become a terrain of ideological and political struggle. A striking difference with the inter-war era is that, as we saw in the preceding chapter, the most important single arena for the advance of the far right is the United States, still the hegemonic capitalist power. It is there that the role of racism in the antagonisms expressed by the far right has been most visible – both in Trump's articulation of anti-Black and anti-migrant racism and Islamophobia and in the riposte represented by the Black Lives Matter (BLM) revolt. But, especially in the form of Islamophobia, racism has played an important part on other continents as well.

This is not the place to explore in any depth the historical relationship between capitalism and racism, but a few points are necessary. In contemporary critical discourse, the connection is thought to be so tight that it is common to talk about 'racial capitalism', a usage that can be traced back principally to Cedric Robinson's very influential *Black Marxism*.[22] The bond between capitalism and racism is indeed profound. I would stress in particular three elements. First, the historical role played by plantation slavery in the development of capitalism in the Americas in the sixteenth and seventeenth centuries provided the context for 'the invention of the white race' (in Theodore Allen's words).[23] The development of biological racism, according to which humankind is a natural hierarchy of inherently superior and inferior groups, served to legitimize the enslavement of Africans despite the increasing prevalence of the principle of universal human equality, which helped to motivate the English, American, and French revolutions. Racism also functioned as a mechanism of social control in Britain's American colonies, dividing the African slaves from white indentured labourers, whose conditions were often little different.

Second, the persistence of racism is not simply a legacy of slavery, important though that is in countries such as the United States and Brazil.[24] Modern industrial capitalism is a global system heavily dependent on flows of migrant workers. Competition in the labour market between 'natives' and migrants creates conditions for the kind of divisions that can be worked up into racial antagonism and can undermine the cohesion and effectiveness of the working class as a collective agent, as Marx already saw in mid-nineteenth century Britain.[25] In his classic analysis of the US South after the abolition of slavery, W. E. B. du Bois points to the political and ideological efforts needed to entrench racial divisions, in this case between 'poor whites' and the former slaves:

> It must be remembered that the white group of labourers, while they received a low wage, were compensated in part by a sort of public

and psychological wage. They were given public deference and titles of courtesy because they were white. They were admitted freely with all classes of white people to public functions, public parks, and the best schools. The police were drawn from their ranks, and the courts, dependent upon their votes, treated them with such leniency as to encourage lawlessness. Their vote selected public officials, and while this had small effect upon the economic situation, it had great effect upon their personal treatment and the deference shown them.[26]

Third, as this example illustrates, racism is closely interwoven with the institutions of the state. This is very visible in the way in which the police tend to operate as a militarized occupation force in racialized communities. But racism is also important to legitimize imperial interventions, as we can see with the growth of Islamophobia as the US 'War for the Greater Middle East' developed. It is in this context that racist ideology has in the past 50 years been reconfigured to affirm the existence of ineradicable cultural differences between groups that prevent them living together in the same society.[27]

*

Racism is therefore institutionalized throughout global capitalism, but it takes particularly virulent forms in the United States. It's enough to recall a few instances: the embedding of slavery in the constitution; the subsequent failures to make the destruction of the slave power in the South the basis for achieving equal citizenship for African Americans, either during Reconstruction (1865–77) or during the Civil Rights movement of the 1960s; or the systematic use of repression (notably a militarized police force and the 'prison–industrial complex') to keep people of colour subordinated.[28] Michael Goldfield has pointed to the peculiar role of the South – still a reservoir of cheap racialized labour long after Emancipation and the abolition of Jim Crow – in limiting the advances of the organized working class in the United States.[29]

One of the most distinctive features of Trump's irruption into the political big time is how he sought to instrumentalize the racial antagonism in order to win and retain the presidency and how, in doing so, he stimulated mass mobilization to end this very antagonism. For the most remarkable and encouraging aspect of the COVID-19 pandemic was the way in which, in the summer of 2020, it was interrupted by the huge wave of protests provoked by the murder of George Floyd at the hands of the police, in Minneapolis, on 25 May. Noam Chomsky stressed the unprecedented scale of these protests:

There was a huge outpouring, nothing comparable in American history. There were huge demonstrations; there was a sense of dedicated solidarity of Black and white people marching together. They were nonviolent overwhelmingly, though the right wing would like you to believe otherwise. There was also enormous public support, with two-thirds of the population supportive of protest. There is nothing remotely like that in US history.[30]

The *New York Times*, reporting in the summer of 2020, confirmed this judgement:

The recent Black Lives Matter protests peaked on June 6, when half a million people turned out in nearly 550 places across the United States. That was a single day in more than a month of protests that still continue to today.

Four recent polls ... suggest that about 15 million to 26 million people in the United States have participated in demonstrations over the death of George Floyd and others in recent weeks.

These figures would make the recent protests the largest movement in the country's history, according to interviews with scholars and crowd-counting experts.[31]

According to one study, in the year after George Floyd's murder, there were 'more than 11,000 demonstrations associated with the Black Lives Matter (BLM) movement ... reported in nearly 3,000 distinct locations'.[32] By comparison, the risings provoked by Martin Luther King Jr's assassination on 4 April 1968 took place in just over a hundred cities – and those, according to Elizabeth Hinton, sparked 'the largest wave of domestic violence since the Civil War' and pushed President Lyndon Johnson to mobilize 20,000 Federal troops, including machine gun placements on the Capitol.[33] Trump's efforts similarly to militarize the state's response to the 2020 protests, symbolized as they were by his theatrical and heavily guarded walk to a church in Lafayette Square on 1 June, may have contributed to the Pentagon's alienation from him, as discussed in the preceding chapter.[34]

Meanwhile, the BLM protests swept around the world. The protests in Britain, apparently the largest outside the United States, produced the symbolic moment on 7 June when the statue of the eighteenth-century slaver Edward Colston was thrown into Bristol Harbour, to the fury of Boris Johnson's right-wing Tory government. The protests' global resonance was shown in their influence on other movements

– for example the tendency of Palestinian activists during the May 2021 Unity Intifada to frame it in terms borrowed from BLM. The Black feminist intellectual and organizer Barbara Ransby explains the significance of the demand for abolition popularized by the risings:

> When we talk about abolition, we do a shorthand; for we're not just talking about abolishing, we're talking about building. Abolition is a potentially revolutionary and radical demand because you're saying we can't just patch up the system that we live under. We have to rethink it, we have to dismantle it, we have to have something fundamentally different. To abolish without building leaves us vulnerable. We have to build new institutions, we have to build new power, we have to build a new system, and we have to become different people in the process.[35]

Anti-racism has thus become a mobilizing force that reaches far beyond the Black community, or indeed the United States. But the BLM protests were not a victory parade; they were an advance that met with powerful pushback. The study cited earlier reports:

The BLM movement has remained overwhelmingly non-violent.

- Approximately 94% of all pro-BLM demonstrations have been peaceful, with 6% involving reports of violence, clashes with police, vandalism, looting, or other destructive activity ...

Police have taken a heavy-handed, militarized approach to the movement, escalating tensions.

- Authorities are three times more likely to intervene in pro-BLM demonstrations than they are in other demonstrations.
- When intervening, they are more likely to use force against pro-BLM demonstrators: 52% of the time, compared to 26% of the time against all other demonstrators.[36]

The police and their unions of course had a vested interest in trying to crush a movement that targets them directly, as in campaigns to 'defund the police'. But they were backed by hit squads of federal agents deployed to selected cities under Trump's 'Operation Diligent Valor'; and they also enjoyed the support of the armed auxiliaries provided by far right groups to attack the protests. New, repressive laws followed the protests, both in many American states and in Britain (see Chapter

2 above). Meanwhile, 'race' has become another front in the culture war. Politicians in other countries have sought to borrow Trump's ploy. Thus the Conservative government in Britain has mainstreamed far right themes, campaigning against wokeism, policing cultural institutions to prevent them from thematizing the historical legacy of imperialism and slavery, and appointing a commission that attacked the very idea of institutional racism at a moment when its reality was being starkly exposed.[37] The denunciations of 'Islamo-leftism' made by Emmanuel Macron's ministers in France and the bitter battles over indigenous rights in the Americas and in Australia are instances of the same polarization.

The BLM explosion is suggestive of how the racial fracture increasingly condenses all the antagonisms of contemporary society. It reflected not simply an unprecedented mass reaction to the continuous pressure that militarized policing places on Black communities. We saw in Chapter 2 how mortality rates in the COVID-19 pandemic have soared among Black and Latinx people in the United States. Vulnerability to the virus and to police violence are two symptoms of how 'race' and class intersect in our societies. The neoliberal restructuring of capitalism has fostered increasing reliance on low-paid and insecure workers, often racialized, in many cases migrants and refugees. The pandemic thrust them into the front line, as 'essential' workers; and this added a new dimension to their precarity, as they risked their very lives in doing their jobs. These experiences surely informed the rebellion in the summer of 2020.

Writing about the July 2014 police murder of Eric Garner, whose unforgettable dying words were 'I can't breathe!' and who was arrested for allegedly selling individual cigarettes, Salar Mohandesi pointed to the connection between precarity and racism:

> Marx tried to explain the historical emergence of this wageless life by showing how capitalism is itself structurally incapable of fully employing everyone who depends on wages to live. By necessity capitalism produces 'a relatively redundant working population, i.e. a population which is superfluous to capital's average requirements for its own valorization, and is therefore a surplus population' ... As Garner's death shows, the production of a surplus population is closely intertwined with racism. The history of capitalism demonstrates that racial categories are constantly incorporated, and in fact reconstituted, by the processes that generate dispossessed, disciplined, terrorized surplus populations.[38]

The intersection of 'race' and class is indeed increasingly a basis of political mobilization. On the one hand, the social and political rise of a Black middle class since the 1960s, and in particular the role it has in managing the urban United States means that, as Keeanga-Yamahtta Taylor points out, 'today, when poor or working-class Black people experience hardship, that hardship is likely being overseen by an African American in some position of authority'.[39] On the other hand, the material impoverishment suffered by working-class people generally in the United States affects whites as well as Blacks, and they too are vulnerable to police violence, albeit not on the same scale as African Americans.

By comparison with the 1960s risings that peaked after King's murder, the BLM protests were non-racial in composition, as Chomsky and many others have stressed. Buchanan, Bui, and Patel observe: 'Unlike with past Black Lives Matter protests, nearly 95 percent of counties that had a protest recently are majority white, and nearly three-quarters of the counties are more than 75 percent white.' No doubt white protesters were strongly motivated by some moral identification with the BLM cause. Indeed, according to the same report, 'the movement appears to have attracted protesters who are younger and wealthier. The age group with the largest share of protesters was people under 35 and the income group with the largest share of protesters was those earning more than $150,000'.[40]

Nevertheless, the BLM rebellion offered a glimpse into how class agency can be remade. This isn't simply because of the trend for people of colour to become a growing percentage of the population – and not just in the United States but in advanced capitalist societies more widely. Insecurity is becoming generalized in the world of work; the determined attempt by British universities to destroy what was once an excellent pensions system for academics, who used to regard themselves as professionals rather than workers, is symptomatic of this process. The experiences of precarious workers and what were once relatively privileged sections of the working class are tending to converge (though not to coincide: Blacks and Muslims, for example, bear an especially heavy weight of racial oppression). Out of this convergence could emerge a new kind of workers' movement, no doubt very different from its predecessors because, to be effective, it would need to address more than straightforward workplace issues or even broader socioeconomic reforms, important though these are.

Given its nature in the twenty-first century, the working class would have to give the different oppressions that weigh down on people

– especially those arising from gender, 'race', sexual orientation, and disability – a strategic importance that they have lacked in the past (insofar as they were addressed at all in any consistent manner). This would be not merely a moral stand but a matter of self-interest, of practical necessity. This necessity is underlined by the way in which the development of globalized production networks creates an interdependence between workers in the South and in the North (while many of the latter come in fact from the South). In unexpected ways, the world working class, which Marx and Engels address at the end of the *Communist Manifesto*, could thus begin to emerge as a collective agent in this age of catastrophe.[41]

Planning for progress or catastrophe

The collective agency on which the BLM revolt offered glimpses is important because the problems we face require political solutions. Relying on what Ronald Reagan called the 'magic of the marketplace' is no longer credible. The global financial crisis marked a turning point; as I argued at the time, states stepped in to prevent another Great Depression.[42] In Chapter 3 of this book we saw how this proved not to be a temporary emergency measure, as central banks used their balance sheets to maintain effective demand and to keep financial markets liquid into, and through, the COVID-19 pandemic. Governments also took major measures to support employment and demand. As after the global financial crisis, once economic recovery started to set in, louder voices were heard, for example those of prominent economists such as Lawrence Summers and Martin Wolf, who called for the 'normalization' of interest rates, particularly in the light of the uptick in inflation. But then came the destabilizing impact of Russia's invasion of Ukraine. The whole thrust of this book has been that such events cannot be seen as exogenous shocks, as mainstream economics affirms; they arise from a multifaceted structural crisis of the entire capitalist system and, more broadly, of the civilization that fossil capitalism has created. We are living what James Galbraith has called 'the end of normal'.[43]

The only question is what shape the 'new normal' will take. One way to bring the choices into focus is by considering the question of economic planning. Planning involves an ex ante coordination of economic activities that is achieved through some form of authoritative political process; markets, by contrast, offer ex post coordination, where the aggregate state of the economy is a consequence of decentralized decisions taken by competing actors. One of the key ideological achievements of neoliberalism was effectively to exile from polite society any discussion of planning, especially on the basis of Friedrich von Hayek's efforts to demonstrate that the market provides the most efficient form of coordination and distribution of knowledge for a complex modern economy; but this achievement was greatly facilitated by what proved to be the terminal crisis of the Stalinist command economy in the Soviet Union during the 1980s.[44] This led G. A. Cohen, one of the most outstanding socialist theorists of our times, to conclude his last book by declaring an impasse: 'Every market economy, even a socialist economy, is a system of predation. Our attempt to get beyond predation have thus far failed. I do not think the right conclusion is to give up.'[45]

The context is very different now. I corresponded with Cohen about his book, in draft as the global financial crisis was beginning to unfold in 2008, but I was unable to persuade him to take seriously the models of democratic planning developed by Pat Devine and Michael Albert (on which a little more follows). Thanks to that crisis and its aftermath, markets no longer seem quite so efficient. But the problem lies much deeper than the dysfunctions and scams inherent in financial markets. The pandemic has showed governments not simply acting as a backstop when markets fail but mobilizing resources to resolve problems – to develop and distribute vaccines in the first place, but also to pursue, say, track-and-trace programmes. Once again, interventions of this kind can't be seen as temporary emergency measures. Even if we manage to duck a new pandemic, the economic disruption caused by climate change will require more of this type of activity.

Above all, to decarbonize economies will require a plethora of decisions about where to reallocate resources to and from. And this is a global process of reorientation. The technologies involved in the provision of renewable energy require intensive resource extraction; to rely on the existing 'planetary mine', with its environmentally destructive and highly exploitive methods of production, would be massively self-defeating.[46] As Thea Riofrancos puts it in a tweet, '[t]he ecomodernist fantasy of ever-cheaper green tech is dead, as "critical minerals" prices boom. We're in a world of increasing geo-economic conflict, market shortages, and costs of energy transition. It's vital to advocate for an energy transition that requires *less* mining.'[47] It is the purest folly to imagine that this kind of problem can be overcome by relying on market mechanisms such as the emissions trading promoted by the European Union.

Planning is thus needed to manage economies, which are likely to become more unstable in coming decades. The important political choice is about the kind of planning we want to have: critically, is it to be one from above or from below? Laurie MacFarlane of the platform openDemocracy warns that the crisis of neoliberalism and the return of the 'politicized economy' can lead to the kind of 'authoritarian capitalism' pioneered in recent decades by China, where ultimate economic control is in the hands of the top echelons of the Communist Party and citizens are subjected to increasingly sophisticated techniques of digital surveillance.[48] The growing resort to emergency measures prompted by the global financial crisis and by the pandemic can harden into a political regime that seeks to minimize disruption but maintains its freedom of manoeuvre and protects capital by reducing democratically elected institutions to a decorative façade. Although this regime would represent a break, it would benefit from the ways in which its neoliberal predecessor sought to immunize economic policymaking against any kind of political accountability. The 'authoritarian statism' that Poulantzas warned us against on the eve of the neoliberal era may in fact be taking shape at its end.[49]

But the kind of ex ante economic coordination we need can be provided in other ways. There already exist models of democratic planning, notably Pat Devine's negotiated coordination, Michael Albert's participatory economics (or Parecon), and Daniel Saros's needs-based socialism.[50] Albert's and Saros's models seek to transfer as much power as possible to the level of workplace councils, which interact with consumers' councils to decide on the allocation of resources and the production of output. Devine's negotiated coordination also requires broad economic parameters (e.g. individual vs collective consumption; social vs economic investment; energy and transport; environmental priorities) to be set through a process of democratic decision-making at the national and international levels. It is only within the framework established by this process that negotiated coordination would go on between producers and communities, on a sectoral, regional, and local basis; and the information required for rational economic decisions would circulate through these interchanges.

But the technological and social conditions for the discussion of alternatives to the market have changed radically with the emergence of platform capitalism: firms such as Amazon and Facebook use the digital infrastructure they provide to amass vast amounts of marketable data about their users. James Meadway argues that these companies represent 'a path out of neoliberalism'. For example, the principle of price as an organizer of economic activity has become increasingly tenuous. The products of the platform giants, at least on the consumer side, tend to work against market mechanisms. Facebook still boasts that 'it is free, and always will be'. There is no consumer market and no price being established, when a product like Facebook is free. Where a product is not obviously free, the platforms have attempted to push their customer base into a subscription model: not organizing a market through price, but creating a continual flow of income, at a fixed rate, from the consumer to themselves.[51]

Evgeny Morozov points to the potential that the digital feedback infrastructure developed by platform capitalism has for democratic planning: 'On the consumption side, the predictive capacity of Big Data can anticipate our preferences better than we can ... suggests that the "feedback infrastructure" can foresee and facilitate the satisfaction of our needs in ways unimaginable to central planners. Such predictive capacity is a function, not of the mysterious workings of the price system, but of the data held by platforms.'[52] He notes that Saros's needs-based socialism seeks to take advantage of the advances in information technology.

In particular, Saros proposes that each individual digitally creates and constantly updates a personal needs profile by selecting from the list of all available use values in an electronic general catalogue; the sum of these choices then guides the allocation of resources among workplace councils and the actual production of use values (for children, it's their parents who would make these choices).[53] Saros's proposal, like Parecon, seems too reliant on atomized decision-making, leaving a vacuum that new forms of bureaucratic power might fill; but one doesn't have to endorse all the details of Saros's proposal to appreciate how it seeks to tap into the current transformations in capitalism to lay the basis for a socialist future. Morozov's half tongue-in-cheek call to 'socialize the means of feedback production' highlights the necessity of taking on big data, not just because of the concentration of economic power they represent but because they have developed technologies that allow us to move beyond capitalism.[54]

One great merit of these models of planning is that they seek not simply to maintain but to increase democracy, both by transferring decision-making as far as possible downwards and by extending the principle of majority rule to the economy. In both respects, they break with liberal democracy, which functions as far as possible to keep the masses passive and to prevent politics from interfering with the functioning of the market. Compare what Adam Tooze wrote in a recent discussion of Keynesianism: 'there are good reasons to defend technocratic government against the unreasoning passions of mass democracy'.[55] This does indeed hark back to Maynard Keynes's intellectual elitism, his belief that 'the economic problem ... the problem of want and poverty, and the economic struggle between classes and nations, is nothing but a frightful muddle, a transitory and an *unnecessary* muddle'.[56] But Tooze's reference point is more indirect, namely Geoff Mann's argument that '[m]odern political economy has always already been Keynesian in this sense: haunted by the memory of revolution and upheaval, and thus by a consciousness of the menace of popular rejection of the existing order, but convinced the right tax tweak or policy fix has the capacity to put off disaster so we can focus on economic bliss once more'.[57]

Mann, interestingly, compares Keynes's political outlook (which he does not himself endorse unconditionally) to Hegel's warning that the mass impoverishment generated by modern civil society threatens to create a 'rabble' (*Pöbel*) that lacks a definite social position or status, 'which in turn makes it much easier for disproportionate wealth to be concentrated in a few hands'.[58] Hegel and Keynes are indeed kindred social thinkers, aware of the political and economic limits of capitalism but committed to overcoming them through the reconciling power of the state.[59] It is worth remembering here that Marx engaged not in political economy but in its *critique*. He thinks that the antagonisms of capitalist society are too profound to be contained by state intervention, and he reconceives of the 'rabble' by casting it as the proletariat, the class on whose labour the system depends, and therefore the class with the power to liberate itself. So the right tax tweak or policy fix won't save us from the unfolding catastrophe. And working people aren't a problem to be managed but potential agents of their own liberation whose collective action can save us all.

The disagreement here is not primarily analytical, or even ethical; nothing has fed the growth of the far right more than a widespread sense of exclusion from the political process.[60] It is thus for reasons not merely of principle but of political necessity that alternatives to capitalism represent an advance in democracy. I noted in Chapter 5 that the left has been much less effective in responding to states' management of the pandemic than the far right. Recovering Marx's original conception of socialism as *self*-emancipation, as working people and the oppressed liberating themselves, is a precondition for the left's regaining the ability to present itself as an alternative.[61] This vision of socialism as a self-governing society should be articulated with a set of demands that meet people's everyday needs in a world that is disrupted by economic instability, pandemic, climate change, and war and makes a rapid transition to a decarbonized economy.

An alliance of the centre and the left?

It is, of course, one thing to say that democratic planning is feasible, quite another to show how it might be achieved. Creating a digital general catalogue seems a bit remote when we face such urgent and multiple existential threats. In concluding this book, I want to make three points about strategy: first, we can't win by allying ourselves with liberals; second, civil disobedience isn't enough; third, violence isn't enough.

The first point is a response to the arguments put forward by Paul Mason. In response to the storming of the Capitol on 6 January 2021, he wrote:

> in the 20th century, faced with fascism, all Marxist parties who actually found themselves on the receiving end found that: (a) anti-fascist violence is not enough – it cannot match fascist violence in its offensive, mobile, mercurial character; (b) you have to call on the state to defend democracy and the rule of law ... Hannah Arendt described fascism as 'the temporary alliance of the elite and the mob'. That's literally what happened on 6 January... The lessons of Europe in the 1930s are that the only thing that beats an alliance of the elite and the mob is a temporary alliance of the centre and the left. And that when that happens, as in France and Spain between 1934 and 1936, you don't only win elections but you can also create a mass popular anti-fascist culture.[62]

This is a disastrously mistaken strategy. To begin with, Mason presents a false dichotomy. Ultimately, only a socialist revolution that ends capitalism can eliminate the threat of fascism. Nevertheless, in the here and now, the defence of actually existing liberal democracy, for all its flaws, is essential. In his critique of the Stalinist Third Period policy, which equated social democracy with fascism, Trotsky displays one of his most brilliant insights by laying stress on the importance of the workers' defending this space – importance, that is, for their own movement:

In the course of many decades, the workers have built up within the bourgeois democracy, by utilizing it and by fighting against it, their own strongholds and bases of proletarian democracy: the trade unions, the political parties, the educational and sport clubs, the cooperatives and so on. The proletariat cannot attain power within the formal limits of bourgeois democracy, but only by taking the road of revolution: this has been proved both by theory and experience. And these bulwarks of workers' democracy within the bourgeois state are absolutely essential for taking the revolutionary road.[63]

Despite the transformations in working-class life in advanced capitalism since the 1930s, it remains essential to defend existing capitalist democracy, for the reasons Trotsky gives. However, he argues that this requires using the methods of class struggle, not of class collaboration. The Popular Front strategy adopted by the Communist International in 1935, after the disastrous failure of its previous policy in Germany, amounted to an alliance between the workers' movement and the liberal bourgeoisie. This is the essence of the approach Mason is advocating, and it, too, would lead to disaster, just as it did in the 1930s.

To see why, let's return to 6 February 1934 in Paris, when the far right marched violently on the French parliament (see Chapter 5). The victory of the leagues in forcing out Édouard Daladier, the Radical prime minister-designate, provoked a more powerful reaction from the left. In their definitive study of 6 February, Brian Jenkins and Chris Millington write:

> The Communist and Socialist Parties immediately denounced the leagues' action as an attempted fascist coup. On 9 February, the Communist Party organised a demonstration as a riposte, during which four men died in violence with police. ... Yet it was on 12 February that the moment of truth for the left came. On that day, the Socialist Party and the CGT [Confédération Générale du Travail] labour union called a general strike. The Communist Party had not planned to join this action. Instead, it continued to condemn its Socialist Party rival as complicit in the killing of workers on 9 February. However, the party could not prevent its members from mixing spontaneously with their Socialist Party counterparts on the streets of Paris. This display of rank and file unity raised hopes for a coalition. Official collaboration was not immediately forthcoming. However, by July 1934, the Socialist and Communist Parties had formed a formal alliance against fascism,

the Rassemblement Populaire. The following year, the coalition expanded to include the Radical Party. This 'Popular Front' enjoyed electoral success in June 1936 when Léon Blum became France's first Socialist Party prime minister.[64]

So 6 February led to further polarization both right and left – the start of what Robert Paxton calls 'the virtual French civil war of the mid-1930s'.[65] But in the immediate, Jenkins and Millington stress, 'the combined Socialist and Communist demonstration of 12 February 1934 was much larger than that of 6 February and, moreover, found greater echo throughout France', through demonstrations and strikes across the country.[66] Unity was to a large extent imposed on the Socialist Party and Communist Party leaderships through pressure from below.[67] However, the extension – proposed by the communist leader Maurice Thorez – of the Rassemblement Populaire to include the Radicals and the formation of the Popular Front were not the natural culmination of this process, as Mason implies. The Socialists and Communists were working-class and nominally Marxist parties. The Radicals, by contrast, constituted the dominant party of the Third Republic. Trotsky describes them as 'that political instrument of the big bourgeoisie that is the best adapted to the traditions and prejudices of the petty bourgeoisie'.[68] Alliance with the Radicals meant in practice subordinating the interests of the working class to those of French capital.

This became visible in May–June 1936, when the electoral victory of the Popular Front stimulated a wave of mass strikes and factory occupations. Eager to reassure panicky financial markets, the new government made ending the strikes its priority; with the Matignon Agreements, it offered some significant concessions, notably a 12 per cent pay increase and a two weeks' paid holiday per year. But the effect was to demobilize workers, while the new government struggled with relentless capital flight, the devaluation of the franc, and rising inflation, which was eroding the gains made in June 1936. The Blum cabinet lasted a year.[69]

Ironically, it was Daladier, the political victim of 6 February, who finally buried the Popular Front; he did so when he replaced Blum's very short-lived second government in April 1938 with a centre-right coalition. Granted the right to rule by decree that parliament had refused Blum, Daladier in many ways continued along the path of Gaston Doumergue's right-wing authoritarian government, which had been brought to office by 4 February. He signed the Munich agreement with Hitler in September 1938, crushed a general strike that November and banned the Communist Party in August 1939. As so often, giving greater executive powers to the state forged new weapons, ready to be used against the left. Jenkins and Millington observe: 'Arguably, in the course of 1938, the French left experienced a similar crushing defeat' – similar, that is, to the ones suffered by the Italian and the German working class before the fascist seizures of power.

> The hopes and energies aroused by the Popular Front movement had been dissipated, its achievements were being rolled back, and a bitter conservative backlash was underway. Daladier's *dictature*, fuelled by virulent anti-Communism and involving the extensive use of decree powers, was increasingly conservative and authoritarian. The Radical Party itself moved similarly to the right, adopting antisemitic and socially regressive positions that cast some doubt on the notion that it was one of the Republic's key defences against fascism.[70]

In the event, it was the German blitzkrieg of May–June 1940 that destroyed the Third Republic, not the French far right. On 10 July 1940, the Popular Front parliament voted full powers to be granted to Marshal Philippe Pétain, whose regime would enthusiastically collaborate with the Nazis and participate in the Holocaust. The liberal journalist William Shirer writes that the vote 'was overwhelming: 569 for, 80 against and 17 declared abstentions. The majority of the Socialists and of the Radical Party, the two parties that had been the mainstay of the Republic for two generations, joined the majority of conservatives to swell the affirmative vote.'[71]

So the experience of France in the 1930s hardly suggests that 'a temporary alliance of the centre and the left' is the way to beat fascism. The centre not only did not hold: it betrayed. This historical judgement is reinforced when we consider the nature of the contemporary 'extreme centre'. Its chief political representatives are Hillary Clinton, Barack Obama, Joe Biden, Tony Blair, Gordon Brown, David Cameron, Angela Merkel, Emmanuel Macron, Matteo Renzi, Mario Draghi, Olaf Scholz. These are the managers of the contemporary neoliberal order. Their failure is the very source of the present crisis. To ally oneself with their likes is to make it even easier than it already is for the far right to present itself as the real challenger to the status quo.

On the eve of Russia's invasion of Ukraine, Mason translated his popular front strategy to the global level:

> Today's conflict, between the globalist, democratic former imperialist countries of the USA and EU, versus [*sic*] the authoritarian,

anti-modernist dictatorships of China and Russia, contains elements of both kinds of war [inter-imperialist and antifascist]. It is rivalry between capitalist power blocks, but it contains numerous just wars of resistance for national liberation and democracy. And, like it or not, it is a conflict between a democratic, socially liberal model of capitalism and an authoritarian, socially conservative one.[72]

Mason's portrayal of the United States and European Union as 'former imperialist countries' is contradicted by the entire analysis I have tried to put forward in this book. More specifically, it ignores how the United States' policy of expanding NATO and the European Union eastwards turned what initially was only a potential conflict between the West and post-Soviet Russia into a glaring antagonism that threatens the ultimate catastrophe (see Chapter 4). Moreover, the history of international popular frontism is hardly encouraging. The alliance against the Axis powers between the Soviet Union and the western liberal democracies during the Second World War led communist parties to pursue broad anti-fascist coalitions, with particular success in countries under Nazi occupation in southern Europe. But at the end of the war substantial revolutionary possibilities were squandered as a result of Stalin's directives to protect the developing carve-up of Europe into Soviet and Anglo-American spheres of influence.[73] The Cold War saw western corporate liberalism confronting eastern state capitalism, a caricature of the radical hopes that had developed in the wartime antifascist movements. Popular frontism today, at least in the version advocated by Mason, seems even less promising, since it ties the fortunes of the left to the preservation of western domination, at the very moment when the tides of history are turning against this.

So what is the alternative? Mason says, rightly: 'Anti-fascist violence is not enough.' However, it's a mistake to put it in these terms, which suggest a simple choice between popular frontism and relying on small groups of anti-fascist street fighters such as the 'Antifa' in the United States that obsess Trump. There's another option – mass mobilization designed to stop the fascists from organizing and marching, and thereby to cut short their development. This is the lesson of the struggle against the British Union of Fascists in the 1930s, the lesson of the Anti-Nazi League in the 1970s, and the lesson of more recent campaigns against diverse fascist organizations – in Britain, against the British National Party, the English Defence League, and the Football Lads' Alliances; and, in Greece, against Golden Dawn.[74]

As Trotsky argued in the 1930s, building a mass anti-fascist movement requires not a popular front, but a united front: it requires bringing together the different political tendencies of the left, reformist and revolutionary, and of working-class organizations more generally, to mobilize against the fascists.[75] This is by no means simple, above all because allying oneself with social democracy opens a bridge to the extreme centre. Moreover, reformists are more liable to appeal for support from the state, which, as the French experience of the 1930s shows, will use its enhanced powers against the left. Yet, without the involvement of serious reformist forces, the ability of anti-fascists to reach deep into the lives and organizations of working people is fatally limited.

Between catastrophe and revolution

So, if, unsurprisingly enough, we can't rely on neoliberal imperialism to prevent further catastrophe, how is change to be achieved?[76] One of the most promising political developments in recent years has been the emergence of mass movements that demand rapid action to decarbonize society, for example the school strikes initiated by Greta Thunberg and the civil disobedience campaigns mounted by Extinction Rebellion (XR), which shut down London for a week in April 2019. These movements are immensely important because they represent a moment of political transition – from despair motivated by the immensity of the threat of climate catastrophe to willingness to take action on a massive scale, together with others.[77]

The justified anger and sense of urgency shared by these activists is well expressed by Andreas Malm:

> To say that the signals have fallen on the deaf ears of the ruling classes of this world would be an understatement. If these classes ever had any senses, they have lost them all. They are not perturbed by the smell from the blazing trees. They do not worry at the sight of islands sinking; they do not run from the roar of the approaching hurricanes; their fingers never need to touch the stalks from withered harvests; their mouths do not become sticky and dry after a day with nothing to drink. To appeal to their reason and common sense would evidently be futile. The commitment to the endless accumulation of capital wins out every time.[78]

The debates about political strategy within the climate movement have an exemplary role because the minimal demands they are making

– in XR's case, net zero greenhouse gas emissions by 2025 – mean bringing the 'endless accumulation of capital' to a sudden juddering halt. They are advocating nothing short of a revolution against fossil capitalism. In this movement, therefore, the universal and the particular – global transformation and specific demands – fuse.

XR's founders justify their strategy of civil disobedience with a political science theory that asserts that peaceful mass protests, if they develop on a sufficiently large scale, will build up economic pressure on the state either to negotiate or to engage in repression. Indeed, even repression is seen as a sign of the state's defeat. Yet the historical experience of civil disobedience movements doesn't support the mechanical law, affirmed by Erica Chenoweth and repeated by XR, that 'it takes 3.5 percent of the population engaged in sustained nonviolent resistance to topple brutal dictatorships'.[79] Where peaceful resistance has succeeded, that has happened, crucially, thanks to other factors. Gandhi's Quit India movement in 1942–4 rapidly spilled over into popular violence, and was contained by intense repression.[80] It was the Indian Navy mutiny of February 1946 that demonstrated that the colonial power could no longer count on the loyalty of the vast military machine it had built up on the subcontinent, and this at a time when British imperialism could no longer milk India financially either, because of the huge debts it had accumulated there during the Second World War.[81]

The Civil Rights struggles in the United States in the 1950s and the 1960s succeeded in forcing the dismantling of the segregationist regime in the South by putting pressure on a federal government that represented a ruling class with little interest in maintaining Jim Crow and that was also fearful of the emergence of more militant Black movements. At about the same time, the National Party government in South Africa ruthlessly crushed the Defiance Campaign of civil disobedience mounted by the African National Congress and its allies. This defeat prompted moves to guerrilla campaigns that were also brutally broken; it took a new cycle of struggle, beginning with the Soweto rising of June 1976 – violent township insurrections, mass strikes, and the rise of a militant Black workers' movement – to force the apartheid regime to the negotiating table.[82]

The case for civil disobedience as an exclusive strategy is further undermined by its failure to address the problem of the state. As Chris Harman argues, there is a structural interdependence between state and capital that reflects state managers' interest in promoting capital accumulation in order to maintain and enhance the capabilities of their states.[83] This explains why states have intervened so massively, since the global financial crisis, to rescue neoliberal capitalism from the consequences of its own dysfunctions. But it also explains why states' coercive and repressive apparatuses – whose powers are being enhanced – have attempted to protect fossil capitalism against climate protesters.

It is inconceivable that social transformation would be achieved without the mobilization of far larger numbers of people than have so far taken part in climate protests. This kind of mobilization is essential if one wants to exert political pressure for rapid reductions in emissions, and also to embolden the activists who sustain these movements. But mass mobilization can also tap into the collective power that, as I have already argued, the organized working class still retains, although its leaders leave it to waste. This process requires changes on both sides: for trade-union leaders, to give up their support for CO_2-emitting industries and, for XR activists, to abandon the pretence that their movement is somehow 'beyond politics' and grapple with reality of class antagonism, so closely interwoven with gender and 'race'. Such a convergence would be a tremendous source of political energy and social power, as we see in numerous mass movements in the South. The Indian farmers' revolt of 2020–1 is one example.

This kind of political radicalization and social deepening could help the climate movement to crack the hard nut of state power. This means revolution in a more classical sense, directed at the state itself. Malm writes dismissively: 'Any argument along the lines of "one solution – revolution" … is now untenable.' [84] But this begs the question of where the kind of disruptive direct action he personally advocates is supposed to lead, particularly since he has rightly argued that halting and dismantling the CO_2 machine demands the highly authoritative intervention of state power.[85] Pulling the emergency cord means seizing political power.

Who would seize power? A mass movement, at the centre of which would be the working poor; and, thanks to the globalization of capital of the past generation, they resemble and depend on one another, on a planetary scale, far more than they did in the past. This is why opposing imperialism and racism is so important today; it confronts the barriers that must be overcome in order to forge a new workers' movement. Thus it is most regrettable that in the United States the Squad – a group of progressive Democratic Congresswomen – has largely gone along with Biden's policy of military aid to Ukraine, leaving it to the libertarian Republican Rand Paul and his like to lead the opposition.

The parallel failures of the reformist left in Europe since the global financial crisis underline the necessity of confronting the system rather than compromising with it.

How likely is it that the collective subject needed to make a revolution will be forged? To put it another way, which will win the race for the future: catastrophe or revolution? The whole point of this book has been to demonstrate that catastrophe, multiple catastrophes are already with us. But the age of catastrophe is also an age of revolt, and therein lies our hope for the future. Indeed, catastrophe can fuel revolt, as we saw with the explosion of BLM out of the first lockdown.

There are also examples on a smaller scale, for example workers' organized efforts, at the height of the pandemic, to protect themselves from COVID-19. Even initial failure can lead to success. An unsuccessful strike, in March 2020, against unsafe working conditions in Amazon's giant JFK8 warehouse on Staten Island, New York led to the victimization of an activist, Christian Smalls, who went on to initiate, together with others, a new, independent Amazon Labour Union (ALU). Two years later, this group's intense grassroots campaign to overcome the divisions of 'race', gender, and age on which the management played paid off when the ALU won a vote to unionize JFK8: it was the first victory of a union against Amazon in the United States.[86] The involvement of Smalls and other former college students in this breakthrough is symptomatic of what according to the *New York Times* is one of the driving forces in the new wave of labour organizing in the United States: 'Over the past decade and a half, many young, college-educated workers have faced a disturbing reality: that it was harder for them to reach the middle class than for previous generations. The change has had profound effects – driving shifts in the country's politics and mobilizing employees to demand fairer treatment at work.'[87]

The sudden visibility that 'essential workers' – often low-paid, precarious, and racialized – gained during the lockdowns underlined the structural power that wage labour continues to possess. For Marx, the significance of the working class lay not in its victimhood but in its potential collective power. Exploitation – the surplus value that workers create – means that capital is dependent on them to keep profits flowing. The restructuring of production during the neoliberal era has led to the decline of the old basic industries in the North, but it has also created new sites of workers' power, above all in the ballooning logistics sector, which provides the material infrastructure for hi-tech platform capitalism.[88] In Italy, for example, primarily immigrant logistics workers, organized mainly into small left-wing unions, have demonstrated in a series of strikes the considerable disruptive power that the development of transnational supply chains across the Mediterranean has given them.[89]

Catastrophe can increase workers' power and combativeness. Beverly Silver has pointed out:

> It was in the context of the escalation of inter-imperialist rivalries and armed conflict in the first half of the twentieth century that workers (especially in metropolitan countries) succeeded in pushing their states toward a more rapid expansion of both workers' rights and broad democratic rights. Yet this socialization of the state had only limited success in retaining workers' loyalties. The horrors and dislocations caused by modern industrialized warfare made such efforts at national social compacts increasingly unstable, eventually unleashing a vicious cycle of war, labour unrest, and revolutionary crises ... whether we might in the twenty-first century return to a situation of escalating and radicalized labour unrest on a world scale is tied to whether we will return to a situation of growing interstate conflict and world war analogous to the first half of the twentieth century.[90]

Silver was writing in the early years of the twenty-first century, but her words have acquired new meaning today. Disastrous though the Russo-Ukrainian War is, it too can fuel revolt. The conflict represents what one commentator has called 'the return of industrial warfare', a protracted slogging match in which the two sides' firepower and their productive capacity to replace the vast quantities of ammunition, artillery rounds, and missiles consumed in the fighting are likely to be decisive.[91] Sustaining Ukraine in NATO's proxy war with Russia will require a substantial expansion of the western munitions industry, the sector that was a key incubator of labour militancy in both world wars.

Between them, Russia and Ukraine produce 30 per cent of the world's wheat, a fifth of the world's maize, and more than half of the world's sunflower oil, while Ukraine is a major source of fertilizers. So the war disrupted the supply of food, especially in the global South, and sent prices soaring. The United Nations warns that the war 'has exacerbated a global cost-of-living crisis unseen in at least a generation', transmitted through rises in the price of food and energy and tighter financial conditions, and hitting populations already weakened by the COVID-19 pandemic, especially in the global South. '94 countries, home to around 1.6 billion people, are severely exposed to at least one dimension of the crisis and unable to cope with it. Out of the 1.6 billion, 1.2 billion or three quarters live in "perfect-storm" countries, meaning countries that are severely exposed and vulnerable to all three dimensions of finance, food, and energy, simultaneously.' The number of food-insecure people worldwide has doubled during the pandemic, going from 135 million to 276 million at the start of 2022, but was projected to rise to 323 million in the course of the same year.[92]

Ngozi Okonjo-Iweala, director general of the World Trade Organization, told the *Guardian*: "'If we don't think about how to mitigate the impact of the war that will be another catastrophe not just this year but next year' ... 'There was a danger of a repeat of the food riots that marked a previous period of rapidly rising prices in the late 2000s,' she added."[93] The inflationary upsurge at the time of the global financial crisis indeed sparked social unrest in about forty countries; over a third of them were in Africa, where currently more than 40 million people face acute food insecurity.[94] These food riots helped to set the stage for the revolutions in Tunisia, Egypt, Libya, and Syria in 2011. In April and May 2022 financial mismanagement by the ruling Rajapaksa dynasty in Sri Lanka forced the government to default on bond payments, as soaring fuel and food prices provoked massive street protests and mass strikes. The brothers Mahinda and Gotabaya Rajapaksa, respectively prime minister and president, were driven from office. The protests – which reflected a lengthy build-up of dissatisfactions, against the background of long-term economic liberalization – were of a scale, intensity, and duration that invited comparisons with the Arab Spring.[95]

Pointing to the interconnection between catastrophe and revolt is not to engage in a *politique du pire* – a 'politics of the worst' – as practised by the German Communist Party in 1932–3, when it expected the Nazi government to crumble rapidly: 'After Hitler, Our Turn!'[96] Rather it is to understand that we now live in a world where one catastrophe succeeds another. Think of the past few years – the pandemic, a global slump worse than the global financial crisis, the war in Ukraine, the escalating geopolitical confrontation. The cost-of-living crisis I have just described is the latest stage in this breakdown of the existing system. Note also how the burden of this breakdown falls on the shoulders of working people and the poor, as we have seen. Growing numbers of people are confronted with drastic deterioration in their material conditions; at the same time the dominant elites are discredited both as a result of their mismanagement of the situation and because they give priority to protecting and enriching themselves.

The more those who have been hit recognize their plight and the fact that it is shared by many others, the more they are likely to be driven to protest and, more importantly, to organize. It is through the development of forms of self-organization by working people and the poor that the basis of a new society can emerge.

The multidimensional character of the crisis that faces humankind thus tends to create fractures that simultaneously represent catastrophe and the possibility of revolt. The geopolitical conflict between Russia, China, and the West, the energy crisis, and rising inflation are a particularly combustible mix, which will bring people onto the streets in more countries than Sri Lanka. The dialectic of revolution and counter-revolution will continue to play. There will undoubtedly be more explosions like the Arab revolutions and BLM. Trying to assign probabilities as to whether these will develop into full-scale revolutions and survive and spread is futile. The terrifying prospects we face demand that everyone become part of the struggle to rescue humankind. As the great Irish Marxist James Connolly put it at the start of the first age of catastrophe, 'the only true prophets are they who carve out the future which they announce'.[97]

Notes

Notes to Introduction

1 See Elaine Kamarck, 'America Needs a COVID-19 Commission', 1 December 2020. https://www.brookings.edu/blog/fixgov/2020/12/01/america-needs-a-covid-19-commission.
2 William H. McNeill, 'Control and Catastrophe in Human Affairs' (with Comments by Charles P. Kindleberger), *Daedalus* 118.1 (1989): 1–15, here p. 1. See also William H. McNeill, *Plagues and Peoples* (Harmondsworth: Penguin, 1979).
3 Gordon Woo, *Calculating Catastrophe* (London: Imperial College Press, 2011).
4 Rosa Luxemburg, *The Junius Pamphlet: The Crisis in German Social Democracy*, in *The Rosa Luxemburg Reader*, ed. by Peter Hudis and Kevin B. Anderson (New York: Monthly Review Books, 2004 [1916]), 313–41, here p. 321.
5 See the discussion of this slogan in Louis Althusser, *History and Imperialism: Writings, 1963–1986*, ed. by G. M. Goshgarian (Cambridge: Polity, 2020), pp. 49–50, 111–13.
6 E. J. Hobsbawm, *Age of Extremes: The Short Twentieth Century, 1914–1991* (London: Weidenfeld & Nicolson, 1994).
7 Walter Benjamin, *Selected Writings*, vol. 4: *1938–40* (Cambridge, MA: Harvard University Press, 2003), p. 392; see Victor Serge, *Midnight in the Century* (New York: New York Review Books, 2014 [1939]).
8 David Harvey, *A Short History of Neoliberalism* (Oxford: Oxford University Press, 2005), p. 31.

9 Fukuyama, Francis, 'The End of History?', *National Interest*, 16 (1989): 3–18.
10 'Flooding Hits Six Million People in East Africa', 6 October 2020. https://www.bbc.com/news/world-africa-54433904.
11 Jean-Paul Sartre, *Search for a Method* (New York: Vintage, 1968), 163n9.
12 Natalia Romé, 'The Normalization of Barbarism', *Crisis & Critique*, 7.3 (2020): 332–59.
13 Theodor W. Adorno, *Negative Dialectics* (London: Routledge, 1973), p. 320.
14 Theodor W. Adorno, *Minima Moralia: Reflections on a Damaged Life* (London: Schocken Books, 1974), p. 55. See Hegel's letter of 13 October 1806 to Niethammer: 'I saw the Emperor – this world-soul – riding out of the city on reconnaissance. It is indeed a wonderful sensation to see such an individual, who, concentrated here at a single point, astride a horse, reaches out over the world and masters it': G. W. F. Hegel, *The Letters*, ed. by Clark Butler and Christiane Seiler (Bloomington: Indiana University Press, 1984), p. 114.
15 Adam Tooze, *Shutdown: How Covid Shook the World's Economy* (London: Penguin, 2021), p. 6.
16 Jem Bendell, 'Deep Adaptation: A Map for Navigating Climate Tragedy', IFLAS Occasional Paper 2, 2018. https://lifeworth.com/deepadaptation.pdf (2nd edn, 2020).
17 Michael Roberts, *The Long Depression* (Chicago, IL: Haymarket, 2016).
18 Tooze, *Shutdown*; Colin Kahl and Thomas Wright, *Aftershocks: Pandemic Politics and the End of the Old International Order* (New York: St Martin's Press, 2021).
19 Tariq Ali, *The Extreme Centre: A Warning* (London: Verso, 2015).
20 US Department of the Treasury, 'Day One Message to Staff from Secretary of the United States Department of the Treasury Janet L. Yellen', 26 January 2021. https://home.treasury.gov/news/press-releases/jy0003.
21 Adam Tooze, *Crashed: How a Decade of Financial Crisis Changed the World* (London: Allen Lane, 2018); Tooze, *Shutdown*.
22 See the critique of Tooze's historiography in Perry Anderson, 'Situationism à l'envers', *New Left Review*, 2.119 (2019): 47–93, and the response in Adam Tooze, 'Chartbook on Shutdown #2: Writing in Medias Res ... History in The Thick of It', 4 September 2021. https://adamtooze.substack.com/p/chartbook-on-shutdown-2-writing-in.

23 Fredric Jameson, *The Political Unconscious: Narrative as Socially Symbolic Act* (London: Methuen, 1981), p. 52.
24 For a full discussion, see Alex Callinicos, *Deciphering Capital: Marx's Capital and Its Destiny* (London: Bookmarks, 2014).
25 Jean-Paul Sartre, *Critique of Dialectical Reason*, vol. 1: *Theory of Practical Ensembles*, ed. by Jonathan Rée (London: Verso, 2004 [1960]), p. 39.
26 Karl Marx, *A Contribution to the Critique of Political Economy* (London: Lawrence & Wishart, 1971), p. 20 (translation modified).
27 Alex Callinicos, 'The Limits of Passive Revolution', *Capital & Class*, 34 (2010): 491–507.
28 Marx, *A Contribution*, p. 20.
29 Throughout this book I put 'race' in quotation marks to highlight that, as Adolph Reed (*The South: Jim Crow and Its Afterlives*, London: Verso, 2022, Apple Books edn, p. 165) felicitously puts it, '"race" has no biological foundation and is a fluid, contextual, and historically contingent notion'.
30 Tooze, *Shutdown*, pp. 301.
31 Edward Luce, 'Changing Is Moving Close to Impossible in America', *Financial Times*, 14 January 2022.
32 Adorno, *Minima Moralia*, p. 247.
33 Benjamin, *Selected Writings*, p. 397.
34 See especially Michael Löwy, *Fire Alarm: Reading Walter Benjamin's 'On the Concept of History'* (London: Verso, 2005).
35 Louis Althusser et al., *Reading Capital: The Complete Edition* (London: Verso, 2015 [1965]), pp. 242, 252.
36 Ibid., p. 254.
37 Louis Althusser, *For Marx* (London: Allen Lane, 1969), p. 100. For further discussion of what is distinctive to conjunctural analysis, see Alex Callinicos, 'Epoch and Conjuncture in Marxist Political Economy', *International Politics*, 42 (2005): 353–63 and Juan Domingo Sánchez Estop, *Althusser et Spinoza: Détours et retours* (Brussels: Éditions de l'Université de Bruxelles, 2022).
38 I am aware of the tensions between the different theoretical sources I use in this book, but I have been persuaded by Jameson's argument that it is possible to recuperate at least some of the substance of apparently divergent critical theories within the framework set by Marxist totalization: see especially chapter 1 in Jameson's *The Political Unconscious*, and the wonderful essays in his *Valences of the Dialectic*, both listed in Select Bibliography.

39 Jameson, *The Political Unconscious*, p. 9.
40 Arno J. Mayer, *The Furies: Violence and Terror in the French and Russian Revolutions* (Princeton, NJ: Princeton University Press, 2000); Walden Bello, *Counterrevolution: The Global Rise of the Far Right* (Rugby: Practical Action Publishing, 2019).
41 Lucia Pradella, *L'attualità del capitale: Accumulazione e impoverimento nel capitalismo globale* (Padua: Il Poligrafo, 2010); and Lucia Pradella, 'Imperialism and Capitalist Development in Marx's *Capital*', *Historical Materialism*, 21.2 (2013): 117–47.
42 Richard B. Day and Daniel Gaido, eds, *Discovering Imperialism: Social Democracy to World War I* (Leiden: Brill, 2011); N. I. Bukharin, *Imperialism and World Economy* (London: Martin Lawrence, 1929); and Henryk Grossman, *The Law of Accumulation and Breakdown of the Capitalist System: Being also a Theory of Crises*, ed. by Rick Kuhn (Leiden: Brill, 2022 [1929]).
43 See especially Alex Callinicos, *Imperialism and Global Political Economy* (Cambridge: Polity, 2009); Alex Callinicos, 'The Multiple Crises of Imperialism', *International Socialism*, 2.144 (2014); and also Chris Harman, 'Analysing Imperialism', *International Socialism*, 2.99 (2003).
44 Max Horkheimer, 'The Jews and Europe', in Stephen E Bronner and Douglas M Kellner, eds, *Critical Theory and Society* (London: Routledge, 1989), 77–94, here p. 78.
45 Nicos Poulantzas, *Fascism and Dictatorship: The Third International and the Problem of Fascism* (London: Verso, 2018 [1970]), Kindle loc. 834.
46 Richard Overy, *Blood and Ruins: The Great Imperial War, 1931–1945* (London: Penguin, 2021).
47 Hannah, Arendt, *The Origins of Totalitarianism* (New York: Harcourt Brace & Co, 1973); see also Nicholas Devlin, 'Hannah Arendt and Marxist Theories of Imperialism', *Modern Intellectual History* (2021), 1–23, doi: 10.1017/S1479244321000603.
48 Karl Marx, *Early Writings*, ed. by Lucio Colletti (Harmondsworth: Penguin, 1975), p. 251 (translation modified).

Notes to Chapter 1

1 Arno J. Mayer, *The Persistence of the Old Regime: Europe to the Great War* (New York: Pantheon Books, 1981), p. 5.
2 For a recent synthesis on the second half of this period, see Richard Overy, *Blood and Ruins: The Great Imperial War, 1931–1945* (London: Penguin, 2021), ch. 10.

3 Ernst Jünger, *A German Officer in Occupied Paris: The War Journals, 1941–1945*, ed. by Elliot Neaman (New York: Columbia University Press, 2019), p. 169.
4 Aimé Césaire, *Discourse on Colonialism* (New York: Monthly Review, 2000) [1955], p. 36.
5 David Harvey, *The New Imperialism* (Oxford: Oxford University Press, 2003) and Alex Callinicos, *Imperialism and Global Political Economy* (Cambridge: Polity, 2009).
6 William H. McNeill, *The Pursuit of Power: Technology, Armed Force, and Society since AD 1000* (Oxford: Blackwell, 1982), chs 7 and 8.
7 Antonio Gramsci, *Selections from the Prison Notebooks* (London: Lawrence & Wishart, 1971), p. 68; Antonio Gramsci, *Quaderni del carcere*, 4 vols, ed. by Valentino Gerratana, vol. 3 (Rome: Einaudi, 1975): Quaderno 19 (X), §24, p. 2018; see also Callinicos, *Imperialism and Global Political Economy*, pp. 144–64.
8 Enzo Traverso, *Fire and Blood: The European Civil War (1914–1945)* (London: Verso, 2016).
9 Tim Harper, *Underground Asia: Global Revolutionaries and the Assault on Empire* (London: Penguin, 2020).
10 Harold R. Isaacs, *The Tragedy of the Chinese Revolution* (Chicago, IL: Haymarket, 2009 [1938]).
11 Mark Mazower, *Dark Continent: Europe's Twentieth Century* (London: Allen Lane, 1998), p. 28.
12 See Nicos Poulantzas, *Fascism and Dictatorship: The Third International and the Problem of Fascism* (London: Verso, 2018 [1970]), an important but not entirely satisfactory discussion. Gramsci developed his own analysis of authoritarian political forms, central to which are the concepts of Bonapartism and Caesarism; for a lucid study, see Francesca Antonini, *Caesarism and Bonapartism in Gramsci* (Leiden: Brill, 2021).
13 Leon Trotsky, *The Struggle against Fascism in Germany* (New York: Pathfinder, 1971), p. 276.
14 For the economic context, see Tobias Straumann, *1931: Debt, Crisis, and the Rise of Hitler* (Oxford: Oxford University Press, 2019).
15 Mayer, *Persistence of the Old Regime*, p. 127. Mayer overstates his case: for better overviews of Europe's contradictions before 1914, see E. J. Hobsbawm, *The Age of Empire, 1875–1914* (London: Weidenfeld & Nicolson,1987) and Norman Stone, *Europe Transformed 1878–1919* (London: Fontana, 1983). On the financial dominance of Britain and France, see Herbert Feis,

Europe: The World's Banker, 1870–1914 (New Haven, CT: Yale University Press, 1930).
16 Ernst Bloch, *Heritage of Our Times* (Cambridge: Polity, 1991 [1935]), Part 2.
17 Robert O. Paxton, *The Anatomy of Fascism* (New York: Alfred A. Knopf, 2004), p. 218.
18 Trotsky, *The Struggle against Fascism in Germany*.
19 Bloch, *Heritage of Our Times*, pp. 2, 108. The concept of a romantic anti-capitalism seems to have been common to Bloch and his friend and rival Georg Lukács: see the discussion in Michael Löwy, *Georg Lukács: From Romanticism to Bolshevism* (London: NLB, 1979). But the early twentieth-century German far right often combined this stance with more positive evaluations of modern technology. Jünger was an exemplary figure in this respect: see Ernst Jünger, *The Worker: Dominion and Form* (Evanston, IL: Northwestern University Press, 2017 [1932]), and Jeffrey Herf, *Reactionary Modernism: Technology, Culture, and Politics in Weimar and the Third Reich* (Cambridge: Cambridge University Press, 1984).
20 John Foot, *Blood and Power: The Rise and Fall of Italian Fascism* (London: Bloomsbury, 2022), p. 136.
21 Trotsky, *The Struggle against Fascism in Germany*, p. 405.
22 Ibid., p. 278.
23 Alex Callinicos, 'Plumbing the Depths: Marxism and the Holocaust', *Yale Journal of Criticism*, 14.2 (2001): 385–414, here 295 and 395–6.
24 Adam Tooze, *The Wages of Destruction: The Making and Breaking of the Nazi Economy* (London: Allen Lane, 2006), ch. 4.
25 Ibid., p. 114.
26 Daniel Guérin, *Fascism and Big Business* (New York: Pathfinder, 1973), ch. 4.
27 This analysis is fully developed in Callinicos, 'Plumbing the Depths'. I was delighted to discover, recently, that it was largely anticipated in a brilliant brief essay by Peter Sedgwick, 'The Problem of Fascism', *International Socialism* 1.42 (1970): 31–4. See also the superb discussion of the radicalization of the fascist regimes in Paxton, *Anatomy of Fascism*, ch. 6.
28 Overy, *Blood and Ruins*, p. 35.
29 On this highly conflictual and unstable carve-up, see James, Barr, *A Line in the Sand: Britain, France and the Struggle that Shaped the Middle East* (London: Simon & Schuster, 2011).

30 For a contemporary analysis, see Alfred Sohn-Rethel, *The Economy and Class Structure of German Fascism* (London: Free Association, 1987).
31 Overy, *Blood and Ruins*, p. 36.
32 Tooze, *Wages of Destruction*, ch. 7.
33 Nicholas Mulder, *The Economic Weapon: The Rise of Sanctions as a Tool of Modern War* (New Haven, CT: Yale University Press, 2022), ch. 9.
34 On the German case, see Mark Mazower, *Hitler's Empire: Nazi Rule in Occupied Europe* (London: Penguin, 2009).
35 Jonathan Haslam, *The Spectre of War: International Communism and the Origins of World War II* (Princeton, NJ: Princeton University Press, 2021), xi–xii.
36 Arno J. Mayer, *Why Did the Heavens Not Darken? The 'Final Solution' in History* (New York: Pantheon, 1990), p. 34.
37 Paxton, *Anatomy of Fascism*, p. 171.
38 For the quotations, see Gramsci, *Selections*, pp. 109, 110 and Gramsci, *Quaderni*, vol. 3, pp. 1767, 1768 from Quaderno 15 (II), §6. On organic crises, see Gramsci, *Selections*, pp. 175–85; Gramsci, *Quaderni*, vol. 3, pp. 1578–89 from Quaderno 13 (XXX), §17.
39 I am indebted here to the interpretation of passive revolution in André Tosel, *Étudier Gramsci: Pour une critique continue de la révolution passive* (Paris: Éditions Kimé, 2016), pp. 121–39. See the pioneering economic study of Fordism in Michel Aglietta, *A Theory of Capitalist Regulation: The US Experience* (London: Verso, 2015) [1979]).
40 Louis Althusser, *Philosophy for Non-Philosophers*, ed. by G. M. Goshgarian (London: Bloomsbury, 2017), p. 120. Compare Paul Mason, *How to Stop Fascism: History, Ideology, Resistance* (London: Penguin, 2021).
41 John Kenneth Galbraith, *American Capitalism: The Concept of Countervailing Power* (Livingston, NJ: Transaction, 1995 [1952]), p. 65.
42 See Kees Van der Pijl, *The Making of an Atlantic Ruling Class* (London: Verso, 1984).
43 Overy, *Blood and Ruins*, p. 872.
44 John Gallagher and Ronald Robinson, 'The Imperialism of Free Trade', *Economic History Review*, 6.1 (1953): 1–13.
45 See especially Neil Smith, *American Empire: Roosevelt's Geographer and the Prelude to Globalization* (Berkeley: University of California Press, 2003); Callinicos, *Imperialism and Global*

Political Economy; and Leo Panitch and Sam Gindin, *The Making of Global Capitalism: The Political Economy of American Empire* (London: Verso, 2012).

46 Michael Kidron, *Western Capitalism since the War* (Harmondsworth: Penguin, 1970); Chris Harman, *Explaining the Crisis: A Marxist Reappraisal* (London: Bookmarks, 1984); Chris Harman, *Zombie Capitalism: Global Crisis and the Relevance of Marx* (London: Bookmarks, 2009); and Joseph Choonara, 'The Monetary and the Military: Revisiting Kidron's Permanent Arms Economy', *International Socialism*, 2.171 (2021): 123–50.

47 David de Jong, *Nazi Billionaires: The Dark History of Germany's Wealthiest Families* (London: William Collins, 2022).

48 Tony Cliff, 'The Nature of Stalinist Russia', in his *Selected Writings*, vol. 3: *Marxist Theory after Trotsky* (London: Bookmarks, 2003).

49 C. Wright Mills, *The Causes of World War III* (New York: Ballantine Books, 1960), pp. 29–30. The revival of Cold War tensions in the 1980s stimulated Marxist explorations of lasting value around the logic of these tensions; see Edward Thompson, 'Notes on Exterminism, the Last Stage of Civilization', *New Left Review*, 1.121 (1980): 3–31; Mike Davis, 'Nuclear Imperialism and Extended Deterrence' (blog), Verso, 11 August 2017, https://www.versobooks.com/blogs/3350-nuclear-imperialism-and-extended-deterrence; Peter Binns, 'Understanding the New Cold War', *International Socialism*, 2.19 (1983): 1–48; and Fred Halliday, *The Making of the Second Cold War* (London: Verso, 1983).

50 David Schmitz, *The United States and Right-Wing Dictatorships, 1965–1989* (Cambridge: Cambridge University Press, 2006), p. 48.

51 See Walden Bello, *Counterrevolution: The Global Rise of the Far Right* (Rugby: Practical Action Publishing, 2019), chs 3–5 (on Indonesia, Chile, and Thailand).

52 Colin Barker, *Festival of the Oppressed: Solidarity, Reform, and Revolution in Poland, 1980–81* (London: Verso, 1986).

53 Giovanni Arrighi, *Adam Smith in Beijing* (London: Verso, 2007), ch. 7.

54 Chris Harman, *The Fire Last Time: 1968 and After* (London: Bookmarks, 1988).

55 Fred Halliday, *Cold War, Third World: An Essay on Soviet-American Relations* (London: Radius/Hutchinson, 1989).

Notes to Chapter 2

1. Arnold Westing, 'War as a Human Endeavour: The High-Fatality Wars of the Twentieth Century', *Journal of Peace Research*, 19.3 (1982): 261–70, here p. 263.
2. William Eckhart, 'War-Related Deaths since 3000 BC', *Peace Research*, 23.1 (1991): 80–6, here p. 82.
3. Ian Angus, *Facing the Anthropocene: Fossil Capitalism and the Crisis of the Earth System* (New York: Monthly Review Press, 2016), Kindle version.
4. Ibid., Kindle loc. 1924.
5. James Barr, *Lords of the Desert: Britain's Struggle with America to Dominate the Middle East* (London: Simon & Schuster, 2018); Helen Thompson, *Disorder: Hard Times in the 21st Century* (New York: Oxford University Press, 2022), esp. chs 1 and 2.
6. Thompson, *Disorder*, p. 41.
7. Angus, *Facing the Anthropocene*, Kindle loc. 2089.
8. Martin Empson, *The Great Climate COP Out: Why COP26 Will Not Solve the Climate Crisis* (London: Socialist Worker, 2021).
9. Andreas Malm, *Fossil Capital: The Rise of Steam Power and the Roots of Global Warming* (London: Verso, 2016), p. 3.
10. Intergovernmental Panel on Climate Change, *Climate Change 2021: The Physical Science Basis: Summary for Policymakers* (Switzerland: IPCC, 2021), p. 14.
11. Alexandra Heal and Camilla Hodgson, 'Where Have Weather Records Been Broken so far in the Past Year?', *Financial Times*, 24 December 2021.
12. Leslie Hook and Steven Bernard, 'Weather Events Cost the US $145bn in 2021 as Climate Change Took Hold', *Financial Times*, 14 January 2022.
13. Martin Empson, 'We Face "Socialism or Extinction" after IPCC's new Climate Change Report', *Socialist Worker*, 3 March 2022, summarizing Intergovernmental Panel on Climate Change, *Climate Change 2022: Impacts, Adaptation, Vulnerability: Summary for Policymakers* (Switzerland: IPCC, 2022).
14. Jem Bendell, 'Deep Adaptation: A Map for Navigating Climate Tragedy', IFLAS Occasional Paper 2, 2018. https://lifeworth.com/deepadaptation.pdf.
15. Ilya Prigogine and Isabelle Stengers, *Order out of Chaos: Man's New Dialogue with Nature* (London: Heinemann, 1984).
16. Bendell, 'Deep Adaptation'.
17. Ibid.

18 United States Army War College, *Implications of Climate Change for the US Army*, 2019. https://climateandsecurity.files.wordpress.com/2019/07/implications-of-climate-change-for-us-army_army-war-college_2019.pdf, pp. 16, 17.
19 Isak Stoddard et al., 'Three Decades of Climate Mitigation: Why Haven't We Bent the Global Emissions Curve?', *Annual Review of Environment and Resources*, 46 (2021): 653–89, here pp. 678–9.
20 Malm, *Fossil Capital*, p. 267.
21 Ibid., pp. 265, 353.
22 See Part 2 in Angus, *Facing the Anthropocene*.
23 Robert Brenner, *The Economics of Global Turbulence* (London: Verso, 2006), p. 26.
24 See e.g. John Bellamy Foster, 'Marx as a Food Theorist', *Monthly Review*, 68.7 (2016): 1–22.
25 E.g. Ian Rappel, 'Natural Capital: A Neoliberal Response to Species Extinction', *International Socialism*, 2.160 (2018): 59–76; Geoff Mann, 'Check Your Spillover', *London Review of Books*, 10 February 2022.
26 Stoddard et al., 'Three Decades of Climate Mitigation', pp. 659–60.
27 Leslie Hook, Camilla Hodgson, and Jim Pickard, 'COP26 Agrees New Climate Rules but India and China Weaken Coal Pledge', *Financial Times*, 14 November 2021.
28 Rainforest Action Network and others, 'Banking on Climate Change: Fossil Fuel Finance Report Card 2019', 20 March 2019. www.ran.org/wp-content/uploads/2019/03/Banking_on_Climate_Change_2019_vFINAL1.pdf.
29 Carol Olson and Frank Lenzmann, 'The Social and Economic Consequences of the Fossil Fuel Supply Chain', *MRS Energy & Sustainability*, 3.6 (2016). https://doi.org/10.1557/mre.2016.7.
30 Stoddard et al., 'Three Decades of Climate Mitigation', p. 662. See also Michael E. Mann, *The New Climate War: The Fight to Take Back Our Planet* (Brunswick, Australia: Scribe Publications, 2021).
31 Damien Carrington and Matthew Taylor, 'Revealed: The "Carbon Bombs" Set to Trigger Catastrophic Climate Breakdown', *Guardian*, 11 May 2022.
32 Gregor Semieniuk et al., 'Stranded Fossil-Fuel Assets Translate to Major Losses for Investors in Advanced Economies', *Nature Climate Change* 12 (2022): 532–8. https://doi.org/10.1038/s41558-022-01356-y.
33 E.g. Nastassia Astrasheuskaya and Henry Foy, 'Polar Powers:

Russia's Bid for Supremacy in the Arctic Ocean', *Financial Times*, 28 April 2019; United States Army War College, *Implications of Climate Change*, pp. 9–11.

34 Stratfor, 'How Renewable Energy Will Change Geopolitics', 27 June 2018. https://worldview.stratfor.com/article/how-renewable-energy-will-change-geopolitics (available on subscription).

35 On geo-economics, see Jim Glassman, *Drums of War, Drums of Development: The Formation of a Pacific Ruling Class and Industrial Transformation in East and Southeast Asia, 1945–1980* (Leiden: Brill, 2018), ch. 1.

36 John Bellamy Foster, *Marx's Ecology: Materialism and Nature* (New York: Monthly Review Press, 2000); John Bellamy Foster, *The Return of Nature: Socialism and Ecology* (New York: Monthly Review Press, 2020); Paul Burkett, *Marx and Nature: A Red and Green Perspective* (Chicago, IL: Haymarket, 2014); Angus, *Facing the Anthropocene*; and Kohei Saito, *Karl Marx's Ecosocialism: Capital, Nature, and the Unfinished Critique of Political Economy* (New York: Monthly Review Press, 2017).

37 Jess Spear, 'Women and Nature: Towards an Ecosocialist Feminism', *Monthly Review*, 15 March 2021. https://mronline.org/2021/03/15/women-and-nature-towards-an-ecosocialist-feminism.

38 Karl Marx, *Capital: A Critique of Political Economy*, vol. 1 (Harmondsworth: Penguin, 1976 [1867]), p. 290.

39 Marx, *Capital*, p. 638; see Lucia Pradella, 'Foundation: Karl Marx (1818–83)', in Alex Callinicos, Stathis Kouvelakis, and Lucia Pradella, eds, *The Routledge Handbook of Marxism and Post-Marxism* (New York: Routledge, 2021), pp. 25–40.

40 Karl Marx, *Das Kapital: Öknomische Manuskripte, 1863–1865*, in Karl Marx and Friedrich Engels, *Gesamtausgabe*, Part 2, '*Das Kapital*' *und Vorarbeiten*, vol. 4.1 (Berlin: Dietz Verlag, 1992), p. 753.

41 Mike Davis, *Old Gods, New Enigmas: Marx's Lost Theory* (London: Verso, 2018), Kindle loc. 3075.

42 Mike Davis, *The Ecology of Fear: Los Angeles and the Dialectic of Disaster* (New York: Metropolitan Books, 1999); Mike Davis, *Late Victorian Holocausts: El Niño Famines and the Making of the Third World* (London: Verso, 2001).

43 For a broader understanding of this interaction, see Richard Levins and Richard C. Lewontin, *The Dialectical Biologist* (Cambridge MA: Harvard University Press, 1985) and Richard C. Lewontin,

The Triple Helix: Gene, Organism, and Environment (Cambridge MA: Harvard University Press, 2000).
44 William H. McNeill, *Plagues and Peoples* (Harmondsworth: Penguin, 1979), pp. 11, 12, and 266.
45 Ole J. Benedictow, *The Complete History of the Black Death*, rev edn (Woodbridge: Boydell Press, 2021), ch. 43.
46 McNeill, *Plagues and Peoples*, p. 185.
47 Laura Spinney, *The Pale Rider: The Spanish 'Flu of 1918 and How It Changed the World* (London: Jonathan Cape, 2017).
48 Kyle Harper, *The Fate of Rome: Climate, Disease, and the End of an Empire* (Princeton, NJ: Princeton University Press, 2017), pp. 19 and 4.
49 Ibid., p. 192.
50 John Haldon et al., 'Plagues, Climate Change, and the End of an Empire: A Response to Kyle Harper's *The Fate of Rome*', *History Compass*, 16 (1), (2), and (3); here 16 (1), p. 3. https://doi.org/10.1111/hic3.12508.
51 Peter Brown, *Through the Eye of a Needle: Wealth, the Fall of Rome, and the Making of Christianity in the West, 350–550 AD* (Princeton, NJ: Princeton University Press, 2012), Kindle loc. 474.
52 Guy Bois, *The Crisis of Feudalism: Economy and Society in Eastern Normandy c. 1300–1550* (Cambridge: Cambridge University Press, 1984); and T. H. Aston and and C. H. E. Philpin, eds, *The Brenner Debate: Agrarian Class Structure and Economic Development in Pre-Industrial Europe* (Cambridge: Cambridge University Press, 1985).
53 Vandana Shiva, *Who Really Feeds the World? The Failures of Agribusiness and the Promise of Agroecology* (Berkeley: North Atlantic Books, 2016).
54 Quoted in Saito, *Karl Marx's Ecosocialism*, p. 210.
55 Rob Wallace, *Big Farms Make Big Flu* (New York: Monthly Review Press, 2016). See also Mike Davis, *The Monster Enters: Covid-19, Avian Flu, and the Plagues of Capitalism* (New York: OR Books, 2020), Apple edn.
56 C. J. Carlson et al., 'Climate Change Increases Cross-Species Viral Transmission Risk', *Nature*, 607 (2022): 555–62. https://doi.org/10.1038/s41586-022-04788-w.
57 Wallace, *Big Farms Make Big Flu*, Kindle locs. 1949–59.
58 Ashley Hagen, 'COVID-19 and the Flu', *American Society for Microbiology*, 7 October 2021. https://asm.org/Articles/2020/July/COVID-19-and-the-Flu. RNA, like DNA, is a nucleic acid

essential to the functioning of living cells; unlike DNA, it typically forms a single strand, and hence does not have the double helix structure of DNA.
59 Davis, *The Monster Enters*, pp. 18–19.
60 Oliver Barnes, Clive Cookson, and Jamie Smyth, 'Scientists Puzzle over Omicron's Origins as Variant Spreads', *Financial Times*, 10 December 2021.
61 Hannah Kuchler, Donato Paolo Mancini, and David Pilling, 'The Inside Story of the Pfizer Vaccine: "A Once-in-an-Epoch Windfall"', *Financial Times*, 30 November 2021.
62 Alexander Zeitchik, 'How Bill Gates Impeded Global Access to COVID Vaccines', *The New Republic*, 12 April 2021.
63 Colin Kahl and Thomas Wright, *Aftershocks: Pandemic Politics and the End of the Old International Order* (New York: St Martin's Press, 2021), p. 34.
64 Visit https://twitter.com/AdamJKucharski/status/1495334479052869634.
65 'Professor Dame Sarah Gilbert Delivers 44th Dimbleby Lecture', University of Oxford News and Events, 7 December 2021, https://www.ox.ac.uk/news/2021-12-07-professor-dame-sarah-gilbert-delivers-44th-dimbleby-lecture.
66 Jonathan Portes, 'Now It's Official: Brexit will Damage the Economy Long into the Future', *Guardian*, 28 October 2021.
67 Alex Callinicos, 'Science Advice is Shaped by Politics', *Socialist Worker*, 27 April 2020.
68 Michel Foucault, *The Birth of Biopolitics: Lectures at the Collège de France, 1978–1979*, ed. by Michel Senellart (Basingstoke: Palgrave Macmillan, 2008), p. 317.
69 Michel, Foucault, *The Punitive Society: Lectures at the Collège de France, 1972–1973*, ed. by Bernard Harcourt (Basingstoke: Palgrave Macmillan, 2015), p. 140. Foucault's struggle to escape from Marxism emerges clearly in these lectures, which, as their editor puts it, maintain 'a silent dialogue with [Edward] Thompson, as well as [with] Althusser,' and indeed 'are far more Marxist-"sounding" than other of Foucault's writings, while formulating clear lines of demarcation, maybe even the clearest he drew, between Marx and himself' (p. 278). One of Foucault's main charges against Marxism is that it hypostatizes the state. Nicos Poulantzas very effectively rebuts this accusation and insists, correctly, that '[t]he [s]tate plays a constitutive role in the existence and reproduction of class powers, and more generally in

the class struggle itself – a fact which refers us back to its presence in the relations of production' (Nicos Poulantzas, *State, Power, Socialism*, London: NLB, 1978, p. 38).
70 Michel, Foucault, *Discipline and Punish: The Birth of the Prison* (London: Allen Lane, 1976).
71 Michel, Foucault, *Security, Territory, Population: Lectures at the Collège de France, 1978*, ed. by Michel Senellart (Basingstoke: Palgrave Macmillan, 2007), pp. 108, 42, 64.
72 Ibid., p. 63.
73 A timely introduction can be found in Adam Kucharski, *The Rules of Contagion: Why Things Spread – and Why They Stop* (London: Profile Books, 2020). For an encyclopaedic and idiosyncratic exploration of modelling, see James R. Thompson, *Empirical Model Building: Data, Models, and Reality* (Hoboken, NJ: John Wiley & Sons, 2011).
74 Nancy Cartwright, *How the Laws of Physics Lie* (Oxford: Clarendon, 1983), p. 153.
75 Rob Wallace, *Dead Epidemiologists: On the Origins of COVID-19* (New York: Monthly Review Press, 2020), Apple edn, pp. 54–5.
76 Roy Bhaskar, *A Realist Theory of Science* (London: Routledge, 2008 [1975]).
77 Wallace, *Dead Epidemiologists*, p. 69.
78 See Peter Linebaugh and Marcus Rediker, *The Many-Headed Hydra: Sailors, Slaves, Commoners, and the Hidden History of the Revolutionary Atlantic* (London: Verso, 2000), pp. 146–7, and Jennifer L. Morgan, *Reckoning with Slavery: Gender, Kinship, and Capitalism in the Early Black Atlantic* (Durham, NC: Duke University Press, 2021).
79 Ian Hacking, *The Taming of Chance* (Cambridge: Cambridge University Press, 1990).
80 See the important study of these trends in Justin Joque, *Revolutionary Mathematics: Artificial Intelligence, Statistics and the Logic of Capitalism* (London: Verso, 2022).
81 Giorgio Agamben, *A che punto siamo? L'epidemia come politica*, expanded edn (Macerata: Quodlibet, 2021), pp. 6–7.
82 See Carl Schmitt, *Political Theology: Four Chapters on the Concept of Sovereignty* (Cambridge MA: MIT Press, 1985), p. 5; Giorgio Agamben, *State of Exception* (Chicago, IL: Chicago University Press, 2005).
83 Haidong Wang et al., 'Estimating Excess Mortality Due to the COVID-19 Pandemic: A Systematic Analysis of

COVID-19-Related Mortality, 2020–21', *The Lancet*, 10 March 2022. For an extended critique of Agamben's views on the pandemic, see Benjamin Bratton, *The Revenge of the Real: Politics for a Post-Pandemic World* (London: Verso, 2021).

84 E.g. Norman Ginsburg, *Capital, Class, and Social Policy* (London: Macmillan, 1979).

85 Quoted in Kahl and Wright, *Aftershocks*, p. 303.

86 On the global financial crisis, see Alex Callinicos, *Bonfire of Illusions: The Twin Crises of the Liberal World* (Cambridge: Polity, 2010), pp. 95–105; on vaccine development, see Kahl and Wright, *Aftershocks*, pp. 291–306.

87 'Job Retention Regimes during the COVID-19 Lockdown and Beyond', 12 October 2020. OECD, 12 October 2020. https://www.oecd.org/coronavirus/policy-responses/job-retention-schemes-during-the-covid-19-lockdown-and-beyond-0853ba1d.

88 Ugo Palheta, 'Fascism, Fascization, Antifascism', 7 January 2021. https://www.historicalmaterialism.org/blog/fascism-fascisation-antifascism. Unfortunately Palheta uses the very problematic concept of 'fascization'. Coined in the Communist International in the early 1930s, when Stalin's policy was to erase the differences between National Socialism and social democracy (which was branded 'social fascism'), the term implies a gradual and peaceful transition to fascism. For a brief critique, see Leon Trotsky, 'Radek Novitiate: What Is Social Fascism?', *The Militant*, 1 October 1930. https://wikirouge.net/texts/en/Radek's_Novitiate._What_is_Social-Fascism%3F.

89 Louis Michel, 'Emmanuel Macron Promised a New French Liberalism: Now He's Crushing It', *Prospect*, 2 March 2021.

90 International Center for Not-For-Profit Law, 'Analysis of US Anti-Protest Bills', ICNL 2022. https://www.icnl.org/post/news/analysis-of-anti-protest-bills.

91 Paul A. Passavant, *Policing Protest: The Post-Democratic State and the Figure of Black Insurrection* (Durham, NC: Durham University Press, 2021), p. 1. Passavant argues that the changes he discusses have to be seen in the context of the shift from Foucault's disciplines – characteristic of nineteenth- and twentieth-century capitalism, where institutions sought to form coherent subjects – to what Gilles Deleuze in a brilliant late essay called the 'societies of control'. Here institutions are in perpetual crisis, subjectivity fragmented, and '[w]e no longer find ourselves dealing with the mass/individual pair. Individuals have become *"dividuals"* and

masses, samples, data, or *"banks"'* (Gilles Deleuze, 'Postscript on the Societies of Control', *October*, 59 (1992): 3–7, here p. 6.
92 Missy Ryan and Dan Lamothe, 'Trump Administration to Significantly Expand Military Response in Washington amid Unrest', *Washington Post*, 1 June 2020.
93 Florian Schmitz, 'Greece: Abandoned to the Flames on Evia', 14 August 2021. https://www.dw.com/en/greece-abandoned-to-the-flames-on-evia/a-58860740?maca=en.
94 Edward White and Eleanor Olcott, 'Closed China: Why Xi Jinping Is Sticking with His Zero Covid Policy', *Financial Times*, 1 February 2022.
95 Chuang, 'Social Contagion: Microbiological Class War in China', February 2020. https://chuangcn.org/2020/02/social-contagion.
96 Michel Foucault, *The History of Sexuality*, vol. 1: *The Will to Knowledge* (London: Allen Lane, 1979).
97 Foucault, *Security, Territory, Population*, p. 47.
98 See Nick Srnicek, *Platform Capitalism* (Cambridge: Polity, 2017), and, for a well-argued but overly optimistic reading of the biopolitics of the pandemic, Bratton, *The Revenge of the Real*.
99 Ulrich Beck, *Risk Society: Towards a New Modernity* (London: SAGE, 1992). For a critique, see Alex Callinicos, *Social Theory: A Historical Introduction*, 2nd edn (Cambridge: Polity, 2007), pp. 301–11.
100 Elizabeth B. Pathak et al., 'Social Class, Race/Ethnicity, and COVID-19 Mortality among Working Age Adults in the United States', *medRxiv*, 24 November 2021, p. 6. https://doi.org/10.1101/2021.11.23.21266759.
101 Ibid., p. 13. There's clearly much more to be said about the conceptualization of class – see especially Erik Olin Wright, *Class Counts: Comparative Studies in Class Analysis* (Cambridge: Cambridge University Press, 2000) – and also about its relationship with 'race'; but this does not diminish the value of Pathak's study (which awaits peer review at the time of writing). I return to 'race' and class in Chapter 6.
102 See 'The Kill Floor', in Wallace, *Dead Epidemiologists*.
103 Erika Solomon, Valerie Hopkins, and Alexander Vladkov, 'Inside Germany's Abattoirs: The Human Cost of Cheap Meat', *Financial Times*, 8 January 2021.
104 Wang et al., 'Estimating Excess Mortality', pp. 7, 13, 17.
105 UN Global Crisis Response Group on Food, Energy and Finance, *Global Impact of the War In Ukraine: Billions of People Face the*

Greatest Cost-of-Living Crisis in a Generation, 8 June 2022. https://news.un.org/pages/wp-content/uploads/2022/06/GCRG_2nd-Brief_Jun8_2022_FINAL.pdf?utm_source=United+Nations&utm_medium=Brief&utm_campaign=Global+Crisis+Response, p. 6.
106 Thanks to Lucia Pradella for this important point.

Notes to Chapter 3

1 Chris Harman, *Zombie Capitalism: Global Crisis and the Relevance of Marx* (London: Bookmarks, 2009), p. 307.
2 Lucia Pradella, *L'attualità del capitale: Accumulazione e impoverimento nel capitalismo globale* (Padua: Il Poligrafo, 2010).
3 Karl Marx, *Capital: A Critique of Political Economy*, vol. 3 (Harmondsworth: Penguin, 1981 [1896]), pp. 357 and 358. On Marx's theory of crises, see Alex Callinicos, *Deciphering Capital: Marx's Capital and Its Destiny* (London: Bookmarks, 2014), ch. 6.
4 Deepankar Basu et al., 'World Profit Rates, 1960–2019', *Economics Department Working Paper Series*, 318 (2022). https://doi.org/10.7275/43yv-c721. See the discussion in Michael Roberts, 'A World Rate of Profit: Important New Evidence', Michael Roberts' Blog, 22 January 2022. https://thenextrecession.wordpress.com/2022/01/22/a-world-rate-of-profit-important-new-evidence. Important signposts in the analysis of falling profitability include Chris Harman, *Explaining the Crisis: A Marxist Reappraisal* (London: Bookmarks, 1984); Harman, *Zombie Capitalism*; Robert Brenner, *The Economics of Global Turbulence* (London: Verso, 2006), a heterodox Marxist interpretation; Andrew Kliman, *The Failure of Capitalist Production: Underlying Causes of the Great Recession* (London: Pluto, 2011); Michael Roberts, *The Long Depression* (Chicago, IL: Haymarket, 2016); and Guglielmo Carchedi and Michael Roberts, eds, *World in Crisis; Marxist Perspectives on Crash and Crisis: A Global Analysis of Marx's Law of Profitability* (Chicago, IL: Haymarket, 2018). Marx's law is strongly disputed by the premier Marxist political economist David Harvey; see for example David Harvey, *The Limits to Capital* (rev edn; London: Verso, 2006 [1982]) and David Harvey, 'Rate and Mass: Perspectives from the *Grundrisse*', *New Left Review*, 2.130 (2016), 73–98. For a rebuttal, see Alex Callinicos and Joseph Choonara, 'How Not to Write about the Rate of Profit: A Reply to David Harvey', *Science and Society*, 80.4 (2016): 481–94.
5 Michael Kidron, *Western Capitalism since the War* (Harmondsworth:

Penguin, 1970); Harman, *Explaining the Crisis*; Harman, *Zombie Capitalism*, chs 4, 5, 7, and 8; and Joseph Choonara, 'The Monetary and the Military: Revisiting Kidron's Permanent Arms Economy', *International Socialism*, 2.171 (2021): 123–50.
6 John Smith, *Imperialism in the Twenty-First Century: Globalization, Super-Exploitation, and Capitalism's Final Crisis* (New York: Monthly Review Press, 2016).
7 Brenner, *Economics of Global Turbulence*, p. 2.
8 Alex Callinicos, *Bonfire of Illusions: The Twin Crises of the Liberal World* (Cambridge: Polity, 2010).
9 Costas Lapavitsas, *Profiting without Producing: How Finance Exploits Us All* (London: Verso, 2013) and Cédric Durand, *Fictitious Capital: How Finance Is Appropriating Our Future* (London: Verso, 2017).
10 Riccardo Bellofiore, 'Marx and the Crisis', paper presented at IIPPE, 1 September 2010. www.iippe.org/wiki/images/2/24/CONF_FINANCE_Bellofiore.pdf. For pioneering analyses see Robert Brenner, *The Boom and the Bubble* (London: Verso, 2002) and Robert Brenner, 'New Boom or New Bubble?', *New Left Review*, 2.25 (2004): 57–100.
11 Michael J. Howell, *Capital Wars: The Rise of Global Liquidity* (London: Palgrave Macmillan, 2020), pp. 17, 25, and 88; also Fig. 3.3, p. 19.
12 Adam Tooze, *Crashed: How a Decade of Financial Crisis Changed the World* (London: Allen Lane, 2018), pp. 79 and 81.
13 Ibid., p. 81.
14 Ibid., pp. 9–10.
15 Ibid., p. 219.
16 Leo Panitch and Sam Gindin, *The Making of Global Capitalism: The Political Economy of American Empire* (London: Verso, 2012).
17 Karl Marx, *A Contribution to the Critique of Political Economy* (London: Lawrence & Wishart, 1971 [1859]), pp. 136–7.
18 Barry Eichengreen, *Hall of Mirrors: The Great Depression, the Great Recession, and the Uses – and Abuses – of History* (Oxford: Oxford University Press, 2015), p. 281.
19 Coen Teulings and Richard Baldwin, eds, *Secular Stagnation: Facts, Causes and Cures* (London: CEPR Press, 2014).
20 James Galbraith, *The End of Normal: The Great Crisis and the Future of Growth* (New York: Simon & Schuster, 2014).
21 David C. Wheelock, 'Comparing the COVID-19 Recession with the Great Depression', *Economic Synopses*, 39 (2020). https://doi.org/10.20955/es.2020.39.

22 International Monetary Fund, *World Economic Outlook, October 2021: Recovery during a Pandemic*, Washington, DC: IMF Publications: Table 1.1, p. 5.
23 Valentina Romei and Chris Giles, 2021, 'UK Suffers Biggest Drop in Economic Output in 300 Years', *Financial Times*, 12 February 2021.
24 Adam Tooze, *Shutdown: How Covid Shook the World's Economy* (London: Penguin, 2021), p. 5.
25 James Meadway, 'Optimism Bias and the Pandemic Economy', Blog, 24 October 2021. https://jamesmeadway.substack.com/p/optimism-bias-and-the-pandemic-economy.
26 See Michael Roberts, 'Fallen Angels', Blog, 6 March 2022. https://thenextrecession.wordpress.com/2022/03/06/fallen-angels.
27 Duncan Foley, 'Marx's Theory of Money in Historical Perspective', in Fred Moseley, ed., *Marx's Theory of Money: Modern Appraisals* (Basingstoke: Palgrave Macmillan, 2005), 36–49.
28 Tooze, *Shutdown*, p. 131
29 Ibid., p. 141.
30 Thomas Stubbington and Chris Giles, 'Investors Sceptical over Bank of England's QE Programme', *Financial Times*, 5 January 2021.
31 Jens van t' Klooster, 'Technocratic Keynesianism: A Paradigm Shift without Legislative Change', *New Political Economy*, 27.5 (2021): 771–87, here p. 772. https://doi.org/10.1080/13563467.2021.2013791. See the valuable theoretical and historical framing in Daniela Gabor, *Revolution without Revolutionaries: Interrogating the Return of Monetary Finance* (Berlin: Bürgerbewegung Finanzwende/Heinrich-Böll Stiftung, 2021).
32 Harold James, *Making the European Monetary Union* (Cambridge, MA: Harvard University Press, 2012).
33 Van t' Klooster, 'Technocratic Keynesianism', pp. 7–8. The sorry tale of the ECB's mishandling of the global financial crisis is told in some detail in Tooze, *Crashed*, Part III.
34 Tooze, *Shutdown*, p. 146; see A. P. Lerner, 'Functional Finance and the Federal Debt', *Social Research*, 10.1 (1943): 38–51.
35 Tooze, *Shutdown*, p. 12. For a presentation of MMT, see Stephanie Kelton, *The Deficit Myth: Modern Monetary Theory and How to Build a Better Economy* (London: John Murray, 2020); for useful critiques, see Doug Henwood, 'Modern Monetary Theory Isn't Helping', *Jacobin*, 21 February 2019 and Michael Roberts, 'The Deficit Myth', Blog, 16 June 2020. https://thenextrecession.wordpress.com/2020/06/16/the-deficit-myth/

36 Helen Thompson, *Disorder: Hard Times in the 21st Century* (New York: Oxford University Press, 2022), pp. 200–9.
37 Van t' Klooster, 'Technocratic Keynesianism', p. 772.
38 Fathimath Musthaq, 'Unconventional Central Banking and the Politics of Liquidity', *Review of International Political Economy*, 2021, here pp. 2, 18, 3. doi: 10.1080/09692290.2021.1997785.
39 Walter Benjamin, *Selected Writings*, vol. 4: *1938–40* (Cambridge MA: Harvard University Press, 2003), p. 392.
40 Van t' Klooster, 'Technocratic Keynesianism', p. 775.
41 Gabor, *Revolution without Revolutionaries*, p. 8.
42 Ibid., p. 11. See Howell, *Capital Wars*, ch. 6, on the repo market.
43 A useful survey is William Davies and Nicholas Gane, 'Post-Neoliberalism? An Introduction', *Theory, Culture & Society*, 38.6 (2021): 3–28; and see also the stimulating discussion in James Meadway, 'Neoliberalism Is Dying – Now We Must Replace It', *openDemocracy*, 3 September 2021.
44 For example, David Harvey, *A Short History of Neoliberalism* (Oxford: Oxford University Press, 2005), ch. 1.
45 Thomas Hobbes, *Leviathan*, ed. by Richard Tuck (Cambridge: Cambridge University Press, 1996 [1651]), p. 107 (= ch. 21). See Isaiah Berlin, 'Two Concepts of Liberty', in his *Liberty: Incorporating Four Essays on Liberty*, ed. by Henry Hardy (Oxford: Oxford University Press, 2002), pp. 166–217.
46 Andrew Woodcock, 'Coronavirus: Boris Johnson Suggests High Coronavirus Infection Rates Are Due to UK's "Love of Freedom"', *Independent*, 22 September 2020.
47 John Stuart Mill, *On Liberty; with The Subjection of Women and Chapters on Socialism*, ed. by Stefan Collini (Cambridge: Cambridge University Press, 1989), p. 95.
48 Hobbes, *Leviathan*, p. 111 (= ch. 21). See Quentin Skinner, *Liberty before Liberalism* (Cambridge: Cambridge University Press, 1998); Quentin Skinner, *Hobbes and Republican Liberty* (Cambridge: Cambridge University Press, 2008); and, for an argument that freedom as non-domination is central to Marx's *Capital*, William Clare Roberts, *Marx's Inferno: The Political Theory of Capital* (Princeton, NJ: Princeton University Press, 2017). Some conceptual nuances are explored in Miguel Vatter, 'Neoliberalism and Republicanism: Economic Rule of Law and Law as Concrete Order (*nomos*)', in Damien Cahill et al., eds, *The SAGE Handbook of Neoliberalism* (London: SAGE, 2018), pp. 370–83.
49 Quinn Slobodian, *Globalists: The End of Empire and the Birth of*

Neoliberalism (Cambridge, MA: Harvard University Press, 2018), p. 2. Two other important critical studies of the origins of neoliberalism are Michel Foucault, *The Birth of Biopolitics: Lectures at the Collège de France, 1978–1979*, ed. by Michel Senellart (Basingstoke: Palgrave Macmillan, 2008) and Pierre Dardot and Christian Laval, *The New Way of the World: On Neoliberal Society* (London: Verso, 2014).
50 Harvey, *A Short History of Neoliberalism*, p. 19.
51 Milton Friedman, 'The Nature of Monetary Policy', *American Economic Review*, 58.1 (1968): 1–17.
52 Samuel Brittan, 'The Economic Contradictions of Democracy', *Journal of Political Science*, 5.2 (1975): 129–59.
53 Slobodian, *Globalists*, ch. 7.
54 Brenner, *Economics of Global Turbulence*, ch. 11. The extent of the break represented by the advent of neoliberalism is often overstated. For a valuable corrective, see Chris Harman, 'Theorizing Neoliberalism', *International Socialism*, 2.117 (2008): 87–121.
55 Harvey, *A Short History of Neoliberalism*, p. 13.
56 Friedman, 'The Nature of Monetary Policy', p. 17.
57 Nigel Lawson, *The New Conservatism* (London: Centre for Policy Studies, 1980), p. 4.
58 For lucid discussions from antithetical ideological perspectives, see Samuel Brittan, *How to End the 'Monetarist' Controversy* (London: Institute of Economic Affairs, 1982) and Nicholas Kaldor, *The Scourge of Monetarism*, 2nd edn (Oxford: Oxford University Press, 1986).
59 Lawson, *The New Conservatism*, p. 4.
60 Edward N. Luttwak, 'Central Bankism', *London Review of Books*, 14 November 1996.
61 James Livingston, *Origins of the Federal Reserve System: Money, Class, and Corporate Capitalism, 1890–1913* (Ithaca: Cornell University Press, 1986).
62 Joseph Halevi, 'The EMS and the Bundesbank in Europe', in Philip Arestis and Victoria Chick, eds, *Finance, Development and Structural Change: Post-Keynesian Perspectives* (Aldershot: Edward Elgar, 1995), 263–91.
63 Shaun Goldfinch, 'Economic Reform in New Zealand: Radical Liberalization in a Small Economy', *Otemon Journal of Australian Studies*, 30 (2004): 75–98.
64 Foley, 'Marx's Theory of Money in Historical Perspective', p. 43.

65 For a sparkling portrait, see Ben Judah, 'The Sphinx Who Reshaped Europe', *The Critic* (May 2021).
66 Tooze, *Shutdown*, p. 15.
67 Ibid., ch. 8.
68 Daniela Gabor, 'Critical Macro-Finance: A Theoretical Lens', *Finance and Society* 6.1 (2020): 45–55, here pp. 51–2.
69 Michał Kalecki, 'Political Aspects of Full Employment', *Political Quarterly*, 14.4 (1943): 322–30, here p. 325.
70 Ibid., p. 326.
71 Michael H. Best and William E. Connolly, *The Politicized Economy* (Lexington, MA: D. C. Heath & Co, 1980).
72 This text can be found at https://twitter.com/jdcmedlock/status/1350143296459341826.
73 Ezra Klein, 'The Best Explanation of Biden's Thinking I've Heard', *New York Times*, 9 April 2021.
74 Visit https://www.whitehouse.gov/briefing-room/statements-releases/2021/03/31/fact-sheet-the-american-jobs-plan.
75 Klein, 'The Best Explanation of Biden's Thinking'.
76 Ibid.
77 Visit https://www.whitehouse.gov/briefing-room/statements-releases/2021/03/31/fact-sheet-the-american-jobs-plan.
78 Cédric Durand, '1979 in Reverse', *Sidecar*, 1 June 2021. https://newleftreview.org/sidecar/posts/1979-in-reverse.
79 On the theory of inflation, see Guglielmo Carchedi, *Frontiers of Political Economy* (London: Verso, 1991), ch. 5 and Michael Roberts and Guglielmo Carchedi, *Capitalism in the 21st Century: Through the Prism of Value* (London: Pluto, 2023), 75–91. Carchedi and Roberts argue that capitalism has a disinflationary tendency as higher productivity reduces the amount of new value (= wages + profits) per unit of output that may be counteracted if the money supply rises sufficiently. There are useful discussions of the present inflation in Cédric Durand, 'Energy Dilemma', *Sidecar*, 5 November 2021. https://newleftreview.org/sidecar/posts/energy-dilemma; in Michael Roberts, 'Inflation: Supply or Demand?', Blog, 19 February 2022. https://thenextrecession.wordpress.com/2022/02/19/inflation-supply-or-demand; and in Adam Tooze, 'Chartbook #122: What Drives Inflation?', Blog, 17 May 2022. https://adamtooze.substack.com/p/chartbook-122-what-drives-inflation?s=r&utm_campaign=post&utm_medium=web.
80 Chris Giles, 'Bank of England's Andrew Bailey Dishes out Tough Love to British Public', *Financial Times*, 3 February 2022.

81 Szu Ping Chan, 'Don't Ask for a Big Pay Rise, Warns Bank of England Boss', 4 February 2022. https://www.bbc.com/news/business-60206564.
82 Kaldor, *The Scourge of Monetarism*, p. 100.
83 Martin Sandbu, 'The Class Warriors of the Bank of England', *Financial Times*, 10 February 2022.
84 Chris Hayes and Carsten Jung, *Prices and Profits after the Pandemic*, IPPR and Common Wealth, June 2022. https://www.ippr.org/files/2022-06/prices-and-profits-after-the-pandemic-june-22.pdf. 'Profit-price spiral' has become a popular phrase; I first heard it from Volkhard Mosler.
85 Colby Smith, 'Fed to Begin "Rapid" Balance Sheet Reduction as soon as May, Says Top Official', *Financial Times*, 5 April 2022.
86 Robert Armstrong and Ethan Wu, 'What the Bond Rout is Telling Us', *Financial Times*, 28 March 2022.
87 Ole J. Benedictow, *The Complete History of the Black Death*, rev edn (Woodbridge: Boydell Press, 2021), p. 891.
88 David Ratner and Jae Sim, 'Who Killed the Phillips Curve? A Murder Mystery', Finance and Economics Discussion Series, 2022. https://doi.org/10.17016/FEDS.2022.028.
89 Joseph Choonara, 'Uncertain Future: Workers in the Pandemic', *International Socialism*, 2.173 (2021): 3–16, here p. 12.
90 Art Preis, *Labor's Giant Step: The First Twenty Years of the CIO: 1936–55* (New York: Pathfinder Press, 1972); Ira Katznelson, *Fear Itself: The New Deal and the Origins of Our Times* (New York: Liveright, 2013); Michael Goldfield, *The Southern Key: Class, Race, and Radicalism in the 1930s and 1940s* (New York: Oxford University Press, 2020).

Notes to Chapter 4

1 'Remarks by President Biden on the American Jobs Plan', 31 March 2021. https://www.whitehouse.gov/briefing-room/speeches-remarks/2021/03/31/remarks-by-president-biden-on-the-american-jobs-plan.
2 Edward Luce, 'For Biden – and America – It's Basically China from Now On', *Financial Times*, 17 September 2021.
3 Antony J. Blinken, 'The Administration's Approach to the People's Republic of China', US Department of State, 26 May 2022. https://www.state.gov/the-administrations-approach-to-the-peoples-republic-of-china.

4 Rana Forohaar, 'It's Not Just the Economy, Stupid', *Financial Times*, 21 February 2022.
5 Thomas L. Friedman, *The World Is Flat: A Brief History of the Globalized World in the Twenty-First Century* (London: Penguin, 2005).
6 Michael Hardt and Toni Negri, *Empire* (Cambridge, MA: Harvard University Press, 2000); for a critique, see Alex Callinicos, 'Toni Negri in Perspective', *International Socialism*, 2.92 (2001): 33–61.
7 Valentina Pop, Sam Fleming, and James Politi, 'Weaponization of Finance: how the West Unleashed "Shock and Awe" on Russia', *Financial Times*, 6 April 2022.
8 'Russia's Invasion of Ukraine Adds to Pressure on Chip Supply Chain', *Financial Times*, 4 March 2022.
9 Katherine Hille, 'TSMC: How a Taiwanese Chipmaker Became a Linchpin of the Global Economy', *Financial Times*, 24 March 2021.
10 Alex Callinicos, *Imperialism and Global Political Economy* (Cambridge: Polity, 2009), chs. 4 and 5. Mazen Labban, *Space, Oil, and Capital* (Abingdon: Routledge, 2008), a study of the oil industry and inter-capitalist competition firmly based in Marxist value theory, offers much of interest on the history of imperialism.
11 Chris Harman, 'The Storm Breaks: The Crisis in the Eastern Bloc', *International Socialism*, 2.45 (1990): 3–93.
12 Labban, *Space, Oil, and Capital*, p. 95.
13 Charles Krauthammer, 'The Unipolar Moment', *Foreign Affairs*, 70.1 (1990–1): 23–33.
14 Peter Gowan, *The Global Gamble: Washington's Faustian Bid for World Dominance* (London: Verso, 1999); Gilbert Achcar, 'The Strategic Triad: The United States, Russia, and China', *New Left Review*, 1.228 (1998): 91–126.
15 E.g. Michael Doyle, 'Liberalism and World Politics', *American Political Science Review*, 80 (1986): 1151–69 and G. John Ikenberry, *Liberal Leviathan: The Origins, Crisis, and Transformation of the American World Order* (Princeton, NJ: Princeton University Press, 2012).
16 See especially Leo Panitch and Sam Gindin, *The Making of Global Capitalism: The Political Economy of American Empire* (London: Verso, 2012).
17 For a contemporary analysis, see Alex Callinicos, *The New Mandarins of American Power: The Bush Administration's Plans for the World* (Cambridge: Polity, 2003) and the damning military

history in Andew J. Bacevich, *America's War for the Greater Middle East: A Military History* (New York: Random House, 2016), Kindle edn.
18 Robert Kagan, 'America's Crisis of Legitimacy', *Foreign Affairs*, 83.2 (2004): 65–87.
19 David E. Sanger, *Confront and Conceal: Obama's Secret Wars and Surprising Use of American Power* (New York: Crown Publishers, 2012).
20 Lucia Pradella and Sahar Taghdisi Rad, 'Libya and Europe: Imperialism, Crisis and Migration', *Third World Quarterly*, 38.11 (2017): 2411–27.
21 Alex Callinicos, 'The Multiple Crises of Imperialism', *International Socialism*, 2.144 (2014): 17–36.
22 David Samuels, 'The Aspiring Novelist Who Became Obama's Foreign-Policy Guru', *New York Times*, 6 May 2016.
23 Bacevich, *America's War for the Greater Middle East*, Kindle loc. 6839.
24 UNCTAD, *Investment Trends Monitor*, January 2022.
25 Hudson Lockett, 'How Xi Jinping is Reshaping China's Capital Markets', *Financial Times*, 12 June 2022.
26 Chris Harman, 'The State and Capitalism Today', *International Socialism*, 2.51 (1991): 3–54.
27 For a more extended discussion of the conflict in the Indo-Pacific, see Callinicos, 'The Multiple Crises of Imperialism'. There is a lucid realist analysis of this conflict by a former Pentagon official under Trump in Elliott A. Colby, *The Strategy of Denial: American Defense in an Age of Great Power Conflict* (New Haven, CT: Yale University Press, 2021).
28 Michael Roberts, 'IIPPE 2021: Imperialism, China and Finance', Blog, https://thenextrecession.wordpress.com/2021/09/30/iippe-2021-imperialism-china-and-finance. See also Michael Roberts and Guglielmo Carchedi, *Capitalism in the 21st Century: Through the Prism of Value* (London: Pluto, 2023), ch. 4.
29 Herbert Feis, *Europe: The World's Banker, 1870-1914* (New Haven, CT: Yale University Press, 1930), pp. 14, 47, 72.
30 Rana Forohaar, 'The Squid and the Whale', *Financial Times*, 25 October 2021.
31 Paul M. Kennedy, *The Rise of the Anglo-German Antagonism* (New York: Prometheus Books, 1980).
32 Sara Sorcher, 'Top US Military Officer Says China's Hypersonic Weapon Test Very Close to a "Sputnik Moment"', *Washington*

Post, 27 October 2021. In 1957 the Soviet Union launched the first satellite, apparently challenging the United States' technological lead. In fact the United States remained way ahead in the arms race: see Theodore Voorhees Jr, *The Silent Guns of Two Octobers: Kennedy and Khrushchev Play the Double Game* (Ann Arbor: University of Michigan Press, 2020), ch. 1.

33 'US looks like Soviet Union from Outside, Qing Dynasty from Inside', *Global Times*, 24 November 2021.

34 See the elegant and perceptive discussion in Marco D'Eramo, 'American Decline?', *New Left Review*, 2.135 (2022): 5–21.

35 Daniel W. Drezner, 'Targeted Sanctions in a World of Global Finance', *International Interactions*, 41.4 (2015): 755–64; Nicholas Mulder, *The Economic Weapon: The Rise of Sanctions as a Tool of Modern War* (New Haven, CT: Yale University Press, 2022): Conclusion.

36 Martin Wolf, 'China Is Wrong to Think the US Faces Inevitable Decline', *Financial Times*, 27 April 2021.

37 John Paul Rathbone, 'Russian Menace Brings Abrupt End to the West's "Peace Dividend"', *Financial Times*, 7 June 2022.

38 Adam Tooze, 'The New Age of American Power', *New Statesman*, 9 September 2021.

39 'NATO 2022 Strategic Concept', NATO, June 2022. https://www.nato.int/nato_static_fl2014/assets/pdf/2022/6/pdf/290622-strategic-concept.pdf.

40 Matthew C. Klein and Michael Pettis, *Trade Wars Are Class Wars: How Rising Inequality Distorts the Global Economy and Threatens International Peace* (New Haven: Yale University Press, 2020), p. 112.

41 Michael Pettis, 'Why Trade Wars are Inevitable', *Foreign Policy*, 19 October 2019. For an earlier stage in this analysis, see Michael Pettis, *The Great Rebalancing: Trade, Conflict, and the Perilous Road Ahead for the World Economy* (Princeton, NJ: Princeton University Press, 2013). Klein and Pettis draw on J. A. Hobson's proto-Keynesian theory of imperialism, which explains great power expansion and rivalry as a consequence of restricted domestic demand caused by the unequal distribution of income. See J. A. Hobson, *Imperialism: A Study*, 3rd edn (London: Allen & Unwin, 1938).

42 Klein and Pettis, *Trade Wars Are Class Wars*, pp. 114–19.

43 Yen Nee Lee, 'These Charts Show the Dramatic Increase in China's Debt', CNBC, 28 June 2021. https://www.cnbc.com

/2021/06/29/china-economy-charts-show-how-much-debt-has-grown.html.
44. Sun Yu and Tom Mitchell, 2022, 'China's Economy: The Fallout from the Evergrande Crisis', *Financial Times*, 6 January 2022.
45. Klein and Pettis, *Trade Wars Are Class Wars*, p. 125.
46. Xi, Jinping, 'Understanding the New Development Stage, Applying the New Development Philosophy, and Creating a New Development Dynamic', *Qiushi*, 8 July 2021. My thanks to Dr Yue Zhou Lin for checking and explaining the original Chinese version of this passage.
47. Adam Tooze, *Shutdown: How Covid Shook the World's Economy* (London: Penguin, 2021), p. 128.
48. Yu and Mitchell, 'China's Economy'.
49. Ibid.
50. Michael Pettis, 'What Does Evergrande Meltdown Mean for China?', *China Financial Markets*, 20 September 2021.
51. Michael Pettis, 'It Won't be Easy for Foreign Firms to Leave China', *China Financial: GlobalSource Partners*, 13 June 2022.
52. See Tony Norfield, *The City: London and the Global Power of Finance* (London: Verso, 2016), ch. 1, 'World Hierarchy'. Norfield ranks states according to five criteria: nominal GDP, ownership of foreign assets, international importance of banking sector, use of currency in foreign exchange transactions, and the level of military spending. Arguably the weight placed on finance (given three different criteria) favours Britain too much, and Russia deserves to be included in what Norfield calls the 'premier league' thanks to its significance as an energy producer and military power. The importance of access to energy in shaping interstate relationships in the twentieth and twenty-first centuries analysed by Helen Thompson, *Disorder: Hard Times in the 21st Century* (New York: Oxford University Press, 2022) suggests that control over access to energy needs to be integrated into any ranking of states' relative power.
53. See the detailed discussion of sub-imperialisms in Alex Callinicos, 'Marxism and Imperialism Today', *International Socialism*, 2.50 (1991): 3–48.
54. Adam Tooze, 'Chartbook #68 Putin's Challenge to Western Hegemony: The 2022 Edition', Blog, 12 January. https://adamtooze.substack.com/p/chartbook-68-putins-challenge-to?fbclid=&s=r. See also Tony Wood, *Russia without Putin: Money, Power and the Myths of the New Cold War* (London: Verso, 2018)

and Ilya Budraitskis, *Dissidents among Dissidents: Ideology, Politics and the Left in Post-Soviet Russia* (London: Verso, 2022).
55 International Energy Agency, 'Energy Fact Sheet: Why Does Russian Oil and Gas Matter?', IEA, 24 March 2022. https://www.iea.org/articles/energy-fact-sheet-why-does-russian-oil-and-gas-matter. On the Russian energy industry since the end of the Cold War, see also Labban, *Space, Oil, and Capital*, ch. 5.
56 Henry Foy et al., 'Russia: Vladimir Putin's Pivot to Africa', *Financial Times*, 22 January 2019.
57 Andrew England and Simeon Kerr, '"More of China, less of America": How Superpower Fight Is Squeezing the Gulf', *Financial Times*, 20 September 2021.
58 Patrick Bond, 'Beyond Sub-Imperial War, "Blood Methane" and Climate-Debt Denialism: South Africa's Pro-Military Lobby Risks Worsening Multiple Injustices in Northern Mozambique', *Thinker*, 90 (2022): 69–80, here pp. 70–1.
59 Vijay Prashad, 'Why the Discovery Of Natural Gas in Mozambique Has Produced Tragedy', *Mail and Guardian*, 3 September 2021; International Crisis Group, 'Winning Peace in Mozambique's Embattled North', *Crisis Group Africa Briefing*, 178 (10 February 2022). https://d2071andvip0wj.cloudfront.net/b178-winning-peace-in-mozambique_2.pdf.
60 Joe Bavier, 'Congo War-Driven Crisis Kills 45,000 a Month: Study', Reuters, 22 January 2008.
61 Thompson, *Disorder*, ch. 2.
62 Claude Serfati, *Le Militaire: Une histoire française* (Paris: Éditions Amsterdam, 2016).
63 Simon Bromley, *American Hegemony and World Oil* (Cambridge: Polity, 1991), p. 86.
64 Thompson, *Disorder*, pp. 55–7.
65 David Harvey, *The New Imperialism* (Oxford: Oxford University Press, 2003), p. 19.
66 International Energy Agency, 'US Energy Facts Explained', EIA 2021. https://www.eia.gov/energyexplained/us-energy-facts/imports-and-exports.php.
67 Thompson, *Disorder*, p. 7.
68 See the extensive documentation in National Security Archive, 'NATO Expansion: What Gorbachev Heard', 17 December 2017. https://nsarchive.gwu.edu/briefing-book/russia-programs/2017-12-12/nato-expansion-what-gorbachev-heard-western-leaders-early.

69 M. E. Sarotte, *Not One Inch: America, Russia, and the Making of Post-Cold War Stalemate* (New Haven, CT: Yale University Press, 2021), p. 87.
70 Ibid., pp. 275 and 464 (for both quotations). For a long-term historical perspective, see Alan Cafruny et al., 'Ukraine, Multipolarity and the Crisis of Grand Strategies', *Journal of Balkan and Near Eastern Studies* (2022). https://doi.org/10.1080/19448953.2022.2084881.
71 Alex Callinicos, *Bonfire of Illusions: The Twin Crises of the Liberal World* (Cambridge: Polity, 2010).
72 Zbigniew Brzezinski, *The Grand Chessboard: American Primacy and Its Geostrategic Imperatives* (New York: Basic Books, 2016 [1997]), pp. 74, 46. It is a symptom of Ukraine's sorry economic history since independence (see Michael Roberts, 'Ukraine: Trapped in a War-Zone', Blog, 14 February 2022, https://thenextrecession.wordpress.com/2022/02/14/ukraine-trapped-in-a-war-zone) that its population subsequently declined to an estimated 43,745,640 in July 2021 (https://www.cia.gov/the-world-factbook/countries/ukraine/#people-and-society).
73 Brzezinski, *The Grand Chessboard*, p. 52.
74 Rob Ferguson, 'Ukraine: Imperialism, War and the Left', *International Socialism*, 2.144 (2014); Yuliya Yurchenko, *Ukraine and the Empire of Capital: From Marketization to Armed Conflict* (London: Pluto, 2018); and Volodymyr Ishchenko, 'Towards the Abyss', *New Left Review*, 2.133/134 (2022): 17–39.
75 By contrast, in the Cuban crisis, the Soviet leader Nikita Khrushchev was willing to lose face in exchange for the major concessions that President John F. Kennedy secretly offered him: see Voorhees, *The Silent Guns of Two Octobers*. The 'eyeball-to-eyeball' moment is in fact a myth: Glenn Kessler, 'An "Eyeball-to-Eyeball" Moment That Never Happened', *Washington Post*, 23 June 2014.
76 Gideon Rachman, 'Russia's and China's Plans for a New World Order', *Financial Times*, 23 January 2022.
77 Xijin Hu, 'Russia a Crucial Partner for China in Deterring US', *Global Times*, 22 March 2022.
78 Baruch Spinoza, *Political Treatise*, 1.4, in his *Complete Works*, edited by Michael L. Morgan (Indianapolis, IN: Hackett, 2002), Kindle loc. 16579.
79 Charles Tilly, *Coercion, Capital, and European States, AD 990–1992* (Oxford: Blackwell, 1993).

80 Visit https://www.youtube.com/watch?v=CVcKx5-mZx4.
81 Wolfgang Munchau, 'Networks of Resistance', EuroIntelligence, 1 May 2022. https://www.eurointelligence.com/column/networks-of-resistance?fbclid=Iw.
82 Mark Mazzetti et al., 'For the US, a Tenuous Balance in Confronting Russia', *New York Times* (19 March 2022).
83 Visit https://www.bloomberg.com/news/videos/2022-03-17/u-s-is-in-a-proxy-war-with-russia-panetta-video.
84 David E. Sanger, 'Behind Austin's Call for a "Weakened" Russia, Hints of a Shift', *New York Times* (25 April 2022).
85 Mark Hertling, 'I Commanded US Army Europe. Here's What I Saw in the Russian and Ukrainian Armies', *The Bulwark* (11 April 2022).
86 John Curtis and Claire Mills, 'Military Assistance to Ukraine since the Russian Invasion', House of Commons Library: Research Briefing 9477, 23 March 2022; John Paul Rathbone, Henry Foy, and Paul Jones, 'Military Briefing: West Raises Effort to Arm Ukraine as Donbas Battle Looms', *Financial Times*, 7 April 2022; Tony Diver, 'Boris Johnson Promises Armoured Vehicles and More Missiles in Secret Meeting with Volodymyr Zelensky', *Telegraph*, 9 April 2022; Felicia Schwarz, '"A Profound Shift": US Boosts Supply of Heavy Weapons to Ukraine', *Financial Times*, 23 April 2022; Felicia Schwarz, 'Joe Biden Asks Congress for $33bn More Aid for Ukraine as Conflict Escalates', *Financial Times*, 28 April 2022; and Felicia Schwarz, 'US to Provide Ukraine with Longer-Range Rocket Systems', *Financial Times*, 1 June 2022.
87 Ben Hall, Henry Foy, and Felicia Schwartz, 'Military Briefing: NATO Brings Back Cold War Doctrine to Counter Russian Threat', *Financial Times*, 30 June 2022.
88 'Remarks by President Biden on the United Efforts of the Free World to Support the People of Ukraine', White House, 26 March. https://www.whitehouse.gov/briefing-room/speeches-remarks/2022/03/26/remarks-by-president-biden-on-the-united-efforts-of-the-free-world-to-support-the-people-of-ukraine.
89 James Meadway, 'Central Banks as Weapons: How the West Learned from the Eurozone Crisis', Blog, 28 February 2022. https://jamesmeadway.substack.com/p/central-banks-as-weapons-how-the?utm=&s=r.
90 Visit https://twitter.com/LevMenand/status/1498650790071779334.
91 Derek Brower, 'US Energy Envoy Asks India to Restrain Russian Oil Purchases', *Financial Times*, 9 June 2022.

92 Helen Thompson, 'Whatever Moscow's Military Defeats in Ukraine, Vladimir Putin Is Winning the Energy War', *New Statesman*, 22 June 2022.
93 Alan Beattie, 'The Dogs Bark, but the Trade Caravan Moves On', *Financial Times*, 22 November 2021.
94 Simeon Kerr, Samer Al-Artrush, and Andrew England, 'Gulf States' Neutrality on Ukraine Reflects Deeper Russian Ties', *Financial Times*, 28 February 2022.
95 David Adler, 'The West vs Russia: Why the Global South Isn't Taking Sides', *Guardian*, 10 March 2022.
96 Katherine Hille, 'China Reverses Roles in Arms Trade with Russia', *Financial Times*, 30 March 2022.
97 James Meadway, 'Twilight of the Greenback: How Sanctions May Hasten the Dollar's Decline', *New Statesman*, 14 March 2022.
98 Serkan Arslanalap, Barry Eichengreen, and Chirna Simpson-Bell, 'The Stealth Erosion of Dollar Dominance: Active Diversifiers and the Rise of Non-Traditional Reserve Currencies', IMF Working Paper, 24 March 2022.
99 Adam Tooze, 'Chartbook #94: Putin's War, China and the Euro-Dollar Trap', Blog, 7 March 2022. https://adamtooze.substack.com/p/chartbook-94-putins-war-and-the-china?s=r. For some different takes on the impact of the geopolitical conflict on globalization, see Robert Armstrong and Ethan Wu, 'Chartbook-Unhedged Exchange #2: The End Of Globalization As We Know It?', *Chartbook*, 31 March 2022. https://adamtooze.substack.com/p/chartbook-unhedged-exchange-2-the?s=r; John Micklethwait and Adrian Wooldridge, 'Putin and Xi Exposed the Great Illusion of Capitalism', Bloomberg, 24 March 2022. https://www.bloomberg.com/opinion/articles/2022-03-24/ukraine-war-has-russia-s-putin-xi-jinping-exposing-capitalism-s-great-illusion?; and Zoltan Pozsar, 'Money, Commodities, and Bretton Woods III', Credit Suisse, 31 March 2022. https://plus2.credit-suisse.com/shorturlpdf.html?v=5lio-WTBd-V.
100 Colin Kahl and Thomas Wright, 2021, *Aftershocks: Pandemic Politics and the End of the Old International Order* (New York: St Martin's Press), pp. 41–2.
101 Ibid., pp. 78–9.
102 Alex Callinicos, 'Iraq: Fulcrum of World Politics', *Third World Quarterly*, 26.4/5 (2005): 593–608.
103 David Deudney and G. John Ikenberry, 'Misplaced Restraint: The

Quincy Coalition Versus Liberal Internationalism', *Survival*, 63.4 (2021): 7–32, here p. 24.
104 Ibid., p. 27.
105 Robert Kagan, 'The Case for a League of Democracies', *Financial Times*, 13 May 2008.
106 'Remarks by President Biden on the United Efforts of the Free World to Support the People of Ukraine'.
107 For a superb demolition of this rhetoric, see Samuel Moyn, 'How to Stop a New Cold War', *Prospect*, 7 April 2022.
108 Tania Greer, 'Xi Jinping in Translation: China's Guiding Ideology', American Moment, 31 May 2019. https://www.americanmoment.org/xi-jinping-in-translation-chinas-guiding-ideology. On the genealogy of 'Mao Zedong Thought', see Nigel Harris, *The Mandate of Heaven: Marx and Mao in Modern China* (Chicago, IL: Haymarket, 2015 [1978]).
109 Cas Mudde, *The Far Right Today* (Cambridge: Polity, 2019), p. 67.
110 Nick Allen and Rozina Sabur, 'Donald Trump Hails Vladimir Putin as a "Genius" over Russia's Invasion of Ukraine,' *Telegraph*, 23 February 2022.

Notes to Chapter 5

1 Joseph Choonara, 'A New Cycle of Revolt', *International Socialism*, 2.165 (2019): 21–36.
2 Cas Mudde, 'The Far-Right Threat in the United States: A European Perspective', *Annals of the American Academy of Political and Social Science*, 699.1 (2022): 101–16, here p. 106.
3 Ugo Palheta, *La Possibilité du fascisme: France, le trajectoire du désastre* (Paris: La Découverte, 2018), ch. 2.
4 Antonio Gramsci, *Selections from the Prison Notebooks* (London: Lawrence & Wishart, 1971), pp. 275–6; Antonio Gramsci, *Quaderni del carcere*, 4 vols, ed. by Valentino Gerratana, vol. 2 (Rome: Einaudi, 1975): Quaderno 3 (xx), §34, p. 377.
5 Chantal Mouffe, *For a Left Populism* (London: Verso, 2018), p. 25. There is an excellent analysis, inspired by Polybius and Machiavelli, of the crisis of liberal democracy since the 1970s, in Helen Thompson, *Disorder: Hard Times in the 21st Century* (New York: Oxford University Press, 2022), Part III.
6 Alex Callinicos, 'The Return of the Arab Revolution', *International Socialism*, 2.130 (2011): 3–32; Anne Alexander and Mostafa Bassiouny, *Bread, Peace, and Social Justice: Workers and the Egyptian Revolution* (London: Zed, 2014).

7 For recent reflections on this experience, see Stathis Kouvelakis, 'Beyond Left-Wing Melancholia: Reflections on a Militant Trajectory', Blog, Verso, 1 April 2022. https://www.versobooks.com/blogs/5316-beyond-left-wing-melancholia-reflections-on-a-militant-trajectory.
8 Kieran Allen, *32 Counties: The Failure of Partition and the Case for a United Ireland* (London: Pluto, 2021).
9 Cas Mudde, *The Far Right Today* (Cambridge: Polity, 2019) and Mark Thomas, 'Fascism in Europe Today', *International Socialism*, 2.162 (2019): 27–63.
10 Berta Joubert-Ceci, 'US Economic Wars and Latin America', in Robin Riley, Chandra Talpade Mohanty, and Minnie Bruce Pratt, eds, *Feminism and War: Confronting US Imperialism* (London: Zed, 2008), 238–42, here p. 240.
11 Probably the most important exception is the initial period of Corbyn's leadership of the British Labour Party, in 2015–17, before it was overwhelmed by the effects of the Brexit crisis and the unprecedented campaign mounted by the mainstream media and the Labour right to destroy Corbyn personally. The broader failure of the radical left is an important subject that I am unable to address here.
12 Mudde, *The Far Right Today*, p. 101.
13 Agnieszka Graff and Elzbieta Korolczuk, *Anti-Gender Politics in the Populist Movement* (London: Routledge, 2022), p. 19.
14 Fredric Jameson, *The Political Unconscious: Narrative as Socially Symbolic Act* (London: Methuen, 1981), p. 52.
15 Ibid., pp. 52, 55, 102.
16 Donald Trump, Inaugural Address, (20 January 2017. https://www.presidency.ucsb.edu/node/320188.
17 Marco D'Eramo, 'Populism and the New Oligarchy', *New Left Review*, 2.82 (2013): 5–28.
18 See the useful discussion in Graff and Korolczuk, *Anti-Gender Politics in the Populist Movement*, ch. 1.
19 Ernesto Laclau, *Of Populist Reason* (London: Verso, 2005).
20 William Callison and Quin Slobodian, 'Coronapolitics from the Reichstag to the Capitol', *Boston Review*, 21 January 2021.
21 Walden Bello, *Counterrevolution: The Global Rise of the Far Right* (Rugby: Practical Action Publishing, 2019), p. 166.
22 Tariq Ali, *The Extreme Centre: A Warning* (London: Verso, 2015).
23 Priya Chacko and Kanishka Jayasuriya, 'Asia's Conservative Moment: Understanding the Rise of the Right', *Journal of*

Contemporary Asia, 48.4 (2018): 529–40; Nicos Poulantzas, *State, Power, Socialism* (London: NLB, 1978), pp. 203–4.
24 Chacko and Jayasuriya, 'Asia's Conservative Moment', p. 534.
25 See Bello, *Counterrevolution*, chs 6 and 7 and the Postscript.
26 My thanks to John Rose for this crucial point.
27 Ed Pertwee, 'Donald Trump, the Anti-Muslim Far Right and the New Conservative Revolution', *Ethnic and Racial Studies*, 43.16 (2020): 211–30, here pp. 212–13.
28 Judith Orr, 'Women and the Far Right', *International Socialism*, 2.163 (2019): 41–64.
29 Pertwee, 'Donald Trump, the Anti-Muslim Far Right and the New Conservative Revolution', pp. 223–4.
30 Quoted in Graff and Korolczuk, *Anti-Gender Politics in the Populist Movement*, p. 122.
31 Kees Van der Pijl, *The Making of an Atlantic Ruling Class* (London: Verso, 1984).
32 Chris Harman, *Class Struggles in Eastern Europe, 1945–83* (London: Pluto, 1983).
33 Mudde, *The Far Right Today*, p. 20.
34 Quotation from Twitter: visit https://twitter.com/CasMudde/status/1513246220260675598.
35 Utsa Patnaik and Prabhat Patnaik, *Capitalism and Imperialism: Theory, History, and the Present* (New York: Monthly Review Press, 2021), p. 307.
36 Enzo Traverso, *The New Faces of Fascism: Populism and Far Right* (London: Verso, 2019), Kindle loc. 557. See also Ugo Palheta, *La Possibilité du fascisme: France, le trajectoire du désastre* (Paris: La Découverte, 2018), an excellent study of the RN that treats fascism only as a danger.
37 Peter Gowan, *The Global Gamble: Washington's Faustian Bid for World Dominance* (London: Verso, 1999).
38 Robert Brenner, 'Escalating Plunder', *New Left Review*, 2.123 (2020): 5–22, here p. 22.
39 Thomas Piketty, Emmanuel Saez, and Gabriel Zucman, 'Economic Growth in the United States: A Tale of Two Countries', Washington Centre for Economic Growth, 6 December 2016. http://equitablegrowth.org/research-analysis/economic-growth-in-the-united-states-a-tale-of-two-countries.
40 'Illness as Indicator', *The Economist*, 19 November 2016.
41 Daniel Lazare, *The Frozen Republic: How the Constitution is Paralysing Democracy* (New York: Harcourt, Brace, 1996).

42 For the text of the US Constitution, visit the National Archives site at https://www.archives.gov/founding-docs/constitution-transcript.
43 W. E. B. Du Bois, *Black Reconstruction in America: An Essay toward a History of the Part Which Black Folks Played in the Attempt to Reconstruct Democracy in America, 1860–1880* (New York: Oxford University Press, 2007); Eric Foner, *Reconstruction: America's Unfinished Revolution, 1863–1877* (New York: Harper Perennial, 2014 [1988]); and Henry Louis Gates Jr, *Stony the Road: Reconstruction, White Supremacy, and Rise of Jim Crow* (London: Penguin, 2019). These are three great studies of Reconstruction and its defeat. For Marx and the Civil War, see Robin Blackburn, *Marx and Lincoln: An Unfinished Revolution* (London: Verso, 2011), and Lucia Pradella, 'Crisis, Revolution and Hegemonic Tradition: The American Civil War and Emancipation in Marx's Capital', *Science & Society*, 80.4 (2016): 454–67.
44 Michelle Alexander, *The New Jim Crow: Mass Incarceration in the Age of Colorblindness* (New York: New Press, 2010).
45 Among the reasons why the label 'white supremacy' is too simplistic are, on the one hand, the growing political muscle of Black Democrats, whose organizing drive delivered Biden, in January 2021, the two Georgia Senate seats – and thereby control over both houses of Congress; and, on the other, the perturbing fact that, in November 2020, 'even as Mr Trump lost ground in white and Republican areas in and around cities – ultimately leading to his election loss – he gained new votes in immigrant neighbourhoods' (Weiyi Cai and Ford Fessenden, 'Immigrant Neighbourhoods Shifted Red as the Country Chose Blue', *New York Times*, 20 December 2020). For a study of how this happened in South Texas, see Mike Davis, 'Trench Warfare: Notes on the 2020 Election', *New Left Review*, 2.126 (2020): 5–32, at pp. 10–15. For excellent critiques of the 'white supremacy' thesis, see August Nimtz, 'The Meritocratic Myopia of Ta-Nehisi Coates', *Monthly Review*, 17 November 2017, https://mronline.org/2017/11/17/the-meritocratic-myopia-of-ta-nehisi-coates, and Adolph L. Reed, Jr, *The South: Jim Crow and Its Afterlives* (London: Verso, 2022).
46 Louis Althusser, *For Marx* (London: Allen Lane, 1969), ch. 3.
47 A detailed analysis of Trump and his relationship to capital and the state can be found in Alex Callinicos, 'The End of the World News', *International Socialism*, 2.153 (2016): 5–22 and Alex Callinicos, 'The Neoliberal Order Begins to Crack', *International*

Socialism, 2.154 (2017): 3–20. There is a penetrating Freudo-Marxist diagnosis of his political style in Eli Zaretsky, 'The Big Lie', *London Review of Books*, Blog, 15 February 2021. https://www.lrb.co.uk/blog/2021/february/the-big-lie.

48 Andrew Edgecliffe-Johnson, 'Trump's Corporate Trouble', *Financial Times*, 30 October 2020.
49 Davis, 'Trench Warfare', pp. 18–19.
50 Davis, 'Trench Warfare', p. 20; Mike Davis and Adam Shatz, 'Catholics and Lumpen-Billionaires', *London Review of Books*, Podcast, 3 November 2020. https://www.lrb.co.uk/podcasts-and-videos/podcasts/lrb-conversations/catholics-and-lumpen-billionaires.
51 'Wall Street/Trump: The Quieter Riot', *Financial Times*, 7 January 2021.
52 Davis, 'Trench Warfare', p. 17.
53 Joshua Chaffin, 'How the Far Right Fell into Line behind Donald Trump', *Financial Times*, 19 January 2021.
54 Edward Luttwak, *Coup d'état: A Practical Handbook* (Cambridge, MA: Harvard University Press, 1968), p. 27.
55 Naunihal Singh, 'Was the US Capitol Riot Really a Coup? Here's Why Definitions Matter', *Washington Post*, 9 January 2021.
56 Timothy Snyder, 'The American Abyss', *New York Times*, 9 January 2021.
57 Alexandria Ocasio-Cortez, 'What Happened at the Capitol', Instagram, 2 February 2021. https://www.instagram.com/tv/CKxlyx4g-Yb/?igshid=1bzenjfdl26xz.
58 Meryl Kornfield, 'Woman Charged in Capital Riot Said She Wanted to Shoot Pelosi "In the Friggin' Brain"', FBI Says', *Washington Post*, 30 January 2021.
59 Todd Frankel, 'A Majority of the People Arrested for Capitol Riot Had a History of Financial Trouble', *Washington Post*, 10 February 2021.
60 Tom Jackman and Spencer Hsu, 'Proud Boys Leader Admits Plan to Storm Capitol and Will Testify against Others', *Washington Post*, 8 April 2022.
61 Rosalind Helderman and Jacqueline Alemany, 'Jan. 6 Committee Blames Trump for "Carnage" at US Capitol', *Washington Post*, 9 June 2022.
62 Paul Mason, 'We Are All Antifa Now!', Medium, 7 January 2021. https://medium.com/mosquito-ridge/we-are-all-antifa-now-726b307e4255. There is a vivid eyewitness account of 6

February in William Shirer, *The Collapse of the Third Republic: An Inquiry into the Fall of France* (New York: Simon & Schuster, 1971), ch. 14.
63 Philip Rucker and Carol D. Leonnig, '*I Alone Can Fix It* Book Excerpt: The Inside Story of Trump's Defiance and Inaction on Jan 6', *Washington Post*, 15 July 2021.
64 Alex Horton et al., 'Milley Defends Calls Made to His Chinese Counterpart, Saying They Were Sanctioned and Briefed across the Administration', *Washington Post*, 28 September 2021.
65 Michael Glennon, *National Security and Double Government* (New York: Oxford University Press, 2014), pp. 6–7.
66 Mike DeBonis and Jacqueline Alemany, 'Trump Sought to Lead Armed Mob to Capitol on Jan. 6, Aide Says', *Washington Post*, 28 June 2022.
67 The fumbling process through which order was restored is reconstructed in Rucker and Leonnig, '*I Alone Can Fix It* Book Excerpt'.
68 Devlin Barrett, Spencer S. Hsu, and Aaron C. Davis, '"Be Ready to Fight": FBI Probe of US Capitol Riot Finds Evidence Detailing Coordination of an Assault', *Washington Post*, 30 January 2021.
69 Andrew Edgecliffe-Johnson, 'US Business Lobby Groups Call for Patience over Election Result', *Financial Times*, 27 October 2020.
70 Andrew Edgecliffe-Johnson, 'US Business Leaders Rue Their "Faustian Bargain' with Trump"', *Financial Times*, 8 January 2021.
71 Snyder, 'The American Abyss'.
72 'Nearly Half of Republicans Support the Invasion of the US Capitol', *Economist*, 7 January 2021.
73 Lauren Fedor, 'Impeachment Dilemma: Republicans Rally behind Trump before Senate Trial', *Financial Times*, 8 February 2021.
74 Snyder, 'The American Abyss'.
75 Lauren Fedor, 'Donald Trump Still Looms over American Politics', *Financial Times*, 4 February 2022.
76 Lauren Fedor, 'Donald Trump's Machine Kicks off 2022 with War Chest of More Than $100mn', *Financial Times*, 1 February 2022.
77 Paul Kane, Josh Dawsey, and Jacqueline Alemany, 'Rep. Liz Cheney Tells Americans Why Jan. 6 Should Terrify Them', *Washington Post*, 10 June 2022.
78 Ugo Palheta, 'Fascism, Fascization, Antifascism', Blog, 7 January 2021. https://www.historicalmaterialism.org/blog/fascism-fascisation-antifascism.
79 Davis, 'Trench Warfare', p. 32.

80 Barbara Walter, *How Civil Wars Start: And How to Stop Them* (London: Penguin, 2022), p. 11. For a perceptive and thoughtful review of Walter's book, see James Meek, 'What Are You Willing to Do?', *London Review of Books*, 26 May 2022.
81 Walter, *How Civil Wars Start*, pp. 142, 138.
82 *Dobbs vs Jackson's Women's Health Organization*, 597 US (2022) (J. THOMAS, concurring, p. 3).
83 James Politi and Stefania Palma, 'Overturning of Roe vs Wade Sets out Right-Wing Path for US Supreme Court', *Financial Times*, 26 June 2022.
84 Scherer, Michael, 'Conservatives on the March: GOP Gains Ground despite Democratic Control', *Washington Post*, 26 June 2022.
85 Jacob Bogage and Christopher Christopher Rowland, 'Chasm Opens between States over Abortion Pills and Out-of-State Care', *Washington Post*, 25 June 2022.
86 Walter, *How Civil Wars Start*, pp. 166–7, 181–2. Compare the superb history of the Civil War in James McPherson, *Battle-Cry of Freedom: The Civil War Era* (Oxford: Oxford University Press, 1988).
87 Walter, *How Civil Wars Start*, pp. 171, 183–4.
88 Stephen Marche, 'Why the US Military Isn't Ready for Civil War', *Foreign Policy*, 4 January 2022.
89 John Locke, *Two Treatises on Civil Government*, edited by Peter Laslett (Cambridge: Cambridge University Press, 1988), Book 2, §49, p. 301.

Notes to Chapter 6

1 Walter Benjamin, *Selected Writings*, vol. 4: *1938–1940* (Cambridge MA: Harvard University Press, 2003), p. 402.
2 Antonio Gramsci, *Selections from the Prison Notebooks* (London: Lawrence & Wishart, 1971), p. 78; Antonio Gramsci, *Quaderni del carcere*, 4 vols. ed. by Valentino Gerratana, vol. 3 (Rome: Einaudi, 1975), Quaderno 10, §17, pp. 2169–70; translation modified. In particular, I have moved the long passage in brackets ('a demonstration …') back to the place where it occurs in the original text.
3 Benjamin, *Selected Writings*, p. 396.
4 See the fine historical account of working-class agency in Mike Davis, *Old Gods, New Enigmas: Marx's Lost Theory* (London: Verso, 2018), ch. 1.
5 Patrick Buchanan, '1992 Republican National Convention

Speech', Blog, 1992. https://buchanan.org/blog/1992-republican-national-convention-speech-148.

6. Agnieszka Graff and Elzbieta Korolczuk, *Anti-Gender Politics in the Populist Movement* (London: Routledge, 2022), p. 164.

7. For excellent guides through this tangled ideological territory, see Sue Caldwell, 'Marxism, Feminism, and Transgender Politics', *International Socialism*, 2.157 (2017): 25–52 and Laura Miles, *Transgender Resistance: Socialism and the Fight for Trans Liberation* (London: Bookmarks, 2020).

8. Judith Butler, *Gender Trouble: Feminism and the Subversion of Identity* (New York: Routledge, 2006 [1990]), pp. 8–9.

9. Graff and Korolczuk, *Anti-Gender Politics in the Populist Movement*, p. 62.

10. See especially Georges Canguilhem, *The Normal and the Pathological* (New York: Zone Books, 1991 [1966]).

11. Richard Lewontin, Steven Rose, and Leon Kamin, *Not in Our Genes: Biology, Ideology, and Human Nature* (New York: Pantheon Books, 1985), p. 282. For more on the conception of biology that underlies this affirmation, see Richard Levins and Richard Lewontin, *The Dialectical Biologist* (Cambridge, MA: Harvard University Press, 1985) and Richard Lewontin, *The Triple Helix: Gene, Organism, and Environment* (Cambridge, MA: Harvard University Press, 2000).

12. Peter Drucker, *Warped: Gay Normality and Queer Anti-Capitalism* (Leiden: Brill, 2015).

13. Judith Butler, 'Merely Cultural', *New Left Review*, 1.227 (1998): 33–44, here p. 41. See especially Lindsey German, 'Theories of Patriarchy,' *International Socialism*, 2.12 (1981): 33–51; Lise Vogel, *Marxism and the Oppression of Women: Toward a Unitary Theory* (Chicago: Haymarket, 2013 [1983]); Johanna Brenner and Maria Ramas, 'Rethinking Women's Oppression,' *New Left Review* 1.144 (1984): 33–71; and Lucia Pradella, 'Foundation: Karl Marx (1818–83)', in Alex Callinicos, Stathis Kouvelakis, and Lucia Pradella, eds, *The Routledge Handbook of Marxism and Post-Marxism* (New York: Routledge, 2021), 25–40.

14. Graff and Korolczuk, *Anti-Gender Politics in the Populist Movement*, pp. 7, 94.

15. Quoted ibid., p. 52.

16. Judith Orr, 'Women and the Far Right', *International Socialism*, 2.163 (2019): 41–64, here p. 56.

17. Judith Butler, 'Why Is the Idea of "Gender" Provoking Backlash

the World Over?', *Guardian*, 23 October 2021; see also Graff and Korolczuk *Anti-Gender Politics in the Populist Movement*, esp. ch. 5.
18 Graff and Korolczuk, *Anti-Gender Politics in the Populist Movement*, pp. 140, 141, 161.
19 Chantal Mouffe *For a Left Populism* (London: Verso, 2018).
20 Erika Guevara Rosas, 'From Mobilization to Solidarity: The Power of Feminist Struggles in Latin America', openDemocracy, 2 December 2021.
21 Miles, *Transgender Resistance*.
22 Cedric Robinson, *Black Marxism: The Making of the Black Radical Tradition*, 2nd edn (Chapel Hill: University of North Carolina Press, 2020 [1983]). Despite the value of Robinson's exploration of the 'Black radical tradition', represented in his book by W. E. B. du Bois, C. L. R. James, and Richard Wright, I have reservations about his overall approach and, more specifically, about his understanding of racism as a transhistorical phenomenon; thus he posits a unitary subjectivity shared by all Black people. Partly because of these problematic essentialist assumptions, reliance on the expression 'racial capitalism' can encourage taking for granted what needs to be established, namely the historically variable relationship between specific versions of capitalism and different forms of racial oppression. It is therefore better to insist that capitalism and racism are analytically distinct, even if, as Gramsci would put it, they are always found together 'organically', in actuality (Gramsci, *Selections from the Prison Notebooks*, p. 160; Gramsci, *Quaderni del carcere*, vol. 2, Quaderno 13 (xxx), §18, p. 591: see Alex Callinicos, 'Imperialism, Racial Capitalism, and Postcolonialism', paper presented to the Oxford Southernizing Criminology Discussion Group, 17 November 2021, https://www.youtube.com/watch?v=eqIVKwPCEUo. This paper draws on Harold Wolpe, *Race, Class, and the Apartheid State* (London: James Currey, 1988). Two valuable recent critical discussions of Robinson are Ken Olende, 'Cedric Robinson, Racial Capitalism and the Return of Black Radicalism', *International Socialism*, 2.169 (2021): 149–77 and Joseph Ramsay, 'Sifting the "Stony Soil" of Black Marxism: Cedric Robinson, Richard Wright, and Ellipses of the Black Radical Tradition', *Socialism and Democracy*, 34.2–3 (2021): 1–31.
23 Theodore Allen, *The Invention of the White Race*, 2nd edn, 2 vols (London: Verso, 2012).

24 Robin Blackburn, *The American Crucible: Slavery, Emancipation and Human Rights* (London: Verso, 2011).
25 Alex Callinicos, *Race and Class* (London: Bookmarks, 1993); Keeanga-Yamahtta Taylor, 'Race, Class, and Marxism', SocialistWorker.org, 4 January 2011. https://socialistworker.org/2011/01/04/race-class-and-marxism.
26 W. E. B. du Bois, *Black Reconstruction in America: An Essay toward a History of the Part Which Black Folks Played in the Attempt to Reconstruct Democracy in America, 1860–1880* (New York: Oxford University Press, 2007 [1935]), pp. 940–1.
27 Martin Barker, *The New Racism: Conservatives and the Ideology of the Tribe* (London: Junction Books, 1981).
28 Michelle Alexander, *The New Jim Crow: Mass Incarceration in the Age of Colorblindness* (New York: New Press, 2010); Keeanga-Yamahtta Taylor, *From #BlackLivesMatter to Black Liberation*, 2nd edn (Chicago, IL: Haymarket, 2021); Elizabeth Hinton, *America on Fire: The Untold History of Police Violence and Black Rebellion since the 1960s* (London: William Collins, 2021).
29 Michael Goldfield, *The Southern Key: Class, Race, and Radicalism in the 1930s and 1940s* (New York: Oxford University Press, 2020). Ira Katznelson, *Fear Itself: The New Deal and the Origins of Our Times* (New York: Liveright, 2013) shows on how the support of segregationist southern Democrats in Congress both enabled and set limits to Roosevelt's New Deal.
30 Noam Chomsky, quoted in George Yancy, 'Chomsky: Protests Unleashed by Murder of George Floyd Exceed All in US History', Truthout, 7 May 2021. https://truthout.org/articles/chomsky-protests-unleashed-by-murder-of-george-floyd-exceed-all-in-us-history.
31 Larry Buchanan, Quoctrung Bui, and Juhal K. Patel, 'Black Lives Matter May Be the Largest Movement in US History', *New York Times*, 3 July 2020.
32 Roudabeth Kishi et al., 'A Year of Racial Justice Protests: Key Trends in Demonstrations Supporting the BLM Movement', ACLED, May 2021, p. 1. https://acleddata.com/acleddatanew/wp-content/uploads/2021/05/ACLED_Report_A-Year-of-Racial-Justice-Protests_May2021.pdf.
33 Hinton, *America on Fire*, p. 26.
34 There is a good overview of the BLM rebellion in Hinton, *America on Fire*, Conclusion.
35 Barbara Ransby, 'Movement for Black Lives', Institute of Race

Relations, 24 July 2020. https://irr.org.uk/article/movement-for-black-lives-an-interview-with-barbara-ransby.
36 Kishi et al., 'A Year of Racial Justice Protests', p. 1.
37 Commission on Race and Ethnic Disparities, *The Report*, March 2021. https://assets.publishing.service.gov.uk/government/uploads/system/uploads/attachment_data/file/974507/20210331_-_CRED_Report_-_FINAL_-_Web_Accessible.pdf.
38 Salar Mohandesi, 'Who Killed Eric Garner?', *Jacobin*, 17 December 2014.
39 Taylor, *From #BlackLivesMatter to Black Liberation*, p. 78.
40 Buchanan, Bui, and Patel, 'Black Lives Matter May Be the Largest Movement in US History'.
41 An important case study of how imperialism, racism, migration, unfree labour, and the drive for self-emancipation interweave in the contemporary world economy is Lucia Pradella and Rosanna Cillo, 'Bordering the Surplus Population across the Mediterranean: Imperialism and Unfree Labour in Libya and the Italian Countryside', *Geoforum*, 126 (2021): 483–94.
42 Alex Callinicos, *Bonfire of Illusions: The Twin Crises of the Liberal World* (Cambridge: Polity, 2010), pp. 95–105.
43 James Galbraith, *The End of Normal: The Great Crisis and the Future of Growth* (New York: Simon & Schuster, 2014).
44 Friedrich von Hayek, ed., *Collectivist Economic Planning* (London: Routledge, 1935); Friedrich von Hayek, *Individualism and the Economic Order* (Chicago, IL: University of Chicago Press, 1948); and Alec Nove, *The Economics of Feasible Socialism* (London: Routledge, 1983).
45 G. A. Cohen, *Why Not Socialism?* (Princeton, NJ: Princeton University Press, 2009), p. 82.
46 Martin Arboleda, *Planetary Mine: Territories of Extraction under Late Capitalism* (London: Verso, 2020).
47 Visit https://twitter.com/triofrancos/status/1508850259274915852.
48 Laurie MacFarlane, 'A Spectre is Haunting the West – the Spectre of Authoritarian Capitalism', openDemocracy, 16 April 2020.
49 Nicos Poulantzas, *State, Power, Socialism* (London: NLB, 1978), Part 4.
50 Pat Devine, *Democracy and Economic Planning: The Political Economy of a Self-Governing Society* (Cambridge: Polity, 1988); Michael Albert, *Parecon: Life after Capitalism* (London: Verso, 2003), Daniel Saros, *Information Technology and Socialist Construction: The End of Capital and the Transition to Socialism* (Abingdon: Routledge, 2014).

51 James Meadway, 'Neoliberalism Is Dying: Now We Must Replace It', openDemocracy, 3 September 2021.
52 Evgeny Morozov, 'Digital Socialism? The Calculation Debate in the Age of Big Data', *New Left Review*, 2.116–17 (2019): 33–67, here pp. 62–3.
53 Saros, *Information Technology and Socialist Construction*, ch. 7.
54 Morozov, 'Digital Socialism?', p. 65.
55 Adam Tooze, 'Tempestuous Seasons', *London Review of Books*, 13 September 2018.
56 John Maynard Keynes, *Essays in Persuasion* (Basingstoke: Palgrave Macmillan, 2010 [1931]), xviii.
57 Geoff Mann, *In the Long Run We Are All Dead: Keynesianism, Political Economy, and Revolution* (London: Verso, 2017), Kindle loc. 5514.
58 Georg Wilhelm Friedrich Hegel, *Elements of the Philosophy of Right*, edited by Allen Wood (Cambridge: Cambridge University Press, 1991), §244, p. 266.
59 Alex Callinicos, *Social Theory: A Historical Introduction*, 2nd edn (Cambridge: Polity, 2007), p. 46; Mann, *In the Long Run We Are All Dead*, Part 2.
60 Elsewhere, for example when writing about the Brexit referendum and Trump's election, Tooze shows a much more nuanced understanding: Adam Tooze, *Crashed: How a Decade of Financial Crisis Changed the World* (London: Allen Lane, 2018), chs 23 and 24.
61 Alex Callinicos, *The Revolutionary Ideas of Karl Marx* (London: Bookmarks, 1983).
62 Paul Mason, 'The Trump Insurrection: A Marxist Analysis', Medium, 12 January 2021. https://medium.com/mosquito-ridge/the-trump-insurrection-a-marxist-analysis-dc229c34cdc1. Mason misunderstands Arendt's argument. Although she does refer to '[t]he temporary alliance between the elite and the mob', she is talking primarily about pro-imperialist movements in the lead-up to the First World War: Hannah Arendt, *The Origins of Totalitarianism* (New York: Harcourt, Brace, 1973), chs 7 and 8, here p. 333. For Arendt, genuine '[t]otalitarian movements are mass organizations of atomized, isolated individuals' with no definite social location (ibid., p. 323). This may be mistaken, as Mason himself plausibly argues, but the two formulations are not equivalent; see Paul Mason, *How to Stop Fascism: History, Ideology, Resistance* (London: Penguin, 2021), pp. 166–8.
63 Leon Trotsky, *The Struggle against Fascism in Germany* (New York: Pathfinder, 1971), pp. 158–9.

64 Brian Jenkins and Chris Millington, *France and Fascism: February 1934 and the Dynamics of Political Crisis* (Abingdon: Routledge, 2015), pp. 126–7.
65 Robert Paxton, *Vichy France: Old Guard and New Order, 1940–1944* (New York: Alfred A. Knopf, 1972), p. 254.
66 Jenkins and Millington, *France and Fascism*, p. 154.
67 Jacques Danos and Marcel Ghibelin, *Juin 1936* (Paris: Maspero, 1972 [1936]), vol. 1, pp. 18–21.
68 Leon Trotsky, *Whither France?* (London: New Park, 1974 [1936]), p. 46.
69 See the classic study of Danos and Ghibelin, *Juin 1936*.
70 Jenkins and Millington, *France and Fascism*, p. 169.
71 William Shirer, *The Collapse of the Third Republic: An Inquiry into the Fall of France* (New York: Simon & Schuster, 1971), p. 952.
72 Paul Mason, 'Learning to Say "Goodbye Lenin": A Critique of the IST Statement on the Ukraine War', Medium, 20 February 2022. https://paulmasonnews.medium.com/learning-to-say-goodbye-lenin-f5f520f0aaef. See also my response: Alex Callinicos, 'Ukraine and Imperialism: Alex Callinicos Replies to Paul Mason', *Socialist Worker*, 21 February 2022. https://socialistworker.co.uk/long-reads/ukraine-and-imperialism-alex-callinicos-replies-to-paul-mason.
73 Fernando Claudin, *The Communist Movement from Comintern to Cominform* (Harmondsworth: Penguin, 1975).
74 For more on strategy against the far right, see Mark Thomas, 'Fascism in Europe Today,' *International Socialism* 2.162 (2019): 27–63 and the testimony of key anti-fascist organizers in Britain – in the 1930s, in Phil Piratin, *Our Flag Stays Red* (London: Lawrence & Wishart, 1978 [1948]); in the 1970s, in Paul Holborow, 'The Anti-Nazi League and Its Lessons for Today', *International Socialism*, 2.163 (2019): 65–83. Also for contemporary Greece, see Petros Constantinou, 'How We Smashed Golden Dawn', *International Socialism*, 2.169 (2021): 77–88.
75 Trotsky, *The Struggle against Fascism in Germany*.
76 The title of this section is shamelessly stolen from that of a Festschrift for Mike Davis. See Daniel Bertrand Monk and Michael Sorkin, eds, *Between Catastrophe and Revolution: Essays in Honour of Mike Davis* (New York: OR Books, 2021).
77 Alex Callinicos, 'Betting on Infinite Loss', *International Socialism*, 2.163 (2019): 3–18.

78 Andreas Malm, *How to Blow Up a Pipeline: Learning to Fight in a World on Fire* (London: Verso, 2020, Kindle loc. 92.
79 Erica Chenoweth, 'It May only Take 3.5% of the Population to Topple a Dictator – with Civil Resistance', *Guardian*, 1 February 2017. There is a detailed monograph that substantiates this claim – Erica Chenoweth and Maria J. Stephan, *Why Civil Resistance Works: The Strategic Logic of Nonviolent Conflict* (New York: Columbia University Press, 2011); but it contains none of the examples cited here and, absurdly, depicts the Iranian Revolution of 1978–9 as a case of 'non-violent resistance', ignoring the insurrection organized by the left and by Islamists in February 1979 that finally broke the Pahlavi regime. The book is a classic case of mainstream 'comparative politics' as practised especially in the United States: the analysis of statistical data serves systematically to delete the specific historical contexts that shape different political struggles. MacIntyre's splendid demolition job on this method still stands. See Alasdair MacIntyre, 'Is a Science of Comparative Politics Possible?', in his *Against the Self-Images of the Age: Essays on Ideology and Philosophy* (London: Duckworth, 1971), 260–79. See also the important critiques of non-violence in Martin Empson, 'Non-Violence, Social Change, and Revolution', *International Socialism*, 2.165 (2020): 57–79 and Malm, *How to Blow Up a Pipeline*.
80 Talat Ahmed, *Mohandas Gandhi: Experiments in Civil Disobedience* (London: Pluto, 2019), ch. 6.
81 Madhusree Mukerjee, *Churchill's Secret War: The British Empire and the Ravaging of India during World War II* (New York: Basic Books, 2010), ch. 11; Utsa Patnaik and Prabhat Patnaik, *Capitalism and Imperialism: Theory, History, and the Present* (New York: Monthly Review Press, 2021), Parts 2 and 3.
82 Alex Callinicos, *South Africa between Reform and Revolution* (London: Bookmarks, 1988); Callinicos, 'Imperialism, Racial Capitalism, and Postcolonialism'; and Wolpe, *Race, Class, and the Apartheid State*.
83 Chris Harman, 'The State and Capitalism Today', *International Socialism*, 2.51 (1991): 3–54; see also Alex Callinicos, *Imperialism and Global Political Economy* (Cambridge: Polity, 2009), pp. 73–93.
84 Andreas Malm, *Fossil Capital: The Rise of Steam Power and the Roots of Global Warming* (London: Verso, 2016), p. 383.
85 Andreas Malm, *Corona, Climate, Chronic Emergency: War Communism in the Twenty-First Century* (London: Verso, 2020).

86 Anna Betts, Greg Jaffe, and Rachel Lerman, 'Meet Chris Smalls, the Man who Organized Amazon Workers in New York', *Washington Post*, 1 April 2022; Angelika Maldonado, 'Here's How We Beat Amazon', *Jacobin*, 2 April 2022.

87 Noam Scheiber, 'The Revolt of the College-Educated Working Class', *New York Times*, 28 April 2022.

88 Kim Moody, *On New Terrain: How Capital Is Reshaping the Battleground of Class War* (Chicago, IL: Haymarket, 2018).

89 Rossana Cillo and Lucia Pradella, 'New Immigrant Struggles in Italy's Logistics Industry', *Comparative European Politics*, 16 (2018): 67–84.

90 Beverly Silver, *Forces of Labour: Workers' Movements and Globalization since 1870* (Cambridge: Cambridge University Press, 2003), p. 174.

91 Alex Vershinin, 'The Return of Industrial Warfare', Rusi, 17 June 2022. https://www.rusi.org/explore-our-research/publications/commentary/return-industrial-warfare.

92 UN Global Crisis Response Group on Food, Energy and Finance, *Global Impact of the War in Ukraine: Billions of People Face the Greatest Cost-of-Living Crisis in a Generation*, 8 June 2022, pp. 2, 3, 10. https://news.un.org/pages/wp-content/uploads/2022/06/GCRG_2nd-Brief_Jun8_2022_FINAL.pdf?utm_source=United+Nations&utm_medium=Brief&utm_campaign=Global+Crisis+Response.

93 Larry Elliott, 'War in Ukraine Could Lead to Food Riots in Poor Countries, Warns WTO Boss', *Guardian*, 24 March 2022.

94 Andres Schipani and Emiko Terazono, '"People Are Hungry": Food Crisis Starts to Bite across Africa', *Financial Times*, 23 June 2022.

95 Ahilan Kadirgamar, 'Interview: Rising Up in Sri Lanka', *International Socialism*, 2.175 (2022): 27–36.

96 C. L. R. James, *World Revolution, 1917–1936*, edited by Christian Høgsbjerg (Durham, NC: Duke University Press, 2017 [1937]), ch. 12.

97 James Connolly, *Labour in Ireland*, vol. 1: *Labour in Irish History*, vol. 2: *The Reconquest of Ireland*, continuous pagination (Dublin: Irish Transport and General Workers Union, 1944), p. 325.

Select Bibliography

Althusser, Louis. *History and Imperialism: Writings, 1963–1986*, edited by G. M. Goshgarian. Cambridge: Polity, 2020.
Althusser, Louis, et al. *Reading Capital: The Complete Edition*. London: Verso, 2015 [1965].
Angus, Ian. *Facing the Anthropocene: Fossil Capitalism and the Crisis of the Earth System*. New York: Monthly Review Press, 2016.
Arendt, Hannah. *The Origins of Totalitarianism*. New York: Harcourt, Brace, 1973.
Bello, Walden. *Counterrevolution: The Global Rise of the Far Right*. Rugby: Practical Action Publishing, 2019.
Brenner, Robert. *The Economics of Global Turbulence*. London: Verso, 2016.
Burkett, Paul. *Marx and Nature: A Red and Green Perspective*. Chicago, IL: Haymarket, 2014.
Callinicos, Alex. *Bonfire of Illusions: The Twin Crises of the Liberal World*. Cambridge: Polity, 2010.
Callinicos, Alex. *Deciphering Capital: Marx's Capital and Its Destiny*. London: Bookmarks, 2014.
Callinicos, Alex. *Imperialism and Global Political Economy*. Cambridge: Polity, 2009.
Callinicos, Alex, Stathis Kouvelakis, and Lucia Pradella, eds. *The Routledge Handbook of Marxism and Post-Marxism*. New York: Routledge, 2021.
Carchedi, Guglielmo, and Michael Roberts, eds. *World in Crisis: Marxist Perspectives on Crash & Crisis: A Global Analysis of Marx's Law of Profitability*. Chicago, IL: Haymarket, 2018.

Davis, Angela Y. *Women, Race & Class*. New York: Vintage, 1983.

Davis, Mike. *The Monster Enters: Covid-19, Avian Flu, and the Plagues of Capitalism*. New York: OR Books, 2020.

Davis, Mike. *Old Gods, New Enigmas: Marx's Lost Theory*. London: Verso, 2018.

Du Bois, W. E. B. *Black Reconstruction in America: An Essay Toward a History of the Part Which Black Folks Played in the Attempt to Reconstruct Democracy in America, 1860–1880*. New York: Oxford University Press, 2007 [1935].

Empson, Martin, ed. *System Change, not Climate Change: A Revolutionary Response to Environmental Crisis*. London: Bookmarks, 2019.

Foster, John Bellamy. *Marx's Ecology: Materialism and Nature*. New York: Monthly Review Press, 2000.

Foster, John Bellamy. *The Return of Nature: Socialism and Ecology*. New York: Monthly Review Press, 2020.

Graff, Agnieszka, and Elzbieta Korolczuk. *Anti-Gender Politics in the Populist Movement*. London: Routledge, 2022.

Gramsci, Antonio. *Selections from the Prison Notebooks*. London: Lawrence & Wishart, 1971.

Harman, Chris. *Zombie Capitalism: Global Crisis and the Relevance of Marx*. London: Bookmarks, 2009.

Harvey, David. *A Short History of Neoliberalism*. Oxford: Oxford University Press, 2005.

Hinton, Elizabeth. *America on Fire: The Untold History of Police Violence and Black Rebellion since the 1960s*. London: William Collins, 2021.

Jameson, Fredric. *The Political Unconscious: Narrative as Socially Symbolic Act*. London: Methuen, 1981.

Jameson, Fredric. *Valences of the Dialectic*. London: Verso, 2009.

Jenkins, Brian, and Chris Millington, *France and Fascism: February 1934 and the Dynamics of Political Crisis*. Abingdon: Routledge, 2015.

Kahl, Colin, and Thomas Wright. *Aftershocks: Pandemic Politics and the End of the Old International Order*. New York: St Martin's Press, 2021.

Klein, Matthew C., and Michael Pettis. *Trade Wars Are Class Wars: How Rising Inequality Distorts the Global Economy and Threatens International Peace* (New Haven, CT: Yale University Press, 2020.

Lazare, Daniel. *The Frozen Republic: How the Constitution is Paralyzing Democracy*. New York: Harcourt, Brace, 1996.

Levins, Richard, and Richard C. Lewontin. *The Dialectical Biologist*. Cambridge MA: Harvard University Press, 1985.

McNeill, William H. *Plagues and Peoples*. Harmondsworth: Penguin, 1979.

Malm, Andreas. *Fossil Capital: The Rise of Steam Power and the Roots of Global Warming*. London: Verso, 2016.
Mann, Geoff. *In the Long Run We Are All Dead: Keynesianism, Political Economy, and Revolution*. London: Verso, 2017.
Mayer, Arno J. *The Furies: Violence and Terror in the French and Russian Revolutions*. Princeton, NJ: Princeton University Press, 2000.
Miles, Laura. *Transgender Resistance: Socialism and the Fight for Trans Liberation*. London: Bookmarks, 2020.
Mudde, Cas. *The Far Right Today*. Cambridge: Polity, 2019.
Panitch, Leo, and Sam Gindin, *The Making of Global Capitalism: The Political Economy of American Empire*. London: Verso, 2012.
Passavant, Paul A. *Policing Protest: The Post-Democratic State and the Figure of Black Insurrection*. Durham, NC: Durham University Press, 2021.
Patnaik, Utsa, and Prabhat Patnaik. *Capitalism and Imperialism: Theory, History, and the Present*. New York: Monthly Review Press, 2021.
Paxton, Robert O. *The Anatomy of Fascism*. New York: Alfred A. Knopf, 2004.
Poulantzas, Nicos, *State, Power, Socialism*. London: NLB, 1978.
Poulantzas, Nicos. *Fascism and Dictatorship: The Third International and the Problem of Fascism*. London: Verso, 2018 [1970].
Pradella, Lucia. *L'attualità del capitale: Accumulazione e impoverimento nel capitalismo globale*. Padua: Il Poligrafo, 2010.
Pradella, Lucia. *Globalization and the Critique of Political Economy: New Insights from Marx's Writings*. London: Routledge, 2015.
Roberts, Michael, *The Long Depression*. Chicago, IL: Haymarket, 2016.
Saito, Kohei. *Karl Marx's Ecosocialism: Capital, Nature, and the Unfinished Critique of Political Economy*. New York: Monthly Review Press, 2017.
Silver, Beverly J. *Forces of Labour: Workers' Movements and Globalization since 1870*. Cambridge: Cambridge University Press, 2003.
Taylor, Keeanga-Yamahtta. *From #BlackLivesMatter to Black Liberation* (2nd edn). Chicago, IL: Haymarket, 2021.
Thompson, Helen. *Disorder: Hard Times in the 21st Century*. New York: Oxford University Press, 2022.
Tooze, Adam. *Crashed: How a Decade of Financial Crisis Changed the World*. London: Allen Lane, 2018.
Tooze, Adam. *Shutdown: How Covid Shook the World's Economy*. London: Penguin, 2021.
Trotsky, Leon. *The Struggle against Fascism in Germany* (New York: Pathfinder, 1971).

Wallace, Rob. *Big Farms Make Big Flu*. New York: Monthly Review Press, 2016.
Wallace, Rob. *Dead Epidemiologists: On the Origins of COVID-19*. New York: Monthly Review Press, 2020.
Wood, Tony. *Russia without Putin: Money, Power and the Myths of the New Cold War*. London: Verso, 2018.

Index

Adorno, Theodor 5, 11
Afghanistan *see* geopolitical antagonisms
Agamben, Giorgio 51
agriculture 33, 40, 43, 44, 59, 126
Albert, Michael 165
Althusser, Louis 11–12, 28, 121, 134, 180n5
anocracy 144
Anthropocene (geologic epoch), 30–31
anti-genderism, 151, 152, 155
anti-neoliberalism *see* revolt; left wing; the far right
Arendt, Hannah 14, 222n.62
AUKUS (Australia, United Kingdom, United States) submarine deal 87, 95, 103
'authoritarian statism' 124–125, 165
autocracy 86, 112, 115–116

banks and banking
  bailouts 66, 70, 132
  speculation 64, 66
  transatlantic system 65–66, 67
  see also central banks
Bello, Walden 12
Bendell, Jem 32–33
Benjamin, Walter 11, 150
Bharatiya Janata Party 125
Biden, Joe 81–82, 83, 86, 88, 91
biopolitics 48, 50
Black Lives Matter protests 14, 54, 118, 123, 159–161, 179
  composition of 162
  militarized approach to 159, 160
'black swan' events, 2
Bloch, Ernst 20, 185n.19
Bolsonaro, Jair 125
Bonapartism 18–19, 21, 22
Buchanan, Pat 151
Butler, Judith 152–153, 155

capital
  internationalization of 130
  limits to 61–62, 69
  'natural' 36
  organic composition of 62, 63
  and the state 16, 92, 133, 165, 174
  and US presidents 135–136, 140, 141
  see also profit, rate of; imperialism
capital accumulation 27, 35, 75, 93, 94, 109
  and the state 27, 174–175
capitalism, crisis of 5–7, 26, 62, 112, 163
  biological 5
  economic 6
  geopolitical 6
  political 6, 10
Capitol, assault on 137–143
  comparison with events Paris, 6 February 1934, 138
carbon-neutral economy 36, 38
carbon trading 36, 37
Carchedi, Guglielmo 93, 201n.79

INDEX

catastrophe 2, 176
  immanent in capitalism 41
  and climate change 4, 5, 9, 30, 32, 39, 59, 173
  COVID-19 as 5, 6, 9, 48, 57
  Gramsci reference to 150
  Marxist approach to 5, 7–8, 9, 11
  period 1914–1945 16, 18–24
  post-1945 3–4, 5–7, 15, 25–26, 28–29, 58–59
  and revolt 176, 177, 178, 179
  ruling class and 58–59
  state response to 53–54, 55–56, 58, 67, 73
  vulnerability to 4–5, 58, 178
  see also fascism
central bankism 77, 78
central banks 61, 66, 70, 71, 72, 73, 92, 110–111
  change in role of 78–79
  currency reserves 113
Césaire, Aimé 15
Chacko, Priya 124–125
Chenoweth, Erica 224n.79
China *see* People's Republic of China; *see also* US–China relations
China Evergrande Group 99
Choonara, Joseph 85, 118
civil disobedience 54, 168, 173, 174
civil liberties, inroads 53, 54–55
class 57, 195n.101
  see also class and race; ruling class; working class
class and race 127, 161, 162, 175, 219n.22
class struggle 150–151 *see also* working class
climate change 35
  adaptation to 37, 38, 94
  bodies (United Nations) 31
  geopolitical implications 36, 38–39
  indicators 30, 31
  inequality and 36
  and infectious diseases 41
  negotiations 36–37
  vulnerability to 32, 33, 102
  see also civil disobedience
CO_2 emissions 31–32, 34–35, 37, 38, 104
  and human intervention 39, 40
  see also greenhouse gas emissions
coal
  and industrialization 34, 36
  industry 36, 37, 39
  limiting use of 36
  power stations 39
  reliance on 83
  see also energy; fossil fuels
Cohen, G.A. 164
Cold War era 27, 28–29
  arms spending during 63
  proxy wars 28
  polarization post- 112, 114
collective action 56, 167
collective agency 157, 163 *see also* working class
collective subject 150, 155, 176
Communist Party of China (CPC) 55, 92, 165
competition 7, 13, 35, 62, 86, 88
  and green energy 104
  economic and geopolitical 6, 8, 9, 13, 16, 27, 86, 87, 88, 93, 94, 100, 102, 109
competitive accumulation 7, 8, 34, 92, 100
cost of living crisis 177–178
counter-revolution 12, 17, 28, 29, 120, 124, 126, 127, 179
  from above or below 19, 21
  in Europe (inter-war period) 18–19
  see also fascism
COVID-19
  and class and race 56, 57, 58
  deaths 2021–2022, 51, 58
  economic outcome of 68, 70–73, 83, 112
  and the far right 122–123
  and freedom 74, 123–124
  government responses to 51–52, 55, 56, 81, 99, 123, 164
  and HIV 45
  immunity 47–48
  mortality rates 57, 58
  and vaccine inequality 45–46, 47, 58
  workers' bargaining power 84–85
  see also modelling
credit 65, 66, 69, 73, 104
Crimea *see* geopolitical antagonisms

Davis, Mike 40–41, 135
debt, 69, 70, 84
  to GDP 69, 98
  Third World 76, 84
debt-driven accumulation *see* People's Republic of China
decarbonization 36, 37, 104, 164, 168

demand 65, 75, 77, 83, 98, 163
  aggregate 52, 61, 65, 79, 130
democratic planning *see* economic planning
Democratic Republic of Congo (DRC) *see* geopolitical antagonisms
deregulation 35, 64, 129, 136
Deudney, David 114–115
Devine, Pat 165
Duterte, Rodrigo 125

economic growth, 61, 64, 68, 98
economic planning 163–166
  and accountability 165
  alternative models 165, 166
  democracy 166–167
  digital feedback 166
emergency measures 81, 163, 164, 165
emergency powers 19, 51, 53, 55
emissions *see* CO_2 emissions; greenhouse gas emissions; methane
energy
  access to 36
  cartel 112
  competition for 103
  imports and exports 100, 104
  prices 39, 83, 84, 111, 177, 178, 179
  reliance on 109
  sanctions 111, 113
  self-sufficiency 36, 104
  see also renewable energy; green transition; fossil fuels; gas, oil, liquefied natural gas
European Central Bank 66, 71, 111, 129
European Union 103, 106, 117, 128, 164, 172
  and COVID-19, 52
exception, state of 51
exogenous shocks 163
exploitation 8
  rate of 64
extreme weather events 32, 33, 69
  and US energy grid 33

the far right 6, 8, 12, 13, 117, 118, 120, 156
  in Britain 128 161, 172
  in Canada 123
  coherence, lack of 147
  composition 128
  response to COVID 51, 59, 122–123
  economic alternatives, absence of 120, 130

  in Europe 117, 128–129, 147
  grassroots networks 130, 131, 136
  ideology 121, 124, 126, 127–129, 130–113, 154
  mainstreaming of 128, 142, 143, 161
  the North 124
  political parties 117, 125, 128–129, 143
  rise of 120, 142, 147, 157, 167, 171
  in the South 124–125
  and ultraconservative religious actors 154
  in US 118–119, 135, 142, 136–137, 138, 146–147, 157
  see also Islamophobia; fascism; racism
Farage, Nigel 122
farming, intensive factory *see* agriculture
fascism 12, 13, 14, 18, 26
  definition 20, 168, 194n.88
  and the far right 127, 128, 130–131
  in Germany, 19–24
  in Italy, 19, 21
  and organized working class 21, 25, 173
  post- 130
  in Spain 19
  in US 139, 143
  violence 21, 168
  see also counter-revolution
Federal Reserve 67, 70, 76, 96
feminism 152, 156
feminists
  trans-critical 153
financial bubbles 3, 64–65
financial crisis of 2007–2009 47, 64, 65–68, 69, 70, 90, 119; *see also* global financial crisis
fiscal policy 70, 99
the Five Powers Defence Arrangement 96
flooding 4
food insecurity 178
food supply 177
Fordism 25
foreign direct investment 91
fossil capitalism 35, 43, 60, 174
fossil fuel interests 37, 39
fossil fuels 34, 105
  access 36
  bank financing of 37
  investment in 38
  reliance on 39, 69, 83, 104, 164
  speculative trading in 37
Foucault, Michel 48–49, 50, 192 n.69
fracking 36, 37, 104

INDEX

freedom 74–75
Friedman, Thomas 87

Gabor, Daniela 72–73
Galbraith, James 68, 163
Galbraith, John Kenneth 68
gas
  emissions 37, 38
  financing and investment 37, 38
  krypton 88
  market for 101, 104
  natural 100, 104
  neon 88
  reliance on 36, 103, 104, 111
  supplies 111
  see also energy; fossil fuels; liquefied natural gas (LNG)
gender 8, 10, 151, 175
  as contested concept 152
  sex and 152, 153
geopolitical antagonisms 87, 88, 99, 113
  Afghanistan 90, 120
  allies in 112, 115, 117
  Crimea 91, 101, 105, 108
  Democratic Republic of Congo (DRC) 102–103
  Georgia 100, 105
  Iran 90, 91, 101, 112
  Iraq 90, 104, 120
  Libya 90, 101, 102
  Middle East 31, 89, 90, 91, 101, 104, 132, 158
  Mozambique 102
  Syria 91, 102
  Turkey 101–2
  Ukraine 83, 88, 101, 105, 106–107, 109–110, 112, 117
  Taiwan 88, 93
  Vietnam 90
  see also US–China relations
Georgia *see* geopolitical antagonisms
global financial crisis 4, 6, 7, 68, 96, 98, 119, 120, 129–130, 132 *see also* financial crisis of 2007–2009
global polarization 112, 114
global warming 31–32, 33
  Arctic 33, 38
globalization 64, 87, 88, 89, 131
governmentality 9, 49, 51, 56
Graff, Agnieszka 153–154, 155
Gramsci, Antonio, 8, 25, 149–150, 184n.12
green transition 83, 104, 105, 164

greenhouse gas emissions 32, 33, 36
Great Acceleration 30, 76
Gross Domestic Product (GDP)
  global 67–69, 92
Gulf States 101

Hardt, Michael 87
Harman, Chris 61, 92, 174
Harper, Kyle 41–42
Hegel, G. W. F. 167
Horkheimer, Max 13

Ikenberry, John 114–115
information technology (IT) companies
  climate change 38
  US owned 96
  see also platform capitalism
imperial expansion, 23–24
imperialism 8, 9, 13, 14, 25
  hierarchy 100
  conceptualization of 16, 88, 100
  and colonial empires 26, 88
  free trade 26–27
  post-Cold War, 88–95, 96
  super-power (1945–1991) 27, 88
  China 92–94
  see also Islamophobia
inequality 58, 59, 82, 132 *see also* COVID-19
inflation 80, 84
  increases 61, 71, 83, 178
  targets 78
interest rates 67, 76, 83, 84, 163
international financial institutions 76, 89
international order 23, 27, 87, 114
  see also liberal internationalism
Iran *see* geopolitical antagonisms
Iraq *see* geopolitical antagonisms
Islamophobia 10, 126, 154, 157

Jameson, Fredric 7, 12, 121, 182n.38
Jayasuriya, Kanishka 124–125
Jenkins, Brian 169–170
Johnson, Boris 128, 143, 161

Kahl, Colin 114
Kalecki, Michal 80–81
Keynes, John Maynard 77, 167
Keynesianism 67, 71, 75–76, 167
  critique of 75, 80
  privatized 65
  technocratic 61, 71–73, 79

King, Martin Luther Jr 159
Klein, Matthew C. 97, 205n.41
Korolczuk, Elzbieta 153–154, 155
Krugman, Paul 68

labour process 8
Laclau, Ernesto 122
left wing 19, 118, 119, 120, 124, 125–126, 156, 167–168
 alliances 168–171
 response to COVID-19 123, 143, 167
 India 126
 Latin America 125–126
Lenzmann, Frank 37
liberal capitalist international order 27, 114
liberal democracy 53, 115, 166–167
 defence of 168–169
liberal internationalism 89, 114, 117
 see also autocracy
liquefied natural gas (LNG) 102
 importing 109, 111
 see also energy; fossil fuels; gas
Lukács, Georg 121
Libya *see* geopolitical antagonisms

Macron, Emmanuel 53, 103, 129, 171
Malm, Andreas 34–35, 175
Mann, Geoff 167
the market 52, 72, 73, 82, 85, 99, 114, 164, 165, 166–167
market discipline 29, 76
Marx, Karl 14
 Capital, 7, 13
 critique of political economy 7, 167
 and natural environment 40, 41, 42
 and profit, 17
 and structure of social whole 8
 and theory of economic crisis 62
 and the working class 176
Mason, Paul 168–169, 171–172, 222n.62
McNeill, William H. 2
Meloni, Giorgia 127
metabolism of labour and nature 8, 42, 69
methane 33, 102
Middle East *see* geopolitical antagonisms
migrants and migration 120–121, 124, 157
military cooperation with Ukraine 110
 see also NATO

Millington, Chris 169–170
modelling 49–51
modernity, late 56–57
money supply 77, 78
Morozov, Evgeny 166
Mouffe, Chantal 119, 120, 156
Mozambique 4, 102
 climate change 4, 102
 liquified natural gas 102
Mushtaq, Fathimath 72

NATO 90, 96–97, 102, 107 110
 expansion 105, 106
National Socialism 20, 23, 24
natural gas 39, 83, 103, 104, 109
 see also liquified natural gas
nature
 commodification of 35, 36
 interaction with 35, 36, 40, 42, 43, 45, 50, 59, 69
 see also metabolism of labour and nature
negative emissions technologies (NETs) 37, 59
negative externalities 35
Negri, Antonio 87
neoliberalism 3, 9
 dimensions of 74–77, 78
 end of 9, 73, 85, 119, 124
 economic policy regime 6, 64, 74, 75–77, 116, 122
 and the state 175
Norfield, Tony 206n.52
nuclear energy 37, 101

oil
 -based energy consumption 31
 control of 31, 90, 103–104, 112
 imports and exports 101, 104, 111
 production 39, 91, 100
 see also energy; fossil fuels
Olson, Carol 37
Overy, Richard 13, 26

Palheta, Ugo 53, 194n.88
pandemics 41, 43
 see also COVID-19
Panitch, Leo 67
Paris, 6 February, 1934 138, 169–170
Passavant, Paul 54, 194n.91
Patnaik, Prabhat 130
Patnaik, Utsa 130
Pettis, Michael 97–98, 205n.41
People's Republic of China 82, 86, 87

allies 101
capitalism 165
climate change 36, 39, 69, 94, 104
debt-driven growth 98, 99
elites view of US and itself 95
energy 91, 103, 104
global financial markets 92
imperialism 92–94
industrial agriculture 44
industrial subsidies 99
investment 92, 97, 98
military capabilities 94–95
nature of the state in 116
property sector 98, 99
production 91–92
reunification of 93
relations with Russia 107–108, 112
wages 97
and western capital 94
see also US–China relations
Pertwee, Ed 12
platform capitalism 166
Popular Front 25, 169–171
popular frontism 171–172, 173
populism 122, 123, 128
populist movement 120
see also the far right
Poulantzas, Nicos 13, 18, 124, 165, 192-3n69
plagues 41–42
policing 53–55
population, surplus 161
population density and disease 42, 43
populations 50
production
  capitalist mode of 2, 7–8, 10, 11, 25, 35, 40, 121, 122, 154
  means of 27, 62
  relations of 7, 8
productive forces 8
profit, rate of 93
  falling 17, 61, 62–63, 68
  maintaining 35
  recovery 64, 65
proletariat 167, 169
Putin, Vladimir 1, 6, 100–101, 105, 106, 111, 116, 117

Quad 96
quantitative easing 67, 70, 71, 83, 104
quantitative tightening 84

race, 8, 121, 122, 151, 161

and class 127, 161, 162, 175, 219n.22
racism, 10, 13, 14, 122, 157, 158
  biological 157
  and precarity 161
  and slavery 157
racist ideology 158
racist–populist parties 128, 129
recession 26, 64, 69, 81
Reed, Jr, Adolph L. 182n29
renewable energy, shift 92
  impact 38–39, 105
  resources required for 39, 164
Republican Party 140, 141, 142
  Trump supporters 133, 136, 141–142
revolt, cycles of 118, 120, 124–126, 175, 176, 177, 178, 179
  see also Black Lives Matter
revolution, 10, 11, 12, 17, 28, 90, 119, 126, 150, 167, 175, 176, 179
  global nature of 17–18
  passive, 25
  see also counter-revolution; fascism; revolt
right wing 74, 117, 136, 144
  parties of 121, 122, 128–129
  regimes 18, 19, 117
  see also anti-genderism; the far right
Roberts, Michael 63, 88, 93, 201 n.79
Robinson, Cedric 219n.22
Roe vs Wade 145–146
ruling class 21, 53, 119, 140, 143, 174,
ruling-class politics in Europe 18
Russia
  and Africa 101
  currency 111
  economy 100
  oil production and exports 100, 111
  influence internationally 101
  and Middle East 101
  natural gas production and exports 100, 104
  nature of the state in 116
  relations with China 107–108, 113
  sanctions 1, 96, 110–111, 113, 114, 116, 117
  significance of Ukraine for 106
  see also geopolitical antagonisms

Salvini, Matteo 154
Saros, Daniel 165, 166
semiconductors 88
sex and gender 152, 153

236 INDEX

shale industry *see* fracking
Sisi, Abdel Fattah, el- 115, 125
socialism as self-emancipation 167, 168
Soros, George 127
Soviet Union 24, 27, 88, 89, 90, 91, 95, 101
sovereignty, theory of 51
stagflation 76, 84
stagnation 68
strikes 29, 80, 81, 84–85, 170, 174, 177, 178
Summers, Lawrence 68
Sunak, Rishi 94
surplus value 62, 78, 93, 176
Syria *see* geopolitical antagonisms

Taiwan 88, 93, 107, 113
   see also geopolitical antagonisms and US–China relations
Taiwan Semiconductor Manufacturing Company 88
technologies, changing 15, 22, 34, 39, 59, 99, 104, 164, 166
   see also renewable energy
Thomas, Clarence 145
Tooze, Adam, 7, 10, 22, 65, 67, 71, 113, 167
totalization 7, 11, 8, 121
trade war 86, 97–98, 135
trans liberation 152, 156
Treasuries (US Treasury bonds) 70
transnational production networks 87
Traverso, Enzo 130–131
Trotsky, Leon 18–19, 21–22, 168–169
Trump, Donald 39, 52, 81, 117, 121–122, 127, 134–137
   and the ruling class 140
   see also US–China relations
Truss, Liz 94
Turkey, role of 101–2

Ukraine
   resources 88, 106, 177
   see also under geopolitical antagonisms
unemployment rate 64, 68, 80–81
United Nations and Ukraine war 112–113
United States (US), 28, 29, 30
   alliances 96–7
   assets 96–97
   coup 137
   civil war potential for 144
   defence spending 96

dollar dominance 113
economic growth 132
economic strategy 81, 82–83
electoral system 133
energy imports and exports 104
and Europe 109
foreign policy 89, 90–91, 95, 108
global output 95
hegemony 67, 68, 81, 89, 90, 95, 96, 108, 113, 120, 131
infrastructure plan 81, 82
military aid to Ukraine 110
and NATO 96-7, 105, 106, 107
polarization in 82, 144–146
politicized economy 81–82
racial oppression, historical 134
real wealth 59
sanctions 96
security policy 139
Supreme Court 145
technology companies 96
unipolarity 89
   see also Federal Reserve; globalization; imperialism; US–China relations
US–China relations 86–87, 88, 89, 90, 91, 92, 94, 96, 99, 107, 108
   China's elites view of US 95
   and conflict with Russia 108

Van der Pijl, Kees 26
Vietnam *see* geopolitical antagonisms

wage–price spiral 83, 84
wages 97
   real 64, 84
Wallace, Rob 43–45, 50
Walter, Barbara 144, 146–147
war-related deaths 30, 102, 103
Washington Consensus 77
Washington elite 122
wealth 5, 58, 59, 65, 67, 87, 167
white supremacy 134, 214n.45
wildfires 4, 32, 55
Woo, Gordon, 2
workers, disorganization of 81, 143
workers' movement 162, 175
workers' power 85, 176–177
workers' struggles 124, 176–177
working class
   and convergence of issues 162–3
   as collective agency 157, 167, 175, 179
   subject 151
Wright, Thomas 114